Health & Economic Status of Older Women

A. REGULA HERZOG • KAREN C. HOLDEN • MILDRED M. SELTZER
EDITORS

Jon A. Hendricks, Editor
SOCIETY AND AGING SERIES

Baywood Publishing Company, Inc.
Amityville, New York

Library of Congress Catalog Number: 87-36910
ISBN: 0-89503-050-0 (Paper)
ISBN: 0-89503-058-6 (Cloth)

Library of Congress Cataloging-in-Publication Data

   Main entry under title:
Health and economic status of older women.
(Society and Aging series; 1)
   Based on presentations made at an invitational
conference held in Ann Arbor, Mich. in 1984.
   Includes bibliographies and index.
   1. Aged women—United States—Economic conditions—
Congresses. 2. Aged women—Health and hygiene—
United States—Congresses. 3. Aged women—Research—
United States—Congresses. I. Herzog, A. Regula
(Anna Regula), 1941-   . II. Holden, Karen C.
III. Seltzer, Mildred M.
HQ1064.U5H36 1989   305.4   87-36910
ISBN 0-89503-050-0

Table of Contents

PART FOUR
CONCLUSION

APPENDICES

PART ONE
Introduction

CHAPTER
1

On Your Marks:
Research Issues on Older Women

Mildred M. Seltzer and Jon A. Hendricks

The topic of gender differences in the life course has lately become much more interesting; at least now we have two sides to the question. Despite the fact that over a decade has passed since some wag noted that any resemblance between white mainstream aging males and anyone else was purely coincidental, the research has been slow to reflect the call for expanded horizons. These shortcomings are finally being addressed. In the future, when one of those interesting historical reviews of the shaping of gerontology is published by a young, upwardly mobile, new professional, it will likely be noted that the period of the mid 1980s brought a new leaf in the annals of our field. Conferences were held, the President of the American Sociological Association used the prerogatives of her office to organize a special plenary session to focus on gender differences in a life span context, and entire volumes were published to rectify the oversights. All of this in spite of the fact that the International Year of the Woman, at the beginning of the decade, neglected to include older women as a priority topic. Times they are a-changing.

As is the case whenever the paradigm gets refurbished, the pendulum swings the other way for a time. The chapters to follow are a case in point; they concentrate on issues not previously given full hearing and make no bones about addressing how the situation of aging women differs from that of anyone else. They represent a major and long-term effort to shed some light where little had previously been shed. The major topics of this book, health and economic issues of older women, encompass large, complex areas. Others might have been chosen; there is no shortage of needed work, but these are two that can serve an invaluable heuristic purpose. This book, intended to fill at least part of the breech, is devoted to a discussion of two specific areas of old women's lives — economics and health. Based on data drawn exclusively from the United States (except in a review of the Shock Bibliographies), information is presented about 1) research issues in these two areas of life; and 2) data sources currently available to address these issues. Specific research questions, where contradictory, are noted. In other instances, attention is called to neglected areas of research as well as some specific research issues that have never been addressed. Items for a future research agenda are identified. A unique feature of this volume is that brief abstracts of data sets mentioned in the body of the text are included in the Appendix.

The book itself is the result of an invitational conference held in Ann Arbor, Michigan in 1984. Conference discussions informed the choice of topics and the identification of research gaps to be considered. This book, however, is not just a report of those discussions. Rather, the material from that conference was used as a "jumping off" place for the discussions to follow. Similarly, the Appendix on data sources was compiled using the comments and discussion of conference participants as a starting point. While the authors recognize and appreciate the rich contributions of the conference participants in drafting the issue agenda and in identifying resources, the authors do not claim to summarize conference deliberations nor to speak for all participants.

The original plan was to publish the material in this book as a special edition of a journal, but there was too much material for a single journal issue. The manuscript lent itself more readily to a book. What is before you now is the final result. The gestation period has been longer than anticipated. As a consequence, the most recent research is not included. This is true of nearly all book-length manuscripts. And, because it was never intended to be a literature review, the omission of this most recent information should not be considered a major drawback of the book. Instead, the authors focus on some major methodological issues, calling attention to some contradictory findings and drawing attention to the need for different and/or more sophisticated approaches to research about old women and, by extension, research about old people in general.

Understand how differences between the sexes operate in the health and economic worlds, and the remainder will be considerably simplified. The research library of gerontology is well stocked; sometimes, however, the questions originally asked seem naive or quaint to those who go back and try to draw implications not thought of by those who fielded the study in the first place. The existing data sources, however, are a gold mine for those who care to prospect for new insights. One of the goals of the following chapters is to show how new questions can be asked of old data. As the two key chapters make clear, thoughtful new conclusions may issue from the effort.

ORGANIZATION OF THIS BOOK

This book is organized in three parts. Part 1 sets the stage for the more focused discussion of health and economic issues in the lives of old women that follows in Part 2. This first section contains papers by both Troll and Reinharz. Their papers – presented as keynote addresses in the conference – provide a historical context for the subsequent material. Both authors issue challenges to those who would focus their research efforts on older women.

The second part of the book contains the substantive discussions of health and economic aspects of women's lives. Herzog develops material on physical and mental health and Holden material on economic aspects. Herzog's discussion is organized around the principal themes of morbidity, mortality, health perceptions, utilization patterns, subjective well-being, reproductive functioning, and related matters. To the extent that the data permit, she casts findings in a comparative light with males and with younger counterparts. Differences and similarities are set in terms of a variety of contexts to see the differences in terms of bioindividual or environmental approaches to the discussion of health. Not included in the present rendering is much of the political economic approach or a discussion of the pitfalls of the medicalization of social problems. This latter is pointed out merely to augment Herzog's cogent presentation of needed redirection in research on women's health.

Holden's summary of economic factors in the lives of older women focuses on questions that only recently have begun to receive any attention at all. Women's pension income, prior to recent rulings, was a nontopic. As Holden makes clear, a couple of longitudinal data sets and some innovative analytic strategies portent major changes in the next few years. One factor, clearly identified as causal in the relative economic well-being of older women, is the extent and structure of benefits accorded women in many pension plans. Among the unanswered questions is whether differences in coverage would actually benefit women to any significant extent. The popular wisdom is that it would, but the jury is still out. If structural factors are considered, that is, where women work and in what types of occupations, additional coverage might bring marginal improvement at best. Similarly, a range of other factors run as crosscurrents in what, at first, seems to be a neat package of inequalities. As is usually the case, waters tend to become muddier the closer we look.

Part 3 contains discussions of research methodologies. Herzog delineates the importance, complexities and problems involved in quantitative research in general and specifically in research about sex differences. Miller reviews some related issues for qualitative research and provides brief descriptions of data sources available for secondary analysis as well as suggested directions for further research. These suggestions are an initial response to Troll's call for a new paradigm.

Following reviews of qualitative and quantitative data sets and some of the methodological pitfalls one is likely to encounter along the way, Seltzer concludes in Part 4 by pointing to the old twins, the ecological and atomistic fallacies. She also reminds us about the extent to which health and financial well-being are intertwined, and about the role of life course transitions on the way to relative poverty or affluence in old age. Perhaps most important of all, Seltzer does point to the connection between individual level economic situations, too heavy a reliance on human capital variables as an explanation, and policy implications. No matter how sliced, the edges run together. The concluding comments reflect hope that those engaged in research about old women will have learned from the past in order to move in some new directions in the future.

BACKGROUND

The conference, "Older Women: Research Issues and Data Sources," was held in Ann Arbor under the joint sponsorship of the Institute of Gerontology, The University of Michigan, and the Scripps Gerontology Center, Miami University. The conference was funded by the National Institute on Aging. The meeting was convened to enhance the quantity and quality of research about older women by bringing together a group of people engaged in such research or other research relevant to understanding older women. Participants represented a variety of academic disciplines, research interests, and perspectives; a list of participants is included in Appendix B. By bringing together those scholars, the conference provided a forum for interdisciplinary discussions of issues related to current and future research about the health and economic status of older women. The conference also provided a forum for exchanging of ideas about future direction in research on older women and for identifying existing data sources for such endeavors. The underlying theme was to encourage greater use of rich, existing data sources for secondary analysis, thereby reducing the need for additional costly and/or duplicative data collection. Consideration was given to problems of secondary analysis of existing data. While attention must be paid to the ways in which the original data are structured, the authors believe that researchers must also use such data in ways that are most amenable to the current issue being researched rather than limiting themselves to those issues defined by the original data collection purposes. By developing and providing a list of large data sets (assembled by Fultz and included in Appendix A), they hope that awareness of the availability and location of these data will increase their use for secondary data analysis.

The decision to focus on two specific aspects of women's late lives was based on knowledge that health and economics are undeniable factors affecting the quality of life in old age. This is true for both men and women. There are, however, major differences between the economic and health conditions of old men and old women and these differences are not always well understood. It is hoped that, as a result of the conference and of this volume, investigators will be stimulated to develop and implement new directions in research.

RESEARCH ABOUT OLDER WOMEN

Although aging processes are universal, there are physical and social aspects in which gender particularly matters. Two important ways in which old women differ from old men are: 1) characteristics and patterns unique to women because they are associated with the reproductive cycle and its management and control; and 2) characteristics and patterns that are more or less common among old women than among other comparison groups. Menopause falls into the first category. Health issues such as longevity and its social consequences are in the second category. One result of women's longevity is the probability that married women will outlive their husbands. Thus, widowhood and its attendant results has long been a research topic of concern to social and behavioral scientists interested in older women. Similarly, researchers have been interested in the incidence as well as the social and psychological consequences of specific conditions such as arthritis, osteoporosis, and urinary incontinence. We also find the apparent prevalence of depression and institutionalization among old women as well as economic issues such as poverty, pension coverage, and work patterns included in the second category. Some of these issues are more amenable to studies using qualitative methods while others lend themselves to more quantitative analyses. Many of them could profit from a creative combination of both approaches.

A number of general issues permeated the work of the conference and the subsequent discussions presented in this volume. Many of these are issues that surface whenever people engage in discussions about research in general, while others pertain to research specifically concerned with sex differences. A fundamental challenge directed to those engaged in research about sex differences is the conflict that may arise between research and social agendas. This challenge is evidenced in Reinharz's paper. She delineates the feminist perspective in research calling attention to ways in which traditional attitudes may influence research. Moreover, prior assumptions about the role of women in society often shape the nature of research undertaken. These assumptions may also undervalue the need for complete data on women or the need for research on sex differences. Additionally, because researchers function within a social climate, issues such as the potential policy implementation of findings and governmental funding preferences may also determine the collection or use of data. Thus, those doing research need to be sensitive to all of the foregoing concerns when undertaking research about old women.

Any discussion about older people in general inevitably begins with a review of what is meant by the words "old," "older," and "aged." Definitions of age differ from one social class to another, between socially constructed categories of race, and between ethnic categories. Moreover, definitions have changed over time and from place to place. In some periods of our history, chronological age was less important than functional status in defining when someone would be considered old by her/himself and by others. One's perception of being old may also be influenced by health status. Chronological age may be a useful proxy in many areas of life but is less important in others. Similar definitional problems arise when considering economic aspects such as designing eligibility for transfer programs for the "aged."

If there is agreement that there is something unique about growing old as a woman, further questions arise as to whether there is something unique about growing old as a minority woman. Until fairly recently, the majority of those studying aging paid little attention to ethnic and racial differences. The absence of Blacks, Hispanics, Orientals and other minority peoples from large samples parallels the exclusion of women from some large samples of aging populations. As we noted above, parallels to these or other groups were often purely coincidental.

During the 1970s, possibly influenced by an increasing emphasis on civil rights and the spread of egalitarian attitudes, those engaged in research about aging began examining the role of ethnicity and race in aging. A literature emerged on the triple jeopardy of being old, black, and a woman. However, as Markides has noted, until recently ethnicity and race have been among the most underdeveloped topics in social gerontology [1, p. 115]. Despite recent accumulation of data, the relative salience and weight of ethnicity, race and sex as well as the interaction effects of these variables are still unclear.

Methodological issues in research are critical. They concern the appropriateness of specific research designs, strategies, and philosophies, sampling issues and measurement concerns, and the relative advantages and uses of quantitative and qualitative research approaches. The importance of cohort effects is raised throughout this publication, reminding the reader that accurate data about today's older women do not necessarily enable us to predict how future cohorts of older women will experience the effects and processes of aging. Predicting future characteristics based solely on knowledge about present ones is not only difficult, it is inappropriate. The short "half life" of research is nowhere more readily apparent than in the field of aging.

Many of the differences between the sexes in old age have extremely important implications for developing legislation and programs, yet there has been a dearth of accurate and integrated research data used in making informed policy decisions. This volume also addresses the need for better information.

In much of the material that follows, old women are compared with old men. Obviously, comparisons could have been made with groups other than old men. For example, old women can be compared with young women or with themselves at earlier times in their lives. Comparisons of old women with other categories of people are also important. Each set of comparisons can provide different insights and raise different research and policy issues.

Although research about gender differences was undertaken in the past, there was not a great deal of it nor was it easily accessible. Articles reporting research about old women were only infrequently published in gerontology journals. Research that was available was limited to a few topical areas and these areas often reflected the kinds of problems discussed earlier in this introductory section.

An examination of the Shock Bibliographies, conducted specifically for this volume, provides information about the kinds and amounts of research about old women. For the period up to and including 1961, for example, a total of 371 entries related to Health Maintenance but only two dealt with older women. Of the 1416 titles listed under "Gerontology, General Orientation," four articles dealt with old women. Of these four, only one, "Grandmothers are guinea pigs" [2], was published in a gerontology journal. There were 1252 articles listed under "Life Expectancy" and of these, thirty-seven dealt with age and sex morbidity and mortality data and an additional ninety-six were public health service reports containing age, race and sex differentials. None of these articles were in gerontology journals. Other categories under which sex differences would presumably be discussed included "Hygiene" (including mental and physical health and listed under "Geriatrics"). Of the 533 titles listed under "Hygiene," three refer specifically to older women. Of the 138 titles dealing with "Sex Differences," one was in a gerontology journal [3]. As is clear from Table 1, the numbers are indeed very low.[1]

There may have been research focusing on sex differences in old age, but we were able to find only five published in journals specifically denoted as gerontology journals during that period of time. This lack does not necessarily reflect a conscious bias against research concerning gender differences but may reflect (equally disconcerting) the lack of quality of the research itself. Seltzer called attention to inadequate and incomplete descriptions of samples of old people some time ago [4]. Sample descriptions often did not specify the numbers of men and women involved in the research. Different research projects operationalized "old" and "young" differently. Frequently other relevant sample characteristics were omitted (e.g., social class, race, rural/urban differences). One can only suppose that earlier researchers considered sex an irrelevant variable in old age and thus never reported what sex the research persons were. As noted earlier, it is also possible that we could not identify early research on older women because these earlier research findings were not indexed to indicate their relevance to older women.

Fortunately, more recent Shock Bibliographies and the American Association of Retired Persons data base show source shifts in emphases in research about

---

[1] For details concerning this and the following two tables, please see the Addendum to this chapter.

Table 1. Research about Older Women and Sex Comparisons by
Selected Subject Headings through 1961

Subject Heading	Total Titles	Titles Referring Specifically to Older Women and Sex Comparisons Number and (Percent)
Gerontology, general orientation	1,416	4 (.28)
Health maintenance	371	2 (.54)
Life expectancy	1,252	133 (11)
Hygiene (physical and mental health)	533	3 (.56)
Sex differences (listed under biology of aging, longevity)	138	51 (37)
Diagnosis and physical examinations	226	4 (1.77)
Geriatrics, general orientation	506	0 (0)
Employment	1,138	43 (3.78)
Retirement	919	7 (.76)
Economic problems	43	0 (0)
Economic status and needs of the aged	201	3 (1.49)
Social Security including "Old Age Assistance"	921	9 (.98)
Widows	7	7 (100)
TOTAL	7,671	226 (2.95)

Source: *Classified Bibliography of Gerontology and Geriatrics,* Volume 1 and Supplements 1 and 2.

older women. These entries are summarized in Tables 2 and 3 respectively. There were no clear increases, according to the Shock Bibliographic listings, in the percentages of publications specifically about women. Similarly, the AARP Ageline Computer Base showed a general decrease in the percentages of articles (by categories) reporting research about older women. There were a few exceptions in this overall trend, "Employment," "Health Status," and "Financial Assistance." These data, however, may be inconclusive because AARP Ageline has used the label "Female" differently since 1982. Superficially, it would appear that whatever increases have occurred have been in somewhat limited areas and/or are not reflected in the data presented here. While intuitively it appears that there has been increased interest about old women, this intuitive reaction may be more a reflection of discussions, meetings, and the mutual reinforcement of those engaged in such research.

Table 2. Research about Older Women and Sex Comparisons by Selected Subject Headings (1962-1977)

Total Number of Titles by Selected Subject Headings/
Titles Specifically Referring to Older Women, Number and (Percent)

Year	Gerontology	Longevity	Geriatrics	Hygiene	Economic Problems	Social Security
1962	108/0(0)	92/3(3.26)	23/0(0)	19/0(0)	134/1(.75)	20/1(5.00)
1963	122/0(0)	109/3(2.75)	21/1(4.76)	17/1(5.88)	114/7(6.14)	43/1(2.33)
1964	142/0(0)	135/2(1.48)	33/0(0)	20/0(0)	120/7(5.83)	29/1(3.45)
1965	128/0(0)	160/6(3.75)	21/0(0)	11/0(0)	136/8(5.88)	27/0(0)
1966	154/0(0)	140/6(4.29)	25/0(0)	30/0(0)	160/5(3.13)	26/1(3.85)
1967	105/0(0)	125/2(1.60)	18/0(0)	24/0(0)	146/1(.68)	34/1(2.94)
1968	138/0(0)	163/4(2.45)	32/0(0)	34/0(0)	144/4(2.78)	39/0(0)
1969	136/1(.74)	189/9(4.76)	40/1(2.50)	28/0(0)	173/6(3.47)	26/0(0)
1970	119/0(0)	91/3(3.30)	31/0(0)	22/0(0)	115/4(3.48)	56/1(1.79)
1971	123/0(0)	142/4(2.82)	27/0(0)	15/0(0)	147/5(3.40)	31/0(0)
1972	195/0(0)	86/2(2.33)	28/0(0)	0/0(0)	162/5(3.09)	32/0(0)
1973	160/0(0)	141/6(4.26)	26/0(0)	18/0(0)	151/1(.66)	34/1(2.94)
1974	126/1(.79)	135/10(7.41)	55/0(0)	10/0(0)	123/5(4.07)	43/1(2.33)
1975	131/0(0)	153/7(4.58)	37/0(0)	20/0(0)	154/9(5.84)	42/2(4.76)
1976	181/2(1.10)	164/12(7.32)	39/0(0)	18/1(5.55)	169/16(9.47)	58/6(10.34)
1977	158/5(3.16)	175/16(9.14)	50/0(0)	17/0(0)	166/6(3.61)	39/1(2.56)
TOTAL	2226/9(.40)	2200/95(4.32)	506/2(.40)	303/2(.66)	2314/90(3.89)	579/17(2.94)

Source: Classified Bibliography of Gerontology and Geriatrics.
Note: The first number in each figure represents the total number of titles under each subject heading; the second number represents the total number of those titles that refer specifically to older women. "Widows" does not appear as a separate subject heading in the 1962–1980 Shock Bibliographies.

11

Table 3. Research about Older Women by Selected Subject Headings (1977–1987)

Subject Heading	All Articles Listed in AARP Data Base	Articles Specifically Pertaining to Older Women, Number and (Percent)		
		Total	1977 to 1981	1982 to April, 1987
Health	4,949	537(10.85)	456/2303(19.80)	81/2646(3.06)
Physical condition	396	110(27.78)	99/206(48.06)	11/190(5.79)
Health status	170	21(12.35)	2/6(33.33)	19/164(11.59)
Mental health	454	107(23.57)	95/263(36.12)	12/191(6.28)
Widows or widowhood	229	110(48.03)	90/105(85.71)	20/124(16.13)
Employment	1,471	274(18.63)	213/714(29.83)	61/757(8.06)
Retirement	2,524	330(13.07)	268/1134(23.63)	62/1390(4.46)
Income adequacy	249	60(24.10)	49/116(42.24)	11/133(8.27)
Income levels	378	145(38.36)	133/185(71.89)	12/193(6.22)
Income	1,730	347(20.06)	301/792(38.00)	46/938(4.90)
Economics	621	111(17.87)	94/323(29.10)	17/298(5.70)
Financial assistance	59	5(8.47)	4/29(13.79)	1/30(3.33)
Social security	826	82(9.93)	69/385(17.92)	13/441(2.95)
Sex differences	307	130(42.35)	49/56(87.50)	81/251(32.27)
TOTALS	14,363	2,369(16.49)	1,922/6617(29.05)	447/7746(5.77)

Source: American Association of Retired Persons (AARP) "Ageline" Computer Data Base.

Note: In 1982, AARP changed the classification system for organizing published titles in the "Ageline" Data Base. The descriptive term female has been used less frequently since 1982. As a result, data in this table indicating higher numbers and percentages of titles appearing between 1977 and 1981 may be a reflection of indexing methods. Caution should be exercised when using these data for comparative purposes.

The significance of sex differences has not only been overlooked in writing, but also in the production of data resources. Some earlier gerontological research is severely limited by the scarcity of data on women. The *Baltimore Longitudinal Study of Aging*, for example, was initiated in 1959, but only included women after 1978. The absence of women from some samples is particularly striking given the fact that their life expectancy is greater than that of men and the resulting fact that the sex ratio disparity increases as the population ages. In other studies in which women were interviewed, the respondent sample was often restricted to special subgroups of women, for example, women who headed their own households as in the *Panel Study of Income Dynamics*. Only unmarried women were interviewed in the *Retirement History Study*. As Herzog notes, implicit assumptions about the nature of men and women influenced the hypotheses tested, the data collected, and ultimately the results obtained. Even now, much research about older women continues to focus on aspects assumed to be of particular importance in women's lives such as caretaking, husbands' retirement, widowhood, and menopause. In general, such research has focused on the negative consequences of these changes. Far less attention has been paid to the potential for growth that may be involved in such changes and events. Moreover, until recently, less attention has been paid to the health or work-related aspects of their own lives that women might identify as significant or on significant aspects of old women's lives as compared to the lives of other categories of people. Thus, although there has been research about old women, much of it has been "flat" in the sense that it does not reflect all aspects of women's lives. Unidimensional analyses show us single stitches rather than complex patterns and traditional patterns rather than those reflecting changed circumstances and lives. As Miller points out, it is qualitative research that is best equipped to provide descriptions of the richness and complexities of individual lives. It is the kind of research that breathes life into the sometimes chilling effects of numbers. It is not, however, an either/or proposition, but rather which method can answer the critical aspects studied.

WHERE DO WE GO FROM HERE?

There has been a shift in the kinds of gender focused research issues thought sufficiently important to examine. To a large extent, we have moved from a description of gender differences in old age to an examination of their sources and the social and psychological implications for the lives of older women. At the same time, there has been an increasing sophistication about research methods. The extent of this shift can be seen in Troll's chapter in which she reviews the history of research interest in older women. The contrast between her chapter and Reinharz's, which delineates a feminist perspective in studying older women, provides evidence of the varying assumptions and concerns underlying different research perspectives in studying old women. While Troll notes that we are still examining some of the same topics related to old woman-hood that we examined a decade or more ago, and often in the same mechanical fashion, there have been many new and rewarding areas of research. There have also been changes in the kinds and numbers of questions asked, for example, questions about the nature of the mother–daughter relationship in late life. It is in these aspects that we find some of the greatest innovations in research about old women. These shifts are occurring with changes in cohorts of researchers — those researchers whose questions and concerns differ from those of their intellectual foremothers, whose subject pools differ from that of their older colleagues, and whose research competencies are increasingly refined.

Few of us can deny that there has been an increase in some kinds of research about old women as well as increased sophistication in the research that is undertaken. There has not, however, been a marked increase in the research in specific areas.

Because the categories of research in the examined bibliographies are not always comparable, it is difficult to draw relevant comparisons over time. Table 4 shows time trends for a few categories of research that were comparable for the earlier and later Shock Bibliographies (i.e., Tables 1 and 2).

This comparison suggests an increase in numbers of articles about "Economic Problems" and "Social Security," a decrease in articles about "Longevity," and virtually no change in the percent of articles about "Hygiene" and "Geriatrics." The decrease in the proportion of articles about longevity suggests a possible shift from biological to social issues.

These changes have been accompanied by increased interest in older women and research about them on the part of legislators, market specialists, and others. However, lest we become complacent about research accomplishments, it is well to remember that old women continue to be a subject of little interest to many, including those who focus their research on women. For example, Henderson examined the extent to which psychologists specializing in the psychology of women study old women, or even include them in samples [5]. She found that

Table 4. A Comparison Between Tables 1 and 2
on Five Selected Subject Headings

Subject Heading	Up to 1961 Number and (Percent)	1962–77 Number and (Percent)
Longevity	51/138(37)	95/2200(4.3)
Geriatrics	0/506(0)	2/506(.4)
Hygiene	3/533(.56)	2/303(.6)
Economic problems	0/43(0)	90/2314(3.9)
Social Security	9/921(.98)	17/579(2.9)

Source: *Classified Bibliography of Gerontology and Geriatrics,* Volume 1 and Supplements 1 and 2.

women over fifty-five were more obvious by their absence in research in the psychology of women than by their presence. Gerontologists may have become increasingly involved in studying old women – psychologists apparently less so. Old women may constitute a statistical majority of the older population, but they continue to be an undersampled minority in some research.

The conference participants and the authors hope that the material in this book will stimulate further interest in research about old women. They hope, too, that the material will suggest important areas for research to some readers while convincing others of the need for additional support for research on older women, providing new ways of looking at traditional research problems, encouraging new work with existing research, and leading to greater inter-disciplinary research on issues related to the economic and health status of older women.

A number of people worked hard to bring the conference and this publication to fruition. Ethel Shanas and Carol Hollenshead provided invaluable guidance in planning and execution. Ginger Maggio and Julie Walton did the actual organizational legwork. Eloise Snyder and Jeanne Miller were responsible for editorial cleanup and Diane Voss and Peggy White for all clerical duties. Nancy Fultz located and screened the data sets. Grant support was received from the National Institute on Aging, and Marcia Ory gave advice, administrative and moral support as Project Officer. Finally, the conference participants themselves were central to the whole process. They are enumerated on a list in Appendix B along with their institutional affiliations as at the time of the conference.

REFERENCES

1. K. S. Markides, Minority Aging, in *Aging and Society: Selected Reviews of Recent Research*, M. W. Riley, B. B. Hess, and K. Bond (eds.), Lawrence Erlbaum, Hillsdale, New Jersey, 1983.
2. H. G. Robinson, Grandmothers Are Guinea Pigs, *Journal of Gerontology, 4*, pp. 245-247, 1949.
3. W. H. Lewis, Jr., Differences in the Rate and Trends of Mortality for Different Age and Sex Groups in Different Eras, *Journal of Gerontology, 8*, pp. 318-323, 1953.
4. M. M. Seltzer, The Quality of Research Is Strained, *The Gerontologist, 15*, pp. 503-507, 1975.
5. J. Henderson, The Representation of Older Women in "Psychology of Women" Research, Unpublished Senior Honors Thesis, Miami University, Oxford, Ohio, 1986.

ADDENDUM
Paul D. Phillips

Nathan Shock's *Classified Bibliography of Gerontology and Geriatrics* was used to determine the volume and types of research pertaining to older women and sex comparisons for the period up to and including 1961. The Shock

Bibliographies represent the most comprehensive compilation of research and writing in aging available; these bibliographies index hundreds of scholarly and academic journals in the physical and social sciences that are pertinent to gerontology and geriatrics. Particular attention was paid to general research in gerontology, health, life expectancy, geriatrics, economic status and problems, employment, and Social Security, as well as all appropriate subheadings. These subject areas encompass the general topics covered in this volume. The total number of titles in each subject area was calculated using the numerical system included in the Shock Bibliographies. Due to the volume of titles, it was not possible to separate articles and books written in English from those written in foreign languages, nor was it possible to translate the content of non-English entries. Therefore, the total number of titles in each subject area reflects *all* entries, a significant number of which are written in languages such as German, Spanish, French, etc. All articles, books, and documents originally appearing in English were examined to determine the volume and types of research and writing specifically about older women and sex comparisons. The total numbers and percentages of titles within each subject heading examined containing a specific reference to women, females, grandmothers, widows, etc., as well as titles referring to sex comparisons have been incorporated into the accompanying tables.

For the period 1962–1977, a title search was conducted using Shock's *Classified Bibliography of Gerontology and Geriatrics* appearing in each issue of the *Journal of Gerontology*. The classification system used in these quarterly updates was condensed to reflect the major subject headings used in the original *Classified Bibliography of Gerontology and Geriatrics* (1951) as well as Supplement One (1957) and Supplement Two (1963). For the period 1962–1977, all English titles under the following subject headings were examined: Gerontology, general orientation; Longevity (including case reports, drugs, heredity, occupation, and sex differences); Geriatrics, general orientation; Hygiene (physical and mental health); Economic problems (including employment, occupation, retirement and pensions); and Social Security. Again, all English titles containing specific references to older women and sex comparisons are included in the accompanying tables.

The Shock Bibliographies were discontinued in 1980. As a result, a computer search was conducted using "Ageline." Ageline is a powerful computer data base in gerontology, geriatrics, and related physical and social sciences which is made possible through the American Association of Retired Persons (AARP). Ageline provides instant access to hundreds of journals, books, and documents in the field of aging. An Ageline computer search was conducted to determine the total number and percentages of articles pertaining specifically to older women in selected subject headings for the period 1977–1987. In addition, the Ageline search was done in a manner that provided the total number of articles pertaining to older women in each subject heading, separating citations appearing before 1982 from those appearing after 1982. To the greatest degree possible, subject headings included in the Ageline computer search parallel subject headings examined in the Shock Bibliographies. Particular attention was given to research on older women and sex comparisons in the areas of health and economic conditions.

CHAPTER

2

Issues in the Study of Older Women: 1970 to 1985[1]

Lillian E. Troll

THE BEGINNING

At the beginning of the 1970s, a group of professional women met in Detroit one Saturday afternoon. Our agenda was to plan the next move in a campaign for achieving industry-supported daycare for children of employed mothers. We saw ourselves as an advanced guard in the service of women's needs. Originally, we had been drawn to each other by common interests in life-span development that led us to try to improve community services for young children, first, and older people, second. I don't know what precipitated it, but that Saturday afternoon as our talk turned to the problems of aging, we found ourselves turning to each other with something like astonishment. We too were growing old! Perhaps we were even old already. Our ages varied across the adult spectrum from the thirties to the fifties, but we discovered that we shared many concerns about our aging, about our aging as women. In these early years of the Women's Movement, when just discovering that we shared concerns as women, this was a heady experience. We were taking a giant step forward — or was it backward?

Following our recognition of ourselves as aging, we launched into a witty, perhaps counterphobic, discussion of ways in which we could make the process of becoming an older woman more pleasant than it seemed to us just then. As a matter of fact, we spent the remainder of that afternoon brainstorming ways to

---

[1] Keynote address, conference "Older Women: Research Issues and Data Sources," Ann Arbor, Michigan, April 13, 1984.

grow old pleasantly. Many of our suggestions sent us into giggles, but we were as serious as we were flippant, and underneath our flippancy was revealed our anxiety.

Several months after this meeting, Joan Israel, probably the most energetic and innovative of our group, came to me with a proposal for a conference on aging women. We agreed that the annual Michigan Gerontological meeting of the Institute of Gerontology, The University of Michigan would be the ideal organization to sponsor it. These annual meetings, originated in the mid-1950s by Wilma Donahue, rivaled the national meetings of the Gerontological Society of America for many years, drawing participants from all over the country. Our proposal was accepted, and Joan and I worked with a team from the Ann Arbor branch of the Institute and with Eva Kahana at Wayne State to organize the program for this 20th annual meeting of the Institute, in 1973. It was a great success! Somewhat to our surprise, the aging of women could be interesting: it did attract an audience.

The proceedings of this meeting were published by the Institute in 1975 under the title, *No longer young: The older woman in America.* Natalie Trager, a leading member of the Ann Arbor team, wrote the introduction, and there were abstracts of selected papers by Pauline Bart, Virginia Allan, Susan Sontag, Caroline Preston, Gordon Streib, Wilma Scott Heide, Harold Feldman, Isabel Burns Lindsay, Wilbur J. Cohen, Harold Sheppard, and Mary S. Calderone; I also had a paper there. The topics covered a range of issues in the status of older women at that time: emotional and social, economic and legal. We talked about the prevailing stereotypes that reflected a "double standard" of aging. We made suggestions for sociological and political mechanisms for change, and what resources women had available for making changes: consciousness raising, cognitive strategies, coping mechanisms, and governmental policies. We did not ignore finances. Nor did we neglect sex and emotions.

I don't believe any of us really planned to make a career out of older women, but Joan Israel came up with a new proposal about a year later; to publish a book on the topic. The unfortunate title of this book became *Looking ahead: A woman's guide to the problems and joys of growing older.* Our original title had been simply *Older women,* but the marketing people at the publisher insisted nobody would want to buy or read a book called *Older women.*

I edited this volume with Joan Israel and her husband, Kenneth, a psychiatrist. First we made an *a priori* list of the major issues in aging as applied to women at that time. I then turned to friends who were researchers in the field of gerontology for "state of the art" papers on these topics. Almost everybody I approached, incidentally, seemed enthusiastic about participating. That book appeared in 1977, and to my surprise, has remained in print for a decade. Although it has had virtually no direct publicity, it continues to sell at a slow pace by word of mouth, although it could very much profit from updating. As the area has gained insight, so too have new generations of investigators.

I should note that "hard" data are meager in that volume. It was very easy to review the accumulated research on older women ten years ago. Actually, our data are still not extensive today. As will be noted in the chapters to follow, inquiry has not been as extensive as we might have hoped.

In the process of editing that volume, the Israels and I made two general decisions. First, we defined "old," deliberately, as from the age of thirty on, believing that women in their thirties were already facing the problems and fears associated with growing older as a woman. This decision was reinforced by our editor at Prentice-Hall, who also wanted us to start at thirty; she was approaching that dreaded birthday herself and "knew all about it."

Our second decision was concerned with which issues to include. Up front, in both the Ann Arbor conference and in *Looking ahead*, was the topic of physical development. By physical development we did not mean, at that time, morbidity or mortality. We were more concerned with appearance, with loss of attractiveness and youthfulness. Mary Calderone's paper on sexuality had been of supreme interest to those who attended the Ann Arbor meeting. *Looking ahead* thus contains four chapters in a section in "The body," all written by women, incidentally: "More than wrinkles," by Ruth Weg, a physiologist; "Sex and the older woman" by Margaret Huyck; "Does youthfulness equal attractiveness" by Carol Nowak; and "Confessions of a 45-year old feminist" by Joan Israel, who discussed her dismay at the incipient changes in her appearance. A vivid underlining to these anxieties revealed by the women writers is the chapter entitled "Those endearing young charms: Fifty years later" by a man; Robert Kastenbaum (even though he co-authored it with Deborah Simonds). Kastenbaum made the point that old women cannot really be said to "have charm," that charm by definition can only be found in young women. We decided to place this essay in the final section of the book, labeled "Power."

Allied to concerns about the body are attitudes toward older women: age biases and age stereotypes. Susan Sontag, who had published her now classic "The double standard of aging" in the *Saturday Review* in 1972, had been our keynote speaker for the Ann Arbor conference. Her point was the prejudice that exists toward old women, but not toward old men. Old women are viewed negatively, old men often are viewed positively. Caroline Preston's paper, "An old bag: The stereotype of the older woman" deals with the same theme. Although it had not been presented at the Ann Arbor conference, it had been included in the proceedings, *No longer young*. In *Looking ahead,* I included my diatribe on age/sex prejudices, originally presented at a Detroit feminist symposium. This short essay, "Poor, dumb, and ugly" has been haunting me ever since. I dig it out of the file drawer every two or three years, amplify it, and deliver it again. What is curious is that each time it seems more relevant than the times before.

Next in salience to physical issues were economic ones. Virginia Allan, Deputy Assistant Secretary of State for Foreign Affairs, had given a paper on the economic and legal status of older women at the Ann Arbor meeting. Two chapters in *Looking ahead,* "Older women and jobs," and "The nitty-gritty of survival" attended to these issues, as did a third, "Older Black women." On the whole, though, economic matters received less attention than they might have at that time, given that the thrust of feminism in the early 1970s was on job and pay equality and on women returning to the economic scene, to schools and jobs. Later in the decade, more elaborate issues like displaced homemakers, equality of pensions, and inequality of retirement income claimed our consciousness. Why we were so sanguine about money ten years ago is not a trivial question, though. Was it because the members of our pioneering group were not welfare mothers? Was it because we took it so much for granted then that women would not earn as much as men, perhaps even should not earn as much as men? I know as a psychologist that even now effectiveness in dealing with money and finances comes much harder to women than does effectiveness in dealing with interpersonal concerns. Assertiveness training can help us stand up to a loss easier than it can help us ask for appropriate payment for services.

Other issues present in our thoughts ten years ago included love, both in its sense of feelings between people and in sex; pleasure, fun, leisure, recreation; helping and being helped. In general, we had less to say in these three general areas than we would now. We certainly said much less than we did in other areas.

What issues did we not attend to? One glaring omission is divorce. We dealt neither with its economic nor with its social consequences. In fact, we paid scant attention to any aspects of family relationships either in the Ann Arbor papers or in *Looking ahead.*

THE PRESENT

Whether or not the present can be considered a watershed year for interest in aging women in our society in general, it has been a "year of the old woman" in my own life. The conference out of which this book evolved is only one of half a dozen in which I have been asked to speak on this topic. In fact, I have been led to begin labeling myself as an "old woman."

Because I have had to focus my attention repeatedly on the topic, it has occurred to me to review the current status of the original issues.

Have any of the early 70s issues diminished in importance? Certainly not those related to appearance, to health and fitness, or to ageism. In spite of Glamorama ads and portraits of charming women aged fifty, the important part of being considered a beautiful (or still beautiful) older woman is to "look young." Full-page pictures of Gloria Steinem and other feminist icons who are now reaching the dreaded fifty (as distinguished from the earlier dreaded age of thirty or forty) attest to their not showing any of the signs of shame: no dry skin, no sagging muscles, no sallow coloring, no wrinkles.

Second, economic issues still plague aging women. While many of the "young old" are in the labor market, their income relative to men remains 59 or 60 cents to the dollar. While pensions are being adjusted in many cases to remove handicaps putatively based upon greater life expectancy, many women who are older now have earned less than men their age over their working years and have had less time to accumulate savings and equity by the time they retire. Women attached to men are much less likely to be included in the below-poverty-line category than those who are widowed, divorced, or never married.

Third, ageist attitudes may have been raised in our collective consciousness but it is still very easy to find their manifestations in media presentations or even in ordinary conversation. The spectre of the persona of the old woman is never very far from view and is trotted out at too regular an interval.

Studies of recreation or leisure are still largely as mechanical as the kinds of recreation available to most older American women. Bingo and other forms of gambling, preferably by machine, predominate. The possibilities for a richer life presented by the surge in higher education for older women, which we treated in two chapters in *Looking ahead,* "Lifelong learning" and "Education as recreation" seem to be decreasing rather than increasing — with the possible exception of elderhostels. Of course, there are more programs at the periphery of the educational establishment than in large university systems. Community colleges and adult education programs have either increased or remained vigorous, while adult students in major universities appear to have declined. Many of the women involved in educational programs *are* looking for enrichment, but it is my impression that more "older women" students — who are more likely to be in their thirties than in their sixties — are looking for speedy routes to corporate jobs rather than a more meaningful life.

Are there any issues that are new today? Yes, I think so, and these seem to be largely in the arena of social relationships. The problems of older women who are caregivers, as well as of those who need care, are receiving more and more attention. "Networking" (a deplorable term) has been increasing as a topic of research over the last few years. Mother–daughter relationships and grandparenting issues abound in the papers, the magazines, novels, radio, and TV. In 1972, more marriages were disrupted by divorce than by death, and the effects of these divorces — their "ripple effect," to use Gunhild Hagestad's term — on older women are notable. If visibility in the public arena is a criterion, the newsworthiness of displaced homemakers threatens to be displaced by grandparents' rights.

Perhaps the most important thing that has happened over the last decade, so far as older women's issues are concerned, is not a shift in the questions asked but rather an enlargement of the kinds and numbers of questions asked. The field, if it can be considered one yet, is becoming more sophisticated. We no longer are ready to assume that an older woman is an older woman is an older woman. This suggests that we are moving away from ageism and stereotype. We can begin to look at variability in all our measures. One chapter on black older women and one on Jewish grandmothers were included in *Looking ahead*, but now we may be ready to consider the much wider varieties of old women's styles and conditions, just in this country alone. Maybe we can even move beyond the level of descriptions of old women in their different ethnic groups, of Black old women, of Hispanic old women, of Italian old women, to more fundamental questions. Thus, what is it about the differences among old women of different ethnic groups that causes the variance we see? Our view of history is also broadening, and we can examine cultural changes as well as cross-cultural diversity. Finally, we can be alert to a need for a double comparison: older women compared with older men and older women compared with younger women.

LOOKING AHEAD

Have we come a long way in research and with reference to ageism and stereotyping of older women? We have moved, in the research arena, to research designs that can help us in answering the kinds of questions raised here. As anthropologists and humanists have entered the field of aging in increasing numbers, we are learning more about cultural diversity and cross-cultural comparisons in women's patterns of aging [3].

We have, however, not come as far in eliminating the double standard of aging, as we have in expanding our research competencies. Standards of beauty continue to be those of the young. Cosmetic ads for women promise to retard aging and eliminate its symptoms. Physicians advertise the availability of cosmetic surgery to remove wrinkles and bags from the faces and bodies of old women. There is seemingly no end to the things that can be fixed; as though they were broken in the first place.

To get back to the group of six women who met in Detroit in 1972, only three of us are now more than superficially involved in the concerns of older women. Nevertheless, the consciousness raising that went on that Saturday afternoon has, I believe, changed us all. But I'm afraid we are not a representative sample. I often find myself in the presence of women when they come to the startling conclusions that they are probably older women. I was struck by this recently in a workshop on older women in New York City. The subject being discussed was business success or opportunities for women in the corporate world. One young woman — she looked young, that is — in the group commented that she was an example of the new cohort of young women who were on the "fast track" in the corporate world. As she was enlarging upon her value for her company because she was a young, energetic, and skilled woman executive, she digressed for a moment to contrast her personality with that of her mother, whom she described as a typical feminine product of the 1950s.

Unlike her own dedication to achievement, her mother's whole life was absorbed in beauty and attractiveness and homemaking skills. Then our group member said, "When my mother was my age — forty-three — she had a face lift — oooh." She paused a full minute and then said, "This is the first time I have ever told anybody how old I am! " She covered her face with her hands, paused again, and said, "I said it! I told you how old I am! " Everybody in the room was silent for a long moment.

Will the time ever come when we can announce our age matter-of-factly? When we can say it without demurring that we are in good health, doing fine, and proud of who we are? When we can say it without fearing attack, without fearing that our listeners will immediately revise their opinion of us? When that time comes, we will truly be in a position to look ahead to the problems and joys of growing older.

REFERENCES

1. Conference on Aging, *No Longer Young: The Older Woman in America,* Proceedings of the 26th Annual Conference on Aging, Occasional Papers in Gerontology #11, Institute of Gerontology, The University of Michigan — Wayne State University, Ann Arbor, Michigan, 1975.
2. L. Troll, J. Israel, and K. Israel (eds.), *Looking Ahead: A Woman's Guide to the Problems and Joys of Growing Older,* Prentice-Hall, Englewood Cliffs, New Jersey, 1979.
3. J. K. Brown, Cross-Cultural Perspectives on Middle-Aged Women, *Current Anthropology, 23,* 1982.

CHAPTER
3

Feminism and Anti-ageism: Emergent Connections[1]

Shulamit Reinharz

The relationship between feminism and a social movement on behalf of older people has not yet been fully explored. When formulating new research questions and examining the assumptions underlying current research, gerontologists should consider this connection. Feminists too should consider this connection in order to refine feminist theory to include all age groups of women. Finally, scholars and activists interested in social movements can benefit from examining possible linkages between feminism and anti-ageism so as to understand processes of social change.

FEMINISM: DEFINITION AND BACKGROUND

The following statement by philosophers Alison Jaggar and Paula Rothenberg provides a straightforward definition of contemporary feminist concerns:

> Feminists are people who demonstrate a commitment to improving women's position in society. Feminist frameworks are systems of ideas, conceptual structures that feminists use in explaining, justifying, and guiding their actions. Typically, a feminist framework is a comprehensive

[1] Adaptation of keynote address, conference "Older Women: Research Issues and Data Sources," Ann Arbor, Michigan, April 13, 1984. I would like to thank the following people for helpful discussions or correspondence concerning this paper: Hortensia Amaro, Denise Connors, Connie Cutter, Paula Doress, Buffy Dunker, Olivia Espin, Karen Fields, Mickey Friedman, Janet Giele, Mary Gilfus, Ruth Jacobs, Kathy Kautzer, Brinton Lykes, Kathy MacPherson, Loraine Obler, Thelma Nason, Robbie Pfeuffer, Karl Pillemer, Paula Rayman, Annette Rickel, Morris Schwartz, Becky Thompson, and Mary Ann Wilner.

analysis of the nature and causes of women's oppression and a correlated set of proposals for ending it. It is an integrated theory of women's place both in contemporary society and in the new society that feminists are struggling to build [1, p. 17].

Given this scope, it should come as no surprise that feminism is not a homogeneous point of view, but rather consists of diverse, even conflicting perspectives. These perspectives are conventionally referred to as radical, liberal, socialist and Marxist [2]. Although for some purposes, it is important to highlight these differences, for the purpose of this discussion of emerging issues for older women, they will be set aside, and feminism will be defined as their sum.

It is also important to note that feminism is not as recent a vintage as may at first appear. It has been a persistent theme in American, and perhaps all, societies, although certain periods have been characterized by greater visibility than others [3]. The current upsurge of interest in America is usually dated to the publication of Betty Friedan's *The Feminine Mystique* in 1963, the subsequent establishment of the National Organization of Women (NOW) which works toward institutional change, and the proliferation of consciousness-raising groups which work toward personal change. Among writers and academics, the current wave has been characterized by an outpouring of research and theory-building which successively includes increasing numbers of social forces and social structures within feminist analyses. Currently, feminist theory attempts to incorporate the entire gamut of known inequities, although some are given more attention than others — sexism, racism, antisemitism, heterosexism, capitalism, elitism, beautyism, et cetera.

What is more recent is the attention being given to ageism, especially the types of ageism levelled at aging women. Since about 1970, each feminist framework mentioned above has been slowly developing a tentative perspective of aging [4-10]. These analyses are embedded not only in an explicit concern with processes of age but within a more complex framework that takes other inequities into account. From a feminist perspective, aging in America must be understood in conjunction with ageism, which in turn abets and is reproduced by diverse forms of sexism, racism, antisemitism, and the many other "isms" that beset us. In combination, these forces allow small social groups to achieve and retain power, wealth, and prestige, while other groups are blamed for their induced inability to possess these social rewards [11, 12].

GROUNDS FOR THE EMERGENCE
OF SOCIAL MOVEMENTS

It is my contention that a social movement to combat ageism will gradually emerge among women, drawing in part on the success and experience of the women's movement. My prediction is based on three facts: first, the historic continuity among social movements; second, the changing consciousness of movement leaders; and third, demographic phenomena.

Even a cursory glimpse at the succession of social movements illustrates that continuity is the general pattern rather than the exception. For example, in 19th century America there were clear and direct links between the abolitionist, temperance, and suffrage movements, whereas in the 1960s there were clear and direct links between the civil rights, black power, anti-Vietnam war, and women's liberation movements [13]. These connections were tangible, not hidden. On a basic level, the rhetoric and institutions of one movement provide a blueprint for the next. For example, at a meeting of women in radio and television in 1964, Muriel Fox, leader of the conference, slipped Betty Friedan a note: "If you ever start an N.A.A.C.P. for women, count me in" [14, p. 61]. Similarly, continuities can be seen currently between the women's movement and the peace or anti-nuclear movement, as has also occurred in the past, and between the women's movement and an anti-ageism movement.

Organizational membership and concerns serve to link one movement with another either by the delineation of specific issues which cross-cut the concerns of two movements, or by integrating the concerns of a second movement as a subtheme in an organization primarily concerned with a different movement. Examples of organizations with cross-cutting concerns are the Alliance for Displaced Homemakers (founded in 1972) and the Older Women's League (OWL, founded in 1980) started by women who had been coordinators of the Task Force on Older Women of the National Organization of Women (NOW). These organizations challenge the relevance of laws against age discrimination to protect older women seeking work and the ability of Social Security to protect the divorced, separated or widowed women who cannot find paid employment. Further examples include the creation of menopause collectives among women who want to understand and define their menopausal experiences, and older-women's consciousness raising groups such as "The Crones of Ottowa," a group of older women "in need of validation of their own worth as knowledgeable and wise women" [15, p. 203]. An example of the integration of women's concerns *into* an age-oriented activist organization is the Gray Panthers' ideology which incorporates feminism as a key component.

Second, there are continuities in personnel. As leaders and members of the feminist movement age, they become increasingly aware of inequities and contradictions concerning aging, and draw on their skills and experiences honed in the women's movement to conceptualize and act on this emergent issue. In the next section, I will offer some examples of increased age-consciousness among aging leaders of the women's movement.

Third, demographics play a role in generating social movements. Concommitant with the women's movement in the US has been an imbalanced sex ratio. As sociologist Laurel Richardson put it:

Demographically, there are simply not enough single men for all the single women. One out of every five females does not have a potential mate. Currently, 40% of American women are single. Due to the shortage of males, as well as to divorce, widowhood, and delayed marriage and remarriage, every woman is likely to be single for a substantial portion of her life [16, pp. 2–3].

When these conditions occurred in England, a women's movement arose there as well.

There were too many women in Britain, as her great days of power and wealth drew towards their close. . . . The fact that there was a large female majority in the population — 1,327,000 in 1911 — coloured the whole outlook of a girl from early childhood onwards. . . . Just over half the female population had a husband, just over a tenth had had one and lost him, through death or divorce. . . . But the really important change at the beginning of the twentieth century, which affected the majority of wives and transformed everyday married life, was the drop in family size. . . . The release from continual child-bearing and child-rearing was the starting-point of women's emancipation. . . . The early twentieth-century women had the time, and the health — and above all the spirit — to agitate for better conditions for themselves, for education, for careers and for the vote [17, pp. 9, 13, 15].

Because of the world-wide demographic transition based on a decreasing birthrate and an increasing survival rate, there is a well-documented and widely recognized increase both in the percentage of, and in the absolute numbers of older people. At the same time, with the shrinking of the family, particularly in industrialized nations, traditional family-based *roles* of the elderly are becoming less time consuming and less central. The energy of elderly people which may formerly have been expended in sheer survival needs and family roles is freed up for investment in societal concerns. Concomitant changes in labor force involvements spell equally germane changes. In a town nearby, there is a group of retired couples who meet regularly for the sole purpose of discussing what retirement is and what it means to them, a format strikingly reminiscent of women's consciousness raising groups. The future import of these and similar transitions, as far as developing an age-based group consciousness is concerned, has scarcely been acknowledged to date.

AGE-CONSCIOUSNESS AMONG FEMINIST LEADERS

In 1949, Simone de Beauvoir published *The Second Sex*. Twenty-one years later, she published a book similar in style and structure, *Old Age*. In her introduction to this study, she makes use, in reference to the old, of her famous concept developed previously in reference to women — the other. She also proclaims a similar remedy to the inequities of "the other's" existence:

> There is only one solution if old age is not to be an absurd parody of our former life, and that is to go on pursuing ends that give our existence a meaning — devotion to individuals, to groups or to causes, social or political, intellectual or creative work. . . . One's life has value so long as one attributes value to the life of others, by means of love, friendship, indignation, compassion [6, p. 601].

Continuities between feminist and anti-ageist consciousness are striking in de Beauvoir's case.

As her fiftieth birthday approached in 1971, Betty Friedan was frightened as she wrote in her diary.

> The fact is, that week I will have my fiftieth birthday, which, I'm ashamed to admit, I dread. I can't seem to come to terms with it. Me, who's never worried about age or tried to hide it; me, who's been so scornful of women who dye their hair, have their faces lifted, let themselves be hoodwinked by advertisers into buying all those products supposed to make them look forever fifteen [14, p. 19].

But by the end of the actual day, she had come to a new realization.

> For me, I guess, women's liberation is only a way station to human liberation: embracing all we are, human body, spirit, mind, is finally the same, woman and man. This is the road I think the young are heading down. On this road, maybe there isn't a generation gap, or even fear and envy between young and old. . . .
> I have gotten over my fiftieth birthday. I'm fifty on this magic day in this age of Aquarius. I'm my age and I feel glorious. What's the point of making it if you can't celebrate being fifty? . . . my body, as it is, is me. I celebrate using it all, finally — my passions of sex and spirit, my guts and vulnerability and glee for life. . . . I have no dread now of what opens ahead [14, pp. 200–201].

Betty Friedan has gone on to pursue gerontological research, writing, and teaching.

Gloria Steinem is now writing that developing a positive attitude towards one's aging as a woman stems not only from the availability of powerful concepts and critical examination, but also from identifying with other aging women.

> A cheerful, seventyish woman with short white curls held back by an orange ribbon, wearing a satiny green leotard that hugs her gently protruding stomach like a second skin. From her, I learn the beauteous curve of a nonflat stomach. I also learn that a great-grandmother can touch her toes with more flexibility than I, and can leave me panting in an aerobic-dance class [18, p. 163].

Gloria Steinem has demonstrated that identification both in her analysis that contemporary "women become more radical as they age," in contrast with men who become more conservative as they age, and also in her insight that this same pattern existed in the past.

> In this country ... the nineteenth-century wave of feminism was started by *older women* who had been through the radicalizing experience of getting married and becoming the legal chattel of their husbands (or the equally radicalizing experience of not getting married and being treated as spinsters). Most of them had also worked in the antislavery movement and learned from the political parallels between race and sex [18, p. 215]. (emphasis added)

Steinem might have found another illustration in black, "middle-aged, bespectacled" Rosa Parks who refused to give up her seat on a Montgomery, Alabama bus to a white man, thereby sparking the modern civil rights movement [14].

BARRIERS TO THE LINKAGE

The links I have sketched above, though vibrant, are also limited. While social movements have always evolved out of each other, they also compete and carefully guard their resources against dilution. They can induce a single-minded concentration that blocks the concerns of other groups. Thus, Laura Olson writes:

> No one ... really has much knowledge of women over 65 and even feminists have, so far, given very little attention to our elder sisters. How many of us, for example, even know that the author of *The Second Sex* has written a second and equally important study, published under the title *Old Age*? [8, p. 201]

Disregard for theory development concerning age is considered by some to be a specific weakness of feminist scholarship [19–21]. Moreover, because of the strength of youth-worship in our society, feminists too suffer from age-phobia and can be expected to have difficulties accepting their own aging. The very development of feminist consciousness among some women stems from a rejection of the world of their mothers. Conversely, some older feminists are now expressing anger toward younger women, including young feminists who forget and neglect their elders [22].

While these tensions and barriers undoubtedly exist, there is no ideology to support them. Statements such as the following written in the context of Black-White relations are equally applicable to the issue of age:

> We need to do more research and writing about the barriers that separate us and the ways we can overcome such separation. ... To build a mass-based feminist movement, we need to have a liberatory ideology that can be shared with everyone [23, p. 161].

In this sense the goals of feminism, while possibly insufficiently attentive at present to the concerns, needs, and experiences of older women, are moving increasingly in that direction, and are completely open to that possibility. Given that this movement exists, it seems vital for gerontologists as researchers and advocates not to close themselves off to their feminist partners who share the same goals but who may use alternate means to achieve them. For just as academic research has played a vital role in sustaining the feminist movement, so too has it already begun to play a role in the emergent anti-ageism movement [24].

IMPLICATIONS FOR RESEARCH

Although feminism has certainly challenged our stereotypes and assumptions about the nature of women, how much has the direction of research really been altered? What has been the impact on specific hypotheses being investigated today? The introductory chapter in this volume by Seltzer and Hendricks takes an initial look at the change in the specific topics on older women that are being addressed. But their analysis must remain rather crude because of the very general categories of research topics that they can cull from the bibliographies they work with. Much work remains to describe change and lack thereof in research on older women.

And how about public attitudes toward older women? How much have they changed during the last decade? Is the American public aware of the growing numbers of older people in this and other societies? And are they cognizant of the predominance of female members in this age group? Related to this are some hotly debated issues of public policy. Who should take care of older women? How should this work be rewarded? Should we strive for economic equality among the elderly? How are resources to be distributed between various deserving age groups such as aged and children? Should eligibility for welfare programs be determined on the basis of age or need? We know very little about the awareness and the attitudes towards such issues. Furthermore, have such attitudes changed over time, and are they responsive to social movements?

Another topic worthy of research attention is whether the self-understanding of older women has changed as a function of the changing demographic characteristics of the population and the changing social climate. We do not know whether older women now perceive more options, or feel better about themselves.

The process and method of social change on behalf of older women needs to be examined. Theory and method for such research were developed and sharpened when the feminist movement, the civil rights movement, and the aging movement were studied. What can be deduced and utilized from that body of research to learn about the struggle of older women?

Many other research topics could be mentioned, and the chapters in this volume contain a multitude of additional suggestions. It is important, though, to realize that knowledge produced by research needs to be implemented. The political process and social movements are means to implement such change. We need to speak out with older women, talking about plight as well as about strength. We need to take our direction from our constituents while providing the information they need. Most of all, we need to join forces with all the other groups who share this concern.

REFERENCES

1. A. Jaggar and P. Rothenberg, *Feminist Frameworks*, McGraw Hill, New York, 1984.
2. S. Cox, *Female Psychology*, Science Research Associates, Palo Alto, California, 1976.
3. M. Schneir (ed.), *Feminism: The Essential Historical Writings*, Vintage Books, New York, 1972.
4. P. Bart, The Loneliness of the Long-Distance Mother, in *Women: A Feminist Perspective*, J. Freeman (ed.), Mayfield, Palo Alto, California, 1979.
5. I. P. Bell, The Double Standard: Age, in *Women: A Feminist Perspective*, J. Freeman (ed.), Mayfield, Palo Alto, California, 1979.
6. S. deBeauvoir, *Old Age*, Penguin, New York, 1970.
7. R. Jacobs, *Life After Forty: Female, Forty – What Next?*, Beacon Press, Boston, Massachusetts, 1979.
8. L. K. Olson, *The Political Economy of Aging: The State, Private Power and Social Welfare*, Columbia University Press, New York, 1982.
9. L. Rubin, *Women of a Certain Age*, Harper and Row, New York, 1979.
10. S. Sontag, The Double Standard of Aging, *Saturday Review*, *55*, pp. 29–38, September, 1972.
11. W. Ryan, *Blaming the Victim*, Vintage Books, New York, 1976.
12. J. Levin and W. Levin, *Ageism*, Wadsworth Publishing Company, Belmont, California, 1980.
13. S. Evans, *Personal Politics*, Random House, New York, 1979.
14. B. Friedan, *It Changed My Life*, Random House, New York, 1976.
15. E. Nett, Women as Elders, *Resources for Feminist Research, 11*: 2, 1982.
16. L. Richardson, *The New Other Women*, Free Press, New York, 1985.
17. R. Adam, *A Woman's Place*, Norton, New York, 1975.
18. G. Steinem, *Outrageous Acts and Everyday Rebellions*, New American Library, New York.
19. M. I. Lewis and R. N. Butler, Why Is Women's Lib Ignoring Old Women? *Aging and Human Development, 3*, pp. 223–231, 1972.
20. N. Datan, The Lost Cause: The Aging Woman in American Feminism, in *Towards the Second Decade*, R. Pore and B. Justice (eds.), Greenwood Press, Westport, Connecticut, 1981.

21. M. M. Fuller and C. A. Martin, *The Older Woman: Lavendar Rose or Gray Panther*, Charles C. Thomas, Springfield, Illinois, 1980.
22. B. MacDonald and C. Rich, *Look Me in the Eye*, Spinsters Ink, San Francisco, 1984.
23. B. Hooks, *Feminist Theory: From Margin to Center*, South End Press, Boston, Massachusetts, 1984.
24. S. Reinharz, Friends or Foes: Gerontological and Feminist Theory, *Women's Studies International Forum, 9*:5, 503–514, 1986.

PART TWO
Economic and Health Issues

CHAPTER 1

Physical and Mental Health in Older Women: Selected Research Issues and Data Sources[1]

A. Regula Herzog

INTRODUCTION

Health represents one of the major nonmaterial resources influencing an individual's quality of life and enabling a person to contribute to his or her own welfare and that of others. Although health problems can have equally debilitating effects among the young, health status increases in importance with age because of the greater likelihood of health problems at this stage of life. People over sixty-five are more likely than younger persons to report activity limitations due to health and physical conditions [1]. About 85 percent report at least one chronic condition [2]; and many consider poor health to be one of their biggest problems [3]. Despite the relative frequency of reported health problems among the elderly, however, most older persons are capable of carrying on their normal daily routines and very few are unable to perform basic physical care activities [4].

The significance of health in older age has implications on many levels. On the individual level — as demonstrated by many studies — it is essential to the

[1] The author would like to thank all the participants of the conference for their invaluable intellectual contribution and Nancy Fultz, Linda George, James House, Jersey Liang, Marcia Ory, William Rakowski, and Lois Verbrugge for critical reading of earlier drafts of this chapter. Special thanks are due to Ethel Shanas who led the workshop in health during the conference. Of course, all remaining errors are the author's responsibility. The writing of this paper was supported by Grant R13 AG03458 from the National Institute on Aging and part of a sabbatical leave.

understanding of morale, ability to function, productivity, economic status, and overall quality of life of the aged. From a societal perspective, it is important to monitor the health status of the aged population as a national resource or liability, and to assess changes in health status over time. Some have argued that future cohorts will be healthier than present ones, resulting in an older population that is less dependent on social welfare and contributes more. Others, of course, have argued that the recent increase in longevity in the United States might result in greater numbers of frail older adults. Thus, from a social policy perspective, an understanding of the extent and form of health problems among the aged, and how increasing longevity affects health status, is critical in planning health service delivery systems and dealing with their economic ramifications.

Older women's and men's physical and mental health differ in significant ways. Epidemiological studies suggest that older men are more likely than older women to report life-threatening diseases such as heart disease, cardiovascular problems and malignant neoplasms [5]. At any age, men's mortality rates are higher than those of women. As a consequence, a sixty-five-year-old man can expect about four fewer years of life on average than can a woman of the same age [4]. On the other hand, older women report higher rates of non-life-threatening illnesses and symptoms, of impairments in physical activity, mobility, or personal care activities [5, 6]. Finally, older women show higher rates of depression [7]. In sum, it appears that older women are more likely to be impaired by their health problems, while older men are more likely to die from them. These rather remarkable health differences between women and men beg for explanations, explanations that will not only illuminate existing sex differences, but contribute to our understanding of what causes good and bad health in general. Health policies might also be different for women and men, promoting life prolongation for men and improving the quality of life for women.

This chapter selectively reviews the physical and mental health of older women in the United States. It identifies existing knowledge gaps within this context, and suggests further research. Specific health topics covered are mortality, global physical health, chronic illness conditions, reproductive functioning, subjective well-being and mental health, health in a life-span perspective, and utilization of health care. Wherever possible, older women will be compared with older men, and sex differences at older ages will be contrasted with sex differences earlier in life. Possible explanations for observed sex differences and age-related variations in these, including work, social relationships, stress, coping, and health behaviors will then be discussed, and issues for further research outlined. The chapter will focus on directions for further research rather than on comprehensive literature reviews. References to data sources relevant for future research are added to each section. More detailed information on the cited data sources may be obtained from Appendix A.

A terminological detail is worth pointing out. Throughout this chapter the term "sex" will be used to denote differences between women and men, without implications as to the nature of the causes — biological or social — of these differences.

CONCEPTUALIZATIONS OF HEALTH

At present, conceptualizations of physical health employed by epidemiological and social researchers take several different approaches that capture various aspects of health and, as noted by Kasl and Berkman, may measure factors other than physical health [8]. The approaches include 1) acute and chronic illness conditions, 2) levels of functional impairment and disability, 3) self-rated health, 4) utilization of health care services, and 5) age at death, and cause of death as reported on death certificates.

Liang, using reports from about 4,000 older persons on chronic illness conditions, functional impairment, and self-rated health, found that the three dimensions were positively but not highly related to each other after measurement error was controlled [9]. Liang's findings confirm the notion that these different conceptualizations of physical health capture different aspects, and must not be viewed as equivalent measures.

These conceptualizations of physical health also yield varying sex differences, as we shall see below. And findings on the effects of health on economic variables vary depending on the specific conceptualization of health used. Such observations reinforce the impression that the different dimensions of health are distinct; and they suggest that future research must pay close attention to what the different conceptualizations do and do not represent, how they relate to one another, how they relate to other concepts of interest, and how they differ by sex.

A similar pattern emerges for the conceptualization of mental health and subjective well-being. Different conceptualizations show varying sex differences, explicated in more detail below. The major approaches to be discussed include 1) depressive disorders and symptoms, 2) suicide, 3) subjective well-being, and 4) cognitive impairment.

Two other limitations of these conceptualizations of physical and mental health should be noted. First, they focus on a global, relatively stable concept of health as indicated by specific health problems or general health assessments, but fail to capture day-to-day, often ill-defined, health problems. Less well-defined problems like feelings of pain and weakness may in fact dominate the health picture among the elderly, and they deserve more attention by researchers [10]. Second, except for the concept of subjective well-being these conceptualizations focus on negative aspects of health — illness conditions, symptoms, or disabilities. Although positive health has become a key concept, health research focuses primarily on what makes people sick, and often fails to differentiate among the relatively healthy [11]. Future research should pay more attention to what accounts for vigor, energy, and a high level of functioning among older men and women, and how those qualities vary across the life span. Many older women and men are in good physical and mental health, and it would be very useful to learn how they survive so well, and what life is like for them.

MORTALITY

One of the greatest health differences between women and men lies in their respective longevity. Women in the United States live on the average about seven years longer than men. This difference has been widening in this century but may have stabilized in the past few years [12, 13]. At any age, men are at greater risk of dying than are women, although the extent of the sex difference and the causes of death vary considerably across age groups [13, 14]. Men are also more likely than women to have serious health problems, including three of the four leading causes of death — diseases of the heart, malignant neoplasms, and injuries [6]. However, when women do eventually die, they die primarily of the same conditions as men (i.e., heart disease, cancer, and stroke) [5]. Also, Blacks are at greater risk of dying at any age, except after age seventy-five when their life expectancy is greater than that of whites [15]. It would seem that the risk factors for mortality and for morbidity from those serious conditions are best examined together, not separately as is often the case.

Much has been said about factors affecting longevity and serious illness. Yet we lack a clear understanding of what accounts for the observed sex differences, and, even on the most general level, the discussion continues about whether biological or sociocultural factors provide more powerful explanations. The importance of sociocultural factors is suggested by the variability of sex differences across different time periods and cultures. The importance of biological factors is suggested by the presence of sex differences in all countries where death from childbirth has been nearly eliminated, and even in many animal species. Unfortunately, investigations seem to focus on either biological or sociocultural factors, depending largely on the disciplinary background of the investigator. The full truth may well be found in combinations of or interactions between biological and sociocultural variables. An example is the interaction between hormone levels and smoking (i.e., risk of death from myocardial infarction is increased disproportionately among women who smoke and take contraceptive hormone supplements). The explanation of the mortality differential seems therefore to be an issue for multidisciplinary research.

Moreover, as noted recently by Nathanson, although many sociocultural and biological variables have been implicated in these sex differences, the literature has barely started to address the significance of such factors in a multivariate, vigorous fashion [16]. This failure may be based, at least in part, on the lack of individual-level data containing measures of all the relevant factors. Specific factors that have been suggested in explanations of sex differences include life style variations such as cigarette smoking, alcohol consumption, injuries experienced on the job and in the automobile, violent and aggressive behaviors, Type A behavior, employment and stress resulting from such employment, marital status, and parenthood. Other sociocultural factors that have been implicated are so-called positive health behaviors such as the utilization of health care services and preventive measures. Biological differences (some of which may be affected by sociocultural factors), such as chromosomal patterns, hormonal and immunological factors, and physiological processes have also been stressed in explanations of sex differences in life expectancy. Reviews of this literature include those of Hazzard; McGill et al.; Nathanson; the U.S. Department of Health and Human Services; Purtilo and Sullivan; and Waldron [16-21].

In an attempt to organize the various sociocultural and behavioral factors, Nathanson advances the interesting hypothesis that women are generally more likely than men to adopt behaviors beneficial to their health, such as preventive health examinations, dental visits, and immunizations; and are less likely to engage in high-risk behaviors such as smoking, drinking, driving, and illegal drug use. She goes on to argue that "for all causes of death where individual risk-taking behavior is clearly involved, rates for men are from two to four times higher than the comparable rates for women" [22, pp. 145-146].

Some other factors found to affect longevity — such as disability, physical exercise, rest, obesity, and satisfaction or happiness — have not been utilized in discussing possible explanations for the mortality differential, because statistics indicate that sex differences are either nonexistent on those factors or are in the opposite direction to the observed mortality differential. If those factors were to change (e.g., if women were to catch up with men on the amount of exercise they get and on how well they control their weight), this might further widen the sex differential in mortality.

Most likely, the explanation of the sex differential lies in a combination of factors rather than in one single factor; and as sex differences on any factor change, the mortality differential may either widen or narrow. Therefore it seems important to consider all factors that have been found to affect longevity when attempting to explain the sex differential in mortality, and particularly its variability across cultures and across time periods. An investigation by Wingard underscores this suggestion [23]. She used a set of sixteen risk factors to explain sex differences in mortality over a nine-year period in the *Alameda County Study* statistically. Some of the risk factors, like smoking and alcohol consumption, disadvantaged men; others, like physical activity and physical health status, disadvantaged women. The joint adjustment for these risk factors did not reduce the mortality differential between the sexes.

We also need to know whether the so-called risk factors have the same effect on women's and men's longevity. For example, there is a suggestion that cigarette smoking may have less impact on the morbidity and mortality of women [24, 25]. If this pattern can be replicated for different factors, then explanation of sex differences may lie in different impacts of factors on men's and women's longevity, rather than in different levels of these.

To complicate the issue even further, there are a few suggestions in the literature that mortality before the age of seventy — sometimes called premature mortality — may be related to a different set of predictors than mortality after seventy [8, 24–26]. After age sixty-five, for example, unlike at earlier ages, cigarette smoking may have little impact on men's cardiovascular disease — one of the leading causes of death [25]. But these suggestions are few, and they are not entirely consistent, since Kasl and Berkman show that a combined index of health behaviors (which includes smoking) measured in the *Alameda County Study* is related to mortality among both older and younger persons. Kasl and Berkman provide further discussion of the risk factors of mortality at various age levels [8], but much more work needs to be done addressing mortality differentials among the elderly.

Data — Several major prospective studies are suited to addressing some of these research issues, because they include measures of some relevant predictors implicated in mortality and serious health conditions, as well as mortality and morbidity information. These studies include the *Baltimore Longitudinal Study of Aging*, the *Alameda County Study*, the *Framingham Heart Study*, the *Rancho Bernardo Study*, the *Duke Second Longitudinal Study*, the *Tecumseh Community Health Study*, and the *Massachusetts Health Care Panel Study*. Only the *Duke Second Longitudinal Study* is released for public use. Access to information from the other surveys must be discussed with the principal investigators. More detailed information on these and other data sources is provided in Appendix A.

GLOBAL PHYSICAL HEALTH

Self-Rated Health

Measures of self-rated health ("How would you rate your health at the present time?") represent some of the most widely used global health measures in social and epidemiological studies in gerontology. Self-rated health relates to some of the critical health outcomes such as subjective well-being [27, 28], and to mortality [29], relationships that may be stronger than the relationships between more objective health measures and these outcomes [27–30]. This is possibly the case because self-rated health reflects objective health status as well as personality characteristics, for example neuroticism [31], denial, or hypochondriasis [32].

Unlike some of the other health measures to be discussed below, older men and women appear to rate their health similarly ([4,5], but see [33] for males reporting worse health). However, there is some evidence that women's self-rated health may be more predictive of their longevity [34] and of their subjective well-being [31] than men's health ratings. These findings suggest that women are better judges of their health than men, a suggestion that deserves more concentrated research efforts.

Data — Measures of self-rated health are included in too many surveys to list them singly; these measures represent probably the most frequently used measure of overall health, particularly in studies that are not primarily focused on health, but need a brief health measure. Examples of some of the data sets listed in the Appendix that contain such a measure are: the *Aging in Manitoba* study; the *Duke Second Longitudinal Study*; some of the *Establishment of Populations for Epidemiologic Studies of the Elderly* (or *EPESE*) studies; the *National Senior Citizen Survey*; the *National Survey of the Aged*; the *Americans View Their Mental Health*; the *Health Interview Survey* (*NHIS*); and the *Retirement History Longitudinal Survey*.

Functional Health and Impairment

Measurements of functional impairment and disability provide operationalizations of health also well suited to assessing overall health status. Thus these measures lend themselves well to gauging the level of health or the degree of impairment in the overall population and to capturing the impact of health on daily functioning, and on quality of life.

Traditional indicators of health impairment include self-reported limitations in activities and major roles due to health conditions, and the number of days spent in bed due to health conditions. Such measures are used in many health surveys, for example the *Health Interview Survey* (*NHIS*), but they are difficult to interpret. People who report being restricted for many days, or spending many days in bed may do so either because they are indeed impaired, or because they are taking care of themselves. Somewhat less ambiguous measures of impairment are measures of the ability to carry out various functions, and dependency on the help of others for carrying these out. Two types of function are generally distinguished. Physical functions (often referred to as Activities of Daily Living, or ADL) include tasks of personal care such as dressing, bathing, grooming, using the toilet, feeding and sometimes mobility. Typical measures include the Katz Index of ADL [35] or the Physical ADL measure in the Older Americans Resources and Services (*OARS*) instrument [36]. Instrumental functions (often referred to as Instrumental Activities of Daily Living, or IADL) include shopping, cooking meals, managing money, or doing housework. Examples include the Philadelphia Geriatric Center (PGC) Instrumental Activities of Daily Living Scale [37] and the Instrumental ADL in the *OARS* instrument [36]. While the former set of functions can usually be carried out by all independent community-dwelling residents, and is more suitable for differentiating persons in long-term care institutions, or pinpointing the need for institutionalization among community-dwelling older adults, the latter functions usually show some variations among elderly living in the community, and thus are suitable for assessing the level of functioning there. (For a comprehensive discussion of the two types of measures and descriptions of many existing scales, see [38]).

On several traditional indicators of impairment, such as the number of days of restricted activity due to health conditions or the number of days spent in bed due to health conditions, older women report higher levels of disability than older men [1]. Whether these differences reflect certain chronic conditions that are more likely to be symptomatic, or a greater propensity among women to take care of themselves, is not known, according to Verbrugge [5].

On measures of physical function, older women report higher rates of impairment than older men [5, 39-41] and black older women report the worst impairment of all [41]. On measures of instrumental functions, the sex differences are apparently not consistent, but little relevant information appears to be published [42, 43]. What accounts for this greater impairment of physical functions among older women? Is it their higher level of chronic symptomatic conditions? Is it their specific conditions, such as musculoskeletal problems, which are most likely of all conditions to affect physical functioning, or the severity of their conditions [5]? Or is it the way women experience and/or evaluate their functional capabilities?

Age and sex comparisons on measures of functional health are problematic. In terms of sex comparisons, many IADL measures include mostly tasks that are traditionally performed by women, and on which women may score as more competent than men for this very reason [37]. In terms of age comparisons, limitations in performances in major life roles such as limitations to work are not appropriate for most older adults who have ceased to work or to perform other measurable life roles, making the measures of ADL and IADL more appropriate for this age group. Thus, commonly used measures are not necessarily equivalent across age levels.

A comprehensive review of existing functional health measures has recently been completed by Stewart, Ware, Brook, and Davis-Avery, and, based on this review, measures in terms of functioning were developed for the *Rand Health Insurance Experiment* that might be applicable for the entire age range [39]. These measures contain components of physical limitations, mobility limitations, self-care limitations, role limitations, and general limitations.

Data — Many studies of elderly adults contain measures of physical functioning; somewhat fewer studies contain measures of instrumental functioning. Physical functioning measures are included, for example, in the *National Survey of the Aged*; in the *National Senior Citizen Survey*; in the *Aging in Manitoba* study; in all the surveys that use the *OARS* instrument, such as, for example, the *Study of Well-Being of Older People in Cleveland* and the *Survey of Older People in Virginia*; in the *Aging Supplement* to the *NHIS*; in the *Massachusetts Health Care Panel Study*; and in the *EPESE* studies. Most of these studies interviewed large numbers of older adults on a comprehensive range of social-gerontological concepts such as activities, mental health, physical health, utilization of health and social services, and personality and sociodemographic characteristics, all of which may be used in further analyses of functional health. Instrumental functions are measured in the *National Survey of the Aged*; in the *National Senior Citizen Survey*; in all the studies that use the *OARS* instrument; in the *Massachusetts Health Care Panel Study*; in some of the *EPESE* studies; and in the *Aging Supplement* to the *NHIS*.

Measures of bed days due to health problems or restricted activity days are included in some of the *EPESE* studies; in the *NHIS* and its *Aging Supplement*; in the *Health and Nutrition Examination Survey* (*NHANES*); and in the *National Survey of Senior Citizens*.

CHRONIC ILLNESS CONDITIONS

Chronic illness conditions are more frequent among older than among younger persons. About 85 percent of persons over sixty-five report at least one chronic condition [2]. The five most common are arthritis, hypertension, diabetes, bronchitis or emphysema, and allergies [5]. Arthritis and hypertension are reported more frequently by older women than by older men, as are diabetes and allergies. Some less frequent conditions are also higher among older women; these include, among others, urinary incontinence and osteoporosis. Summing up all chronic conditions, Nathanson and Lorenz suggest somewhat lower rates of chronic conditions among older women than older men [44], while Verbrugge concludes that older women report higher rates of chronic conditions than do older men [5]. The latter author further specifies that the chronic conditions of older women are more often symptomatic but seldom fatal, while those of older men, although fewer in number, are more often fatal.

Several measures that probe the presence of specific chronic conditions exist. Measurement of conditions is problematic, because unlike functional health measures which the respondent can answer based on his or her own experiences, valid measures of chronic conditions require accurate diagnosis by a physician, the communication of that diagnosis to the patient, the patient's understanding of the diagnosis, and the patient's correct recall of the diagnosis at the time of the interview. The information on chronic illness conditions has further drawbacks for the assessment of overall health status, because it is difficult to aggregate that information into a global assessment of health, as the level of severity varies considerably across and within conditions.

Particular difficulties in using these (and other) health data for the examination of sex differences are that they are usually based on personal reports in surveys (rather than medical examinations), that they are more often collected from women who serve as "reporters" for all family members than from men, and that they are sometimes defined in terms of actions such as seeking of health care or reducing role involvement and activity level. At present it is not established to what extent observed sex differences in health are due to differences in these forms of reporting.

A difficulty in understanding health among the elderly is that most official health statistics report prevalence and incidence for specific illness conditions and research efforts focus on the etiology, treatment, and effects of specific diseases. Yet the older person's daily health picture undoubtedly consists of combinations of illness conditions [45]. Little systematic information is available about the multiplicity of illness conditions experienced in older age and how they may interact.

Data — Many data sets on older adults contain measures of various self-reported illness conditions. Most of these measures are in the form of a checklist or a series of questions. Sometimes open-ended questions are used. Data sets include, for example, all the studies that utilize the *OARS* instrument such as the *Study of the Well-Being of Older People in Cleveland* or the *Survey of Older People in Virginia*, the *National Senior Citizen Survey*, all the *EPESE* studies, the *Aging Supplement* of the *NHIS*, and the *Aging in Manitoba* study. The large health surveys sponsored by the National Center for Health Statistics — the *NHIS* and the *NHANES* — also contain information on specific self-reported illness conditions. Although the latter surveys sample the entire population, they are sufficiently large to permit separate analyses of older subgroups and, of course, they permit cross-sectional age comparisons.

Several of these surveys are longitudinal, including the *Duke Second Longitudinal Study*, the *Study of the Well-Being of Older People in Cleveland*, and the *EPESE* studies. Longitudinal studies permit a more appropriate investigation of causes and consequences of certain illness conditions, although the period over which they extend may not be long enough to capture all precursors of chronic conditions.

We now turn to a more thorough discussion of research issues related to a few of the specific illness conditions that are more prevalent among older women than older men: arthritis, osteoporosis, and urinary incontinence.

Arthritis

Arthritis is one of the most painful and disabling chronic conditions, and must therefore have a negative impact on the quality of life of the older person with arthritis [5, 46, 47]. Among the elderly, the characteristic pain, stiffness, and swelling in joints may affect the ability of the afflicted person to walk, climb stairs, bend, lift, reach over the head, or to control fine motor coordination. These physical disabilities, in turn, are related to the more complex abilities to move about in one's home and neighborhood, to live independently, and to carry out one's work and social obligations. Ehrlich points out how critical environmental and societal characteristics such as proper architectural design, occupational adjustments, and eligibility rules for assistance programs and the like, are in integrating persons with arthritis into society and preventing their social disability [47].

There are several types of arthritis, which differ in their etiology and symptomatology [48]. Among them, the most common are: osteoarthritis, a degenerative joint disease that is clearly associated with aging but need not be symptomatic, and rheumatoid arthritis, a chronic, inflammatory joint disease that can appear at any age, and produces the more serious effects. Arthritis — most likely largely in the form of osteoarthritis — is one of the most common illness conditions reported by older Americans, with older women reporting the condition more frequently than older men [5]. That the sex difference is a real one and not an artifact of reporting style and symptom recognition (to be discussed below) is indicated by Davis in a study of the relationship between self-reports of osteoarthritic symptoms and radiographic evidence of osteoarthrosis in a large sample of adults twenty-five through seventy-four years of age [49].

The etiology of arthritis is not well understood, although biological and environmental factors have been implicated. Thus, whether the higher prevalence among women is caused by their biology, the specific stresses that they experience, or an interaction between those two sets of factors is not known. Understanding the sex differences in arthritis and potential prevention, treatment, management and societal reactions to it should be of high priority for the investigation of this major illness of the elderly female.

Data — The data from the *Aging Supplement* of the *NHIS*, from studies using the *OARS* instrument, and from the *Duke Second Longitudinal Study* may be particularly useful for examining the effects of arthritis, because, in addition to a rather extensive assessment of health and social-behavioral concepts, these data sets also contain a measure of self-reported arthritis. The *Massachusetts Health Care Panel Study* is another good data base for investigating the effect of arthritis, since this data set contains self-report as well as observational measures of arthritic symptoms along with measures of other relevant concepts. Moreover, this study and some of the studies using the *OARS* are longitudinal in design and therefore particularly well suited for establishing the direction of causal relationships. The *NHANES* also contains self-reports of arthritic symptoms together with radiographic evidence. Finally, a data base sponsored by the American Rheumatism Association Medical Information System (*ARAMIS*) should be mentioned here.[2] It provides detailed longitudinal patient information,

---

[2] Note that this data base is not included in the Appendix.

collected systematically at various sites and controlled for quality. The medical information in this data set has recently been complemented by social-behavioral information. (For more information on *ARAMIS* refer to Fries [50].)

Osteoporosis

Osteoporotic bones break more easily; thus osteoporosis — loss of bone mass — contributes significantly to the incidence of bone fractures among the elderly. Fractures and, in particular, hip fractures are felt to be a significant cause of mortality, institutionalization, and mental deterioration among the elderly, since they may require lengthy periods of bed rest, immobility, and lack of stimulation, even though in recent years new techniques of pinning and replacing hips may have reduced the incidence of serious complications. For detailed discussions of osteoporosis, see Avioli; Giansiracusa and Kantrowitz; Kelsey, Pastides, and Bisbee; and the National Institutes of Health Consensus Conference Statement [51-54].

The risk of developing osteoporosis increases with age, particularly among women. It is estimated that 29 percent of women and 18 percent of men between forty-five and seventy-nine have osteoporosis [51]. Among women, the loss is often accelerated for several years after menopause. Unfortunately, at present there are no simple diagnostic tools to establish the risk for early forms of osteoporosis.

Suggested treatment and prevention for osteoporosis includes estrogen replacement therapy, calcium intake, and modest weight-bearing exercises. While estrogen replacement therapy remains somewhat controversial, its effectiveness for the prevention of osteoporosis in women is well documented. (For more detail on estrogen replacement therapy see below.) The value of such suggested alternative approaches to prevention and treatment as calcium intake and exercise has not been established, but these treatments deserve more attention among researchers. The latter approaches highlight factors that are associated with life style and preventive health behaviors, factors that are often neglected by traditional medicine. We need to learn more about the effects of nutrition and exercise among elderly women, and about the conditions and personal characteristics that are conducive to proper nutrition and sufficient physical exercise.

Data — Information on recent falls, broken bones, and osteoporosis as a condition is collected in the *Aging Supplement* to the *NHIS*. Information on broken bones is also available in some of the *EPESE* studies.

Urinary Incontinence

The prevalence of urinary incontinence — involuntary urine loss — appears to increase substantially with age [55]. The consequences of this condition may be quite disabling. Urinary incontinence is said to cause social isolation and depression among the elderly [56, 57], and to increase the risk of institutionalization [58].

Currently there are a few good prevalence estimates for community-dwelling elderly Americans; European and American figures that do exist suggest a prevalence of 15 to 30 percent for community samples of elderly adults [55, 58, 59]. Moreover, the figures indicate that the prevalence is higher among older women than older men [55, 58, 59], highlighting urinary incontinence as yet another health condition that predominates among older women. Despite these indications that chronic urinary incontinence is widespread among the elderly, and may have disabling consequences, rigorous investigations of its prevalence, causes, course, and consequences in community samples are much needed in this country, and the condition deserves more research attention.

Data — Several data sources contain information that may prove useful for investigating prevalence and/or incidence of urinary incontinence, and its causes, course, and consequences. They include the *Aging Supplement* to the *NHIS*; the *EPESE* project in East Boston which includes a specific component project on urinary incontinence, and other *EPESE* projects containing a few relevant questions; all surveys using the *OARS* questionnaire such as the *Study of the Well-Being of Older People in Cleveland* and the *Survey of Older People in Virginia*. While the *EPESE* project in East Boston contains detailed information on frequency, duration, and forms of urinary incontinence, the other studies contain only a few questions that essentially probe the presence of any problems related to urinary incontinence. The *Study of the Well-Being of Older People in Cleveland* is longitudinal, permitting assessment of incidence, causes, and consequences of urinary incontinence.

Perceptions of and Responses to Illness Conditions

As the foregoing discussion suggests, we know a fair amount about illnesses prevalent among older men and women, about their functional disabilities, and about their rating of their overall health. But we know much less about their subjective perceptions of specific illness symptoms [60]. How do people come to identify and label their health problems? How do they identify symptoms? Do the elderly view certain symptoms as part of a disease process, or simply attribute them to aging, to a newly emerging state, or to a preexisting condition? For example, chest pain may be considered as heartburn instead of as a warning signal for heart disease; or bone pain, which could signal a fracture or bone cancer, may be attributed to rheumatism [61]. Prohaska, Leventhal, Leventhal, and Keller provide some evidence that older adults are less likely to view general weakness and aches as symptoms of illness than are younger people [62].

And how do elderly people think about specific illness conditions? The health belief model proposes several dimensions, including the "perceived susceptibility" to the illness and its "perceived severity" [63, 64]. Leventhal and his colleagues provide a more general discussion of cognitive representations of illnesses by including such concepts as identity of the illness, its cause, its course, and its health consequences [65]. They suggest that older adults have a greater tendency than younger adults to view themselves as susceptible to illnesses and to view illnesses as serious [62].

We also need to know more about the effects that such health and illness perceptions have on how older people deal with their health and illnesses. Do they view themselves as ill or disabled as consequence of a perceived condition, engage in preventive health behaviors, seek professional health care, resort to self-care, or refrain from any action? Of particular importance with regard to aging: are elderly who attribute perceived symptoms to aging less likely to seek medical care than those who attribute symptoms to a specific condition? Perception and interpretation of symptoms and cognitive representation of the illness have been proposed as important early steps in the process of preventive health behaviors and of seeking health care [61, 62, 64].

More generally, it would be very helpful to learn more about how older people think about possible management and cures for health problems. Which illness symptoms do they think require medical attention, which ones self-care only, and which ones require no action? Which treatments do they think are effective? Where did they learn about those treatments? The health belief model emphasizes views about the benefits of and barriers to available treatments along with susceptibility to and severity of the illness as important factors in explaining the utilization of health care. (See Rakowski for a discussion of health beliefs and their application in gerontological research [60].)

Of particular importance in the context of this paper are differences in how men and women perceive their health, how they report it, and what action they take about it. Some investigators have argued that women are more sensitive to symptoms than are men, more willing to report them, more willing to assume the sick and weak role (which may be viewed as more closely linked to the typical female than the typical male role), and more likely to seek a doctor's care. If so, these sex differences might suggest alternative explanations to real health differences for the higher rates of conditions and impairments reported by women than men, and for the higher numbers of women in many studies of health and mental health that are based on clinical populations. On the other hand, we might recall the findings of the study by Davis that showed no sex differences in reporting of an objectively defined osteoarthrosis condition among adults aged twenty-five through seventy-four [49]. Similarly, Wingard reports a number of studies that examined the correspondence between self-reported health indicators and objective health information for the entire adult age range, and identified few systematic sex differences for this age range [13]. If we were to conclude — with more research in hand than we presently have — that the sex differences in morbidity are largely due to an artifact of sex differences in illness perception and reporting, then the question would still remain as to whether men or women are better perceivers and/or reporters of their actual health: that is, whether women overreport, or men underreport the extent of their illnesses.

The understanding of the dynamics of sex differences in self-reports is of utmost importance because most population-based sample surveys use self-reports for the measurement of illness conditions and functional health. Unless we know that the sex differences do not just reflect differences in reporting, perceptional styles, and care behaviors, we cannot interpret observed sex differences as differences in health.

We also need more research on sex differences that are *not* based on self-reports. More work comparing self-reports with physicians' diagnoses and clinical and laboratory tests would also be useful, using for example the data from the *NHANES* surveys. (For an example of such a study see Davis [49].) Qualitative, unstructured data could also provide very useful insights into how people think about their health.

Data — Unlike measures of functional health and self-reported illness conditions, measures of perception of and response to symptoms are much less developed and rarely used in existing surveys.

Physical Examination Measures

Results of clinical examinations and laboratory tests are often heralded as objective measures of health and physical functioning, and as less contaminated by subjective perceptions, evaluations, and actions than self-report information. A major government survey, the *NHANES*, collects such information in conjunction with survey information.

Despite the relatively high validity of these measures for identifying specific physical mechanisms and diagnoses, they are not easily aggregated into an overall assessment of illness or impairment [32]. Neither do these measures lend themselves easily to standard social science data reduction techniques, because the specific measures cannot necessarily be assumed to represent a common underlying concept (i.e., illness or impairment), and distributions are often highly skewed. Careful consideration must thus be paid to the conceptualization and use of physical examination and laboratory data as measures of health status in social science investigations.

Data — Several data sources contain information from physical examinations and laboratory tests. These include studies of the aged such as the *Duke Second Longitudinal Study* and studies of a wider age range as illustrated by the *Framingham Heart Study*, the *Baltimore Longitudinal Study of Aging*, the *Tecumseh Community Health Study*, the *Rancho Bernardo Study*, and the *NHANES*.

REPRODUCTIVE FUNCTIONING

Some aspects of women's health are uniquely female, i.e., menstruation, pregnancy, childbirth, menopause, and illness conditions of the female organs; and a substantial part of women's health care utilization patterns relates to the management of those conditions. Menopause is the obvious health-related event unique to middle-aged and older women. Although menopause is an example of a research area that could benefit from a biosocial approach, most existing research takes either a purely biomedical or a purely social-behavioral view [66]. The biomedical model reduces menopausal symptoms to direct or indirect effects of estrogen reduction in the body without attention to personal and social meanings of the event. In this model estrogen reduction is understood as a deficiency produced by the aging system: hence the use of estrogen replacement therapy. The social behavioral models — without much attention to the undisputed biological mechanisms — view menopausal symptoms as results either of a failure to adjust to the loss of fertility or of external stresses which confront women about the time of menopause.

While the biomedical approach focuses on the universality of the event, the social-behavioral approach emphasizes variations between women of different personalities or different socioeconomic backgrounds. For example, in Westernized societies, menopause is often viewed by the public as signaling the beginning of old age [67], but, in some other cultures, menopause signifies the end to an uncontrollable series of child-bearing, and a release from highly restricted lifestyles [68, 69]. Such cultural differences in the significance of menopause may well affect women's perceptions of the event and their reactions to it [69]. In addition, "true" biological variations may result from cultural differences in diet, obesity, exercise, parity, or sleep and rest patterns, health status, and prior health care [66].

Several recent reviews suggest that little consensus exists about the presence and frequency of menopausal symptoms among women in Westernized societies, a fact which might be attributable to methodological problems of the existing studies to be detailed below [44, 70, 71]. At this point, the only consensus that seems to emerge is that hot flashes and night sweats are frequent concomitants of menopause, both of which might reflect a common underlying vascular mechanism. But not even these symptoms are reported universally by menopausal women.

McKinlay and McKinlay, in reviewing the literature on menopause, specify a series of methodological limitations in existing surveys of menopause symptoms [70]. These include: samples that consist mostly of clinical populations; retrospective designs and associated problems of accurate recall; and subjective nature of the menopausal experience making objective assessment difficult, particularly across culturally divergent subgroups. In addition to a call for better methodology, McKinlay and McKinlay list a number of issues that require further attention by researchers: 1) the average age at menopause, and factors that account for variation in this age; 2) the physiological and psychological symptoms associated with menopause, and how they vary across populations and subgroups of the population; 3) how frequently, and for how long those symptoms occur; 4) whether the symptoms organize into a syndrome (i.e., occur together); and 5) how those symptoms are affected by the type of menopause (natural or artificial), by other events that tend to take place about the time of menopause, by past events and past symptomatology, and by personality and social characteristics. A study of a sample of 2,000 community-dwelling women who are approaching or experiencing the climacteric is currently being conducted by McKinlay and McKinlay, and might soon yield answers to some of these questions.

Use of estrogen for the control of specific symptoms associated with the menopause represents a mix of benefits, risks, and unknowns that are summarized in the report on a Consensus Development Conference organized by the National Institutes of Health in 1979 [72]. On the positive side, it appears established that estrogens can alleviate vasomotor symptoms (i.e., hot flashes and sweating) and atrophy of the vaginal walls, and prevent loss of bone mass if administered shortly after menopause. Beneficial effects of estrogen use have also been suggested, but not established, for urinary tract symptoms, cardio-vascular disease, and aging of the skin. On the negative side, the main risk of estrogen use is endometrial cancer, although this cancer is often curable. The risk for endometrial cancer increases with the duration of estrogen use, but no relationship with dosage has yet been established conclusively. Risk of breast cancer and cardiovascular disorders have apparently not been established. Recent reports suggest that for some women the negative effects can be reduced when an estrogen is administered in combination with a progestogen [73]. Much research regarding outcomes, proper dosage level, and alternative treatments has yet to be done. For additional discussions of estrogen replacement therapy see e.g. Judd et al. [74].

Data — Although these issues require further research, not much relevant data appear to be contained in the data sets listed in this publication. Some of the *EPESE* studies include information on the timing of menopause and estrogen use.

MENTAL HEALTH

Depression

Affective disorders and particularly depression are the most frequent functional psychiatric disorders among the elderly [75]. However, detailed descriptions of prevalence patterns of depression by age and sex are complicated by the different definitions and conceptualizations of depression. For discussions of the conceptualization of depression in older age see Blazer; Gurland; Gurland and Toner; and Klerman [76–79]. Briefly, depression can be defined as an affective disorder identified by a clinical diagnosis, or the Diagnostic Interview Schedule utilized in the *Epidemiological Catchment Area Program (ECA)* studies [80]; or as depressive symptoms more typically reported in an interview. Depressive symptoms may include psychological symptoms such as dysphoric mood or low self-esteem, and psychosomatic symptoms such as loss of appetite, sleep disorders, loss of energy, difficulty concentrating, or general slowing of response. Among the aged, these psychosomatic symptoms may also reflect purely physical problems, which adds a special complication to the conceptualization and estimation of prevalence of depression in older age. Moreover, differing cutoff points on various measures of depressive symptoms may lead to different prevalences. In brief, various conceptual issues still beleaguer the efforts to establish prevalence of depression in older age.

Age patterns in depression seem to vary by definition of depression. For example, major depressive disorders in the clinical sense show lower prevalences among persons over sixty-five than among middle-aged adults, while depressive symptoms show higher prevalences [7, 77]. Measures of psychosomatic symptoms appear to show a clearer age-related increase than do measures of psychological symptoms [76]. Sex differences, however, are confirmed with great consistency. Women have higher rates of depression than men on all measures [7, 77, 81–84].

There are some suggestions in the literature that sex differences in depression are less pronounced among older adults [77, 79, 85, 86]. However, Weissman and Klerman in their classic review from the mid-1970s maintain that the sex differences in depression hold across all age levels [84]. Their conclusion is supported by the recent findings from the *ECA* studies [7]. Support for the hypothesis that sex differences in depression are reduced among the aged is thus inconclusive.

Even less is known about incidence rates at older ages and how late-onset depression differs from depression that prevails through to old age from earlier in life.

Data – Some of the best data on depression will be the data from the *ECA* studies, once they become available. Both depressive symptoms and depression as a major disorder are measured in these studies, using the Diagnostic Interview Schedule based on the DSM-III taxonomy. The *ECA* studies are not national in coverage, but were conducted on community samples at several sites, thus providing at least some basis for generalization. At some of the sites, older adults were oversampled, thus permitting more reliable and detailed analysis of this age group. Although the *ECA* studies measure most of the psychiatric disorders in great detail, they are less rich in measures of potential explanatory concepts. (For a more detailed description of the *ECA* studies see Regier et al. [80].)

Most other surveys measure depression exclusively by symptoms checklists. They include surveys of the aged such as the *EPESE* studies and studies of a wider age range like the study *Americans View Their Mental Health*, the *NHANES*, and the *Framingham Heart Study*.

Suicide

Suicide, particularly among the aged, is thought to be related to depression [87], and may serve as a behavioral indicator of depression and demoralization. Using suicide as a measure of depression avoids some of the problems of self-reported measures. Suicide rates, however, yield different patterns by age and sex than depression measures, and, based on this recognition, their use as indicators of depression may be questioned.

In the United States, suicide rates among older white men are several times higher than rates among older white women and reflect the most substantial sex difference in suicides over the entire age range [88, 89]. This difference results from the fact that male rates continuously increase across the entire age range, while female rates stay lower than those of males at all age levels and peak among middle-aged women. The age pattern for men largely holds when cohorts are examined over time, suggesting that at least the male age differences reflect an aging effect rather than a cohort difference [88]. Suicide rates among older Blacks are generally lower than those among older Whites, the race differences being particularly marked among older men [89].

An examination of the relationship between depression and suicide for the two sexes seems called for. This might best be done by following up a large sample survey (in which depression was measured) with the National Death Index. Of course, such a study would carry some of the same problems as many of the studies of suicide, namely that suicide rates are based on death registries, and therefore considerable underreporting is likely. The underreporting may be more substantial for the older age groups, since at this age illnesses are usually present, and may be substituted as a more acceptable cause of death than suicide [90]. Underreporting may be especially true for women [91, 92]. Moreover, even if properly reported, as pointed out by Atchley these figures include only suicides of persons who overtly acted to kill themselves [88]. Among the elderly in particular, suicide by inaction (failing to observe medical regimens, failing to take prompt action upon recognition of symptoms) may be a relevant form of "passive" suicide requiring attention.

Suicide attempts are considered to follow a different motivational pattern than successfully committed suicides, the former presumably representing more a cry for help than a desire to die. Some have questioned whether this is equally true for the aged [87]. Attempted suicide is thought to be even more closely related to depression among the elderly than completed suicide [87]. Sex differences in attempted suicide are quite consistent with the sex patterns suggested for depression: women attempt suicide more frequently than men [89,

93]. One might also assume that reporting accuracy for suicide attempts is even more problematic than that for completed suicides.

Subjective Well-Being

A fairly recent but rather voluminous literature exists on what is called subjective well-being or subjective indicators of quality of life. These measures were developed as a reaction to the negative definition of mental health in terms of absence of extreme psychological distress and focus instead on a differentiation of the positive side of mental health — range of satisfactions as compared to absence of dissatisfaction, range of happiness as compared to absence of feeling blue and depressed. Unlike the depression measures, measures of satisfaction and happiness rarely show any sex differences for either the aged or the entire age range, particularly when health and socio-economic differences are controlled for, although Spreitzer and Snyder's findings differ slightly [83, 94-97].

A few words are in order on related measures that have a rather long-standing tradition in gerontological studies — morale measures. Many of these are conceptualized as multidimensional measures, including depression and anxiety questions along with questions on happiness and satisfaction and sometimes even measures of social contacts and other more marginal aspects of the concept of mental health. Sex differences on these measures are not remarkable either [98] but vary somewhat more according to the predominant ingredients of the scale and the control variables that were used. For example, one of the studies that found significant zero-order sex differences in morale used scales that contain depression- and anxiety-type measures [99]. Another study of adults from twenty to sixty by Bradburn, using the Affect Balance Scale, finds a similar sex difference, which appears to be due to the questions measuring negative affect [100]. (See, however, a study by George which did not find a sex difference on the Affect Balance Scale among elderly after controlling for socio-economic and health factors [101]; this was also true for [99].)

Data — Data on subjective well-being — variously labeled life satisfaction, morale, or subjective well-being and measured by a number of different questions and scales — are fairly readily available. Such measures are included in the *National Senior Citizen Survey*, the *Myth and Reality of Aging*, the *National Survey of the Aged*, some of the *EPESE* studies, the studies that utilize the *OARS* instrument, the *Aging in Manitoba* study, and the *Ohio Longitudinal Study*. They are included in the following studies of the full age range: the *General Social Survey*, the *Quality of American Life*, the *Quality of Canadian Life*, and the *NHANES*.

To summarize, different indicators of affective mental health — depression, suicide, suicide attempt, and subjective well-being — appear to yield varied sex differences among the elderly, a finding reminiscent of the various forms of sex differences observed for indicators of physical health. Until we understand how these different indicators relate to each other, and how they relate to a definition of mental health, we will not know how to interpret the resultant findings about sex differences.

Cognitive Impairment

Intellectual and cognitive impairments increase with age, in their more serious forms creating hardship for affected individuals and their families and enormous financial burdens for families and the public. Although a definitive diagnosis is not possible without an autopsy, the most common cause of severe cognitive impairment in older age is thought to be Alzheimer's Disease, which involves organic changes in the brain. In the absence of autopsy results, which show large numbers of neurofibrillary tangles and senile plaques in the cerebral cortex, epidemiologic investigations of cognitive impairment in older age must rely on behavioral, psychological, and clinical operationalizations. These include psychological tests of cognitive impairment such as the Short Portable MSQ [102] and the Mini-Mental State Examination [103] as well as psychological tests of learning and memory, psychiatric evaluations, and laboratory tests. For detailed discussions of test procedures and related problems see the *Report of the Secretary's Task Force on Alzheimer's Disease*; Kane and Kane; and Miller [38, 104, 105].

Because of the difficulties inherent in the operationalization, rigorous prevalence and incidence studies are few, and their findings are not entirely consistent. (For reviews of existing studies see Kay and Bergmann; Neugebauer; and Blazer [106-108].) Neugebauer asserts that rates for severe cognitive impairments as identified by clinical diagnoses of senile and arteriosclerotic psychoses in community surveys of the elderly do not differ by sex [107]. Similarly, recently reported findings from the *ECA* studies which used the Diagnostic Interview Schedule and the DSM-III taxonomy to assess mild and severe cognitive impairment show no sex differences at any age level [7]. However, other recent evidence suggests that women over 80 may have higher rates of cognitive impairment than men of the same age [106, p. 43; 109, p. 108]. The lack of comparable measures, the difficulty in entirely controlling for women's higher ages in published data,[3] and the comparatively small numbers of persons in the highest age brackets undoubtedly contribute to the inconsistency in these findings. At present, the only factor that is consistently found to be related to cognitive impairment is age [7, 104, 109]. Clearly, we need more information on sex- and age-specific prevalence and incidence in cognitive impairment, as detailed in the *Report of the Secretary's Task Force on Alzheimer's Disease*. The development of standardized diagnostic assessment

---

[3] Women are older than men, even within older age groupings of say 10-year brackets.

techniques is of prime importance to this objective. We also need to know how these impairments relate to the organic symptoms of Alzheimer's disease, and about the time of onset and the course of the impairments and associated risk factors [104].

Data — Measures of cognitive functioning and impairment are available in the *EPESE* studies, in the *ECA* studies, and in all the studies using the *OARS* instrument. A series of questions on self-reported memory performance is included in the *Aging Supplement* to the *NHIS* and in one of the *EPESE* studies. A memory test for the less seriously impaired elderly is included in one of the *EPESE* studies; an intelligence test for the normal range of adult persons is included in the *General Social Survey*.

Relationship Between Physical and Mental Health

The interrelationship between physical and mental health is complex and not well understood. Many studies examine either physical or mental health as an outcome, but fail to investigate the connections between them, and how life circumstances may express themselves in one or the other or both.

In studies where the direct relationship between indicators of mental and physical health has been examined, the relationship is usually a positive one. For example, happiness, depression, and intelligence are related to morbidity and longevity [23, 26, 110, 111]. It is also suggested that self-reported health is related to subjective well-being [27, 28, 31] and that physical illness underlies many depressions and suicides in older age [87, 108, 109, 112]. Most likely, the relationship is one of mutual causation [113].

Some have found mental and physical health to be more closely related among older women than older men. For example, Okun and George report that neuroticism and self-rated health are stronger predictors of subjective well-being among older women than older men [31]. Wingard reports that life satisfaction predicts mortality among women but not among men [34]. Gurland observed that disability affects women's depression more strongly than men's, a difference that he found to diminish among the very old [114]. These findings could benefit from more concerted research efforts.

It has also been argued that mental and physical health indicators should be more closely interlinked among the aged than among other age groups (e.g., Kane and Kane [38]). Little relevant evidence for this argument exists, however. One intriguing exception is a recent study by Aneshensel, Frerichs, and Huba that shows the contemporaneous impact of illness on depression to be greater among persons over forty-five than among younger persons, particularly those under the age of thirty [113].

Problems that have plagued studies on the interrelationship between physical and mental health include operational confounding between measures of physical and mental health (see Haug, Belgrave, and Gratton for an example and discussion of such confounding [115]); reliance on cross-sectional study designs that do not permit the establishment of the direction of causation; a lack of attention to potential underlying factors that could produce a spurious association between physical and mental health (see Okun and George, for an example of the potential underlying factor of neuroticism [31]); and failure to specify and investigate the process by which the influence takes place. Blazer; Lipowski; and Zautra and Hempel propose a number of mechanisms for explaining the links between physical and mental health which might be worth investigating [30, 108, 116].

Data — Data sets that could prove particularly useful in addressing the inter-relationship between mental and physical health are the *EPESE*, the *Aging Supplement* of the *NHIS*, the studies using the *OARS* methodology, and the *NHANES* studies, although the latter study includes persons only up to the age of seventy-four.

In most of the data sources mentioned in this section on mental health, age comparisons can only be conducted in a cross-sectional manner because the data were collected from an adult cross-section at one point in time. Longitudinal data sets that permit an assessment of age change, and repeated cross-sections from different time periods that permit tracing of cohorts, are needed. Unfortunately, few of the data sets currently available include measures of depression or of subjective well-being. Longitudinal studies that also include women as well as men are, among others, the *Ohio Longitudinal Study*, the study of the *Well-Being of Older People in Cleveland*, the *Duke Second Longitudinal Study*, the *Framingham Heart Study*, the *ECA* studies, and the *EPESE* studies. Repeated cross-sections include the *NHIS*, the *NHANES*, the *Quality of American Life* surveys, and the *Americans View Their Mental Health* surveys.

HEALTH IN A LIFE-SPAN PERSPECTIVE

As indicated by our previous discussions, a fair amount is known about the prevalence of chronic conditions among women and men, about the prevalence of their impairments, and how sex differences on these illness indicators vary by age. In most cases, however, the relevant health data have been collected at only one time, without any information about what led up to a given health problem or status. Although we know that current health or illness represents an accumulation of a lifetime of health and health practices, we lack data about lifetime prevalence and the life-course of health and illness conditions, of disabilities and related health behaviors. We need to investigate the minor symptoms and complaints that, later on, may lead to major problems such as disability or chronic conditions. We need to know whether women's greater sensitivity to symptoms and earlier recognition — if indeed true — account for their greater readiness to seek care, and whether this, in turn, has beneficial effects for their health and longevity in older age. We need to learn how stable certain symptoms, disabilities or conditions are, and what accounts for potential temporal variation. We need to know how different conditions affect each other. We need to know how risk factors encountered throughout life impact morbidity and mortality in older age. And we need to know how interventions such as professional care or self-care affect the course of illness and impairment. Most important, we need to understand how those sequences may differ for women and men and how they may account for the substantial sex differences in health and longevity observed in middle and older age.

We also need to know how the individual learns to perceive his or her health; how experiences with earlier conditions affect perceptions of conditions at later times; and the point at which an individual decides to label him- or herself disabled, and how this affects future health. Differences in the ways of perceiving and handling illness may start early on with differing patterns of parental caring for the health of offsprings and themselves. With regard to women's higher symptom reporting and physician visits, it has been argued that women, through the management of reproductive functions, are taught a more systematic attention to their bodies and symptoms. It has also been suggested that in this society being sick and taking care of one's health problems as well as one's family's health problems is more consistent with the female than the male role and that girls acquire their attitudes toward illness as part of their learning of the female role. More systematic work regarding these hypotheses is needed.

Finally, we know very little about health changes during the final part of life and how they eventually lead to death. How do theories of "compression of morbidity" or "terminal drop" translate into the everyday lives of older adults? How do final years or months look? Do they differ between men and women?

SEX CROSSOVER

A special case of a life-span perspective with implications for mental health is the proposition originally stated by Neugarten and Gutmann that women become more assertive and independent as they grow older, while men become more nurturant and expressive, leading to a rapprochement between the sexes [117-119]. This proposition has had much attention in social gerontology, although it has not yet received sufficient investigation to be considered an established fact.

Neugarten and Gutmann based their conclusion on responses from projective personality techniques. In a more recent piece in the *Annual Review of Gerontology and Geriatrics*, Troll and Parron reviewed the evidence that can be brought to bear on Neugarten's and Gutmann's proposition [120]. The evidence these authors present consists largely of studies of small samples of one or both sexes dealing with changes experienced with age measured by a variety of methods. Few direct comparisons of men and women at different age levels seem to exist today. Based on the available evidence, Troll and Parron give the hypothesis a cautious affirmation, but research directly relevant to this hypothesis is clearly called for. We need to know whether the decline in sex differences, implied by the hypothesis, can be reliably shown for different samples and varying operationalizations of expressiveness and assertiveness. If such a sex difference can be reliably demonstrated, we would like to know whether the phenomenon reflects an effect of aging or of cohort. More specifically, we need to learn what might explain the effect. The hypothesis is often undergirded by the notion that sex-role differences are more distinct at younger ages, when women are more likely to tend to home and children and men to work, than at older ages, when role behaviors may become blurred.

The proposition sometimes takes on a more general tenor, claiming declining sex differences on a wide range of psychological, behavioral, and health characteristics. Earlier in this paper we noted some suggestions that sex differences in depression and mortality might be reduced among the aged. Others have suggested that sex differences in health status are smaller among older adults, as compared to those who are younger. Could such declining differences in physical and mental health and mortality, if true, also be a result of the declining role differentiation?

Data — Data sets that are suited to examining such life-span issues must be longitudinal. The most obvious data sets are the *Duke Second Longitudinal Survey*, the *Alameda County Study*, the *Rancho Bernardo Study*, the *Tecumseh Community Health Study*, the *Framingham Heart Study*, the *Baltimore Longitudinal Study of Aging*, and the *EPESE* studies. All of these studies deal primarily with physical health. Extended longitudinal studies on mental health are rare, although the *ECA* studies will eventually provide a longitudinal sequence.

UTILIZATION OF HEALTH CARE SERVICES

Utilization of health care is often used as yet another indicator of health, although these measures are not a pure reflection of illness (or "need" in the terminology of the health care utilization model proposed by Andersen) but also represent psychological and sociodemographic (or "predisposing"), and financial and other access (or "enabling") factors [121, 122]. Of course, aside from their use as health measures, health care utilization patterns have societal and personal significance. Their societal impact derives from the fact that they have enormous economic implications as health care costs continue to escalate. The personal significance of utilization patterns is demonstrated by the import of institutional care, which may exact a heavy toll from individual residents in terms of relinquished independence and a loss of control over daily affairs.

A considerable part of women's use of health services is related to reproductive behaviors and sex-specific conditions. Among middle-aged and older women a major reason for hospitalization is prolapsed uterus, while the two major preventive health care measures for which they visit a physician's office are the Pap smear and breast examination [44]. Excluding sex-specific reasons for physician visits, women of all ages still visit doctors' offices more often than men, although this sex difference declines with increasing age [44]. In fact, several studies have found few sex differences in health service utilization among the elderly, particularly after health status or need is controlled [123-126], although Verbrugge provides a somewhat different assessment [14].

Hospitalization rates seem to show no sex difference either, when sex-specific reasons are controlled among adults past forty-five, although a difference is found among those younger than forty-five [44, 125, 126]. In sum, physician visits and hospitalizations among the elderly appear to show few sex differences aside from those that can be explained in terms of their health profiles.

On the other hand, nearly three-quarters of nursing home residents are women; thus nursing home residency emerges as another issue of particular relevance to research on older women [127]. Why does this predominance of older women in nursing homes occur? Research has just started to pinpoint the general risk factors for institutionalization. The suggestions are that major functional disabilities (particularly feeding and urine control), mental disorders, living alone, poverty, and old age contribute to admission to an institution [128-130]. Women's higher admission to nursing facilities may possibly be explained by the fact that they have more of the implied risk factors. For example, women live longer, they are more likely to live alone, to be poor, and to have functional impairments and limiting conditions. Or, women's higher nursing home admission may just be a function of their predominance at the age level when nursing home admission becomes reasonably frequent. Verbrugge discusses health care service utilization by older women and men [14].

Further studies on risk factors for nursing home admission and on reasons for the sex difference in such admissions would be very useful. These studies should go beyond a comparison of persons living in institutions (for any amount of time) with persons living in the community, so as not to confound reasons for entrance into an institution with the effects of institutionalization. Rather, studies of risk factors for institutionalization should be longitudinal in design, following a representative sample of community-dwelling older adults over time, including the determination of eventual institutionalization.

As in the case of health indices, the various indices of health care utilization are mostly examined in isolation from one another. Much could be gained by looking at all health care services in combination. Questions such as the following ought to be asked: Are older persons who end up in institutions those who have never gone to the doctor before and thus eventually have developed a serious enough condition to warrant institutionalization? Or, on the contrary, are those older persons with regular physician care the ones who end up most readily in institutions? We need to look at the progression through the various forms of health care services and the connections among them rather than focusing on health service use — however broadly these services are defined — at one point in time.

One of the most basic questions regarding health care is its outcome, that is, whether, and in which ways health care improves health and longevity. Do women have fewer serious health problems than men and live longer because they are more willing to submit to a physician's care and/or enter the medical care system at an earlier point?

Another aspect of the health care system that has received little attention is the use of health services for mental health problems by the elderly. Elderly persons are less likely than younger age groups to utilize outpatient mental health services or mental health professionals, even if in need [108, 131, 132]. They are also less willing or able to report mental health problems such as depressive symptoms, or they report them in the form of physical complaints [76, 78]. General practitioners and health care organizations must, therefore, be very sensitive to disguised messages about potential mental health problems among elderly patients. It is not clear that the medical and the nursing professions are ready for this challenge, nor that they are properly trained for it. Furthermore, women use mental health services more readily than men after a recent mental health disorder, although a good part of their greater utilization is sought from general medical providers rather than mental health professionals [132].

More information is also needed about attitudes of the medical establishment toward the aged, toward the nature of their ailments, and toward their care. For example, what values guide the care of the elderly? Do physicians strive to prolong life or to alleviate suffering and improve the quality of life? With regard to older women, we would like to know whether physicians treat older men and women presenting with the same complaint in the same way, and whether they prescribe more psychotropic drugs or more painkilling medication to women than to men [14, 133]. Women do appear to receive more extensive services, more frequent laboratory tests and more thorough follow-up care, even after medically relevant factors are controlled [134]. But, in general, there is little evidence so far to support the suggestion that women do get different treatment than do men [13, 134].

Although much health care for the elderly is currently covered by public resources under Medicare/Medicaid, several common items are usually not covered including prescription drugs, glasses and hearing aids, routine examinations, footcare, long-term home care, and institutional care through

Medicare. Such lack of coverage has more serious consequences for older women than for men because older women are more frequent users of these items and because they have fewer financial resources than do older men [14].

Finally, little attention has been paid to older adults' self-care. How frequently do older adults resort to self-treatment and medication or the advice of nonprofessionals? What factors contribute to the decision not to seek a physician's care for a particular symptom or complaint? Whose advice do they follow instead? Brody, Kleban, and Moles provided a useful start when they examined the actions taken by a small nonrepresentative group of elderly persons in response to symptoms of pain, weakness, and mental distress, most of which were not reported to a health care professional. They report that the most frequent action taken in response to pain and digestive problems was use of medication: a majority of the medications represented over-the-counter drugs. Other self-care actions that they report include applied temperature treatments, applied preparations, rest, and exercise, depending in frequency on the specific symptom for which they were administered [135]. Although these authors do not report on sex differences, there are good reasons to believe that women's self-care behaviors differ from those of men. As reported above, older women are more likely than men to have chronic conditions that are symptomatic and many of their symptoms might be treated by self-care actions, as suggested by Brody et al.'s study. Also, as women are presumably socialized to be more attentive to their own and their families' health, they may be more attuned to and familiar with various self-care actions.

Data — Several data sets contain information on physician visits and hospitalizations, including the *NHIS* and its *Aging Supplement*, the *NHANES*, the *National Senior Citizen Survey*, the *National Survey of the Aged*, the *Massachusetts Health Care Panel Study*, the *EPESE* studies, the *ECA* studies, the studies using the *OARS* instrument, the *National Ambulatory Medical Care Survey*, the *National Medical Care Expenditure Survey*, the *National Medical Care Utilization and Expenditure Survey*, the *National Survey of Access to Medical Care*, and the *Survey of Health Services Utilization and Expenditures*. Information on visits to mental health professionals is available in the *ECA* studies, in the *Massachusetts Health Care Panel Study*, in some of the *EPESE* studies, in the studies using the *OARS* instrument, and in the study *Americans View Their Mental Health*, although the latter study does not contain many older people, being a survey of the entire adult age range with a total sample size of about 2,250 adults. The *ECA* studies further contain information on in-patient mental health care use. Drug use is assessed in the *Massachusetts Health Care Panel Study*, in the *EPESE* studies, and in the studies using the *OARS* instrument.

Prior stays in a nursing home are assessed in the *Aging Supplement* to the *NHIS*, in the *Massachusetts Health Care Panel Study*, in the *National Senior*

Citizen Survey, and in the studies that use the *OARS* instrument. In order to establish causes of institutionalization, longitudinal surveys that assess institutionalization are needed. The *Massachusetts Health Care Panel Study* — now approaching its fourth follow-up after about ten years — is one suitable example of such a study; others are the *EPESE* studies that follow respondents over a six-year span; the *Study of the Well-Being of Older People in Cleveland* that covers a span of nine years; and the *Alameda County Study*. The *Aging Supplement* of the *NHIS* is also considering a follow-up of a large national probability sample of elderly to determine subsequent institutionalization.

SOME FACTORS CONTRIBUTING TO THE SEX DIFFERENCES IN HEALTH

Sex differences in physical and mental health discussed so far might be a result of factors that themselves differ by sex, such as different work patterns, different amounts and forms of stress, different coping mechanisms, different social relationships, and different preventive health behaviors. Thus, the remaining pages of this chapter will outline some concepts that may be used to explain some of the sex differences in physical and mental health discussed so far; the focus, however, remains on questions and issues for further research rather than on a comprehensive literature review.

Work

The relationship between work and health has not been a major concern in traditional research on women's lives, in part because of the presumed marginal significance of work for women. Following the well-documented influx of women into the work force during recent decades, a flurry of research has appeared that examines the significance of work and changing roles of women on their health.

A stress orientation predominates in much of the research on work and the health of women: to hold employment outside the home and meet traditional family responsibilities is presumed to create role conflict or role overload and therby produce chronic stress and worsening mental and physical health. Interestingly, comparisons of employed and non-employed women, most of them young, seldom support this notion [13, 44, 136-141]. In light of these findings, some recent research emphasizes the positive effects obtained through employment such as prestige, marital power, economic resources, social contacts, stimulation, or self-esteem [141, 142].

Middle-aged and older women may also face multiple demands from family and work, experiencing the stress and related health effects presumed in studies of younger women. A majority of today's middle-aged women are in the work force, and about 10 percent of the women over sixty-five remain in the work force

[140, 143]. At the same time, many of these women have old parents or sick husbands who need their regular assistance, or grown children who still require economic and other support. The number of these "women-in-the-middle" is likely to increase in the future [144–146]. We know little about role conflicts and role overload for these middle-aged and older women, how they deal with these situations, and how their health and mental health is affected by them. Do these women stop working when the demands for the care of older parents become overwhelming? Are working middle-aged and older women more likely to institutionalize their severely impaired parents than are non-working women? How does a middle-aged or older woman decide between full-time care for a confused parent and for a husband recovering from a heart attack? How do these women cope with these conflicts, at a time when their own health and energy may have become frail? These are problems that probably exceed conflicts and overload encountered by young working mothers in terms of ethical dilemmas and long-term hopelessness. Yet they have received comparatively little research attention.

Recent gerontological research has addressed retirement among women – after an almost exclusive focus on men in earlier retirement research. Unlike research on women's work, though, the emphasis in retirement research has been on work as a positive factor in people's lives and consequently on retirement from work as a negative event. Again, this orientation has not been generally confirmed since many elderly persons, men as well as women, experience no negative health effects as a consequence of retirement [8, 147, 148].

However, a simple comparison between employed and non-employed women in a cross-sectional study, or between retired and employed women, as conducted by many investigators in these research traditions, is not sufficient to pinpoint the effect of employment or retirement on women because of a possible selection bias. That is, healthier women could have chosen employment while less healthy women stayed home or retired. In other words, the direction of causality may go from physical and mental health status to employment status instead of from employment status to health status. The introduction of very careful controls into cross-sectional designs or longitudinal data are needed for disentangling these effects.[4] (See also Holden's discussion of work and health in her paper on economic status in this volume.)

The effect of employment on health may also vary by occupation and working conditions [149]. Research therefore needs to focus on specific occupations and working conditions, rather than on employment as a global category. Research on women's employment and retirement usually contrasts all employed or retired women with all housewives but does not differentiate between occupations; between part-time and full-time work; between white-

---

[4] Even in longitudinal studies, a select group is often examined. For example, an examination of the longitudinal impact of retirement at the age of sixty-five removes the persons who retire early, and who are thus likely to be different in health and economic status. Such a study thus applies only to parts of the population [148].

collar, blue-collar, and pink-collar jobs; or between specific conditions of occupations such as the flexibility and control the employee can exert, the time pressure and quantity of work demands, the responsibility for others, the sufficiency of resources, and the amount of stimulating and satisfactory work activity or job satisfaction. Yet we know from studies of men's work that conditions like these are related to men's mental and physical health [149, 150].[5] Likewise, the effects of specific occupations on retirement adaptation of men and women are not well understood [8].

Some recent studies have begun to remedy these shortcomings, and these studies provide useful research paradigms. They demonstrate cognitive, behavioral, and health correlates of specific work conditions and further suggest that the strengths of these relationships are not different for men and women [152, 153].

A number of occupational hazards and diseases are likely to be more prevalent among women than men, because of women's concentration in very different occupations [154, 155], a situation that has changed very little in recent decades. Stellman describes a number of hazardous factors that characterize many of the female-dominated jobs. They include various sources of occupational stress such as underutilization of skills, underpayment, lack of autonomy and control over the work environment, and responsibility for the welfare of others. In addition, Stellman specifies chemical exposure among nurses, laboratory technicians, textile workers, beauticians, and laundry workers; ergonomic considerations such as excessive sitting among clericals, certain types of operators, and dressmakers, and excessive standing among waitresses, nurses, clerks, and teachers; injuries among hospital workers and lab technicians; and infections among health care workers, social workers, dental hygienists, and laundry workers. All these occupational categories contain a disproportionate number of female employees [156].

A particularly interesting job category is clerical work. A large part of the female labor force works in clerical jobs; moreover, many of the middle-aged and older women who have returned to work after rearing children are in clerical jobs. This must be particularly difficult at a time when clerical work is going through a major technological change; word processing and computer technology require an entirely new set of skills from these women. Moreover, clerical work is subject to underutilization of skills, lack of control, role ambiguity and role conflict, and minimal chances for advancement [157]. Some intriguing findings from the *Framingham Heart Study* suggest that clerical jobs may indeed be more stressful for women between the ages of forty-five and sixty-four, particularly when combined with responsibilities in other roles and an unsupportive supervisor [139].

---

[5] This is not to imply that there are no problems in studies conducted on men only. Most of these are cross-sectional in design and thus may reflect a selection bias as men with particular dispositions choose particular kinds of occupations [151].

Of particular importance to older women are the long-term health effects of such working conditions. Existing studies speak primarily to contemporaneous work and health effects as observed in cross-sectional data. Yet many health effects become symptomatic only after a considerable period of time, after lifelong patterns of work and family participation. Does stress from multiple roles in younger years lead to compounded health problems in older age? Or do women learn how to deal with multiple roles? More generally, what are health outcomes of various sequences and combinations of roles and situations? In reviewing a broad and diverse literature with particular attention to middle-aged women, Giele proposes that it is less a particular sequence of roles that makes for adaptability and healthy outcomes than the flexibility that certain women maintain in the sequencing of their life roles [158]. She views sufficient education, work, and family experiences as a critical prescription for maintaining flexibility and avoiding foreclosure of options at an early point in life. This is an intriguing proposition that deserves some direct tests. Longitudinal data sources that include occupational, family, and health information are required.

Data — Many of the data sources listed in Appendix A contain information on current labor force participation of the survey respondents. Often such information consists of the current employment status, the number of hours worked, and the type of occupation; sometimes a very detailed categorization of occupation is provided along with the type of industry in which the occupation is located. Information on employment and occupational history, and specific aspects of the job are less readily available, unless a study focuses primarily on work or retirement. In the latter case, the study most likely will lack comprehensive information on health. One study that contains fairly detailed information on work history and retirement and also assesses health status in fair detail is the cross-sectional *National Survey of the Aged, 1975* by Shanas. Other surveys that focus on work are the *Harris 1978 Retirement and Pension Survey* and the *Quality of Employment Survey*. A longitudinal survey that collected comprehensive information on the transition from work to retirement among a sample of fifty-eight through sixty-three-year olds — the *Retirement History Longitudinal Survey* — contains only a little information on health and, further, selected only unmarried women for interviewing. A regional longitudinal survey — the *Ohio Longitudinal Study* by Atchley — contains information on perceptions of and attitudes toward retirement, in addition to measures of subjective well-being and health.

Social Relationships

Social relationships have beneficial effects on mental health, physical health, and longevity among the general population as well as among the elderly [159–164]. But social relationships can also be stressful, as for example when they put demands on the person and interfere with goal-directed behaviors [108].

Several recent reviews have noted a certain confusion in conceptualization and measurement of such terms as social relationships, social support, social networks, or social integration, and have proposed conceptualizations that should clarify and inform further research on the nature of the relationship between social relationships and health [159, 165, 166]. According to these authors, at least three dimensions of social relationships can be distinguished: 1) the existence and frequency of social relationships; 2) the structure of these relationships, including their quality; and 3) the support provided through these relationships. Existence and frequency represent the most commonly investigated dimension of social relationships. They utilize measures such as marital status, frequency of contacts with relatives and friends, membership in voluntary associations, or frequency of church attendance. The study of structural characteristics of social relationships derives largely from social network analysis and includes such characteristics as the number of social relationships a person maintains, the geographic proximity among the various "participants" in the relationships, the reciprocity of supports and obligations among participants, or the extent to which participants know each other. Other structural aspects of importance are qualitative characteristics such as closeness, intensity, or trust. The dimension of support is of relatively recent origin, referring to the emotional, instrumental, and informational aids that are obtained from and provided for persons with whom social relationships are maintained. The existence and characteristics of social relationships may be viewed as the vehicle through which social support can be (but is not necessarily) obtained and given.

Since social relationships of older women and older men differ substantially, this fact may be important in explaining sex differences in physical and mental health. Older women are more likely to be widowed than are older men, but they have larger numbers and more diverse sets of persons to whom they feel close [165], and they are more likely to have a close relationship in the form of a confidant [167, 168]. Whether older women also have more contact with relatives and receive more aid, appears inconclusive according to a recent review by Atchley and Miller [169]. Blacks have been found to draw on a more varied pool of helpers than whites and to be more likely to substitute one helper for another as they approach old age [170]. Finally, women are more likely to provide help and support to others, including their husbands, their aging parents, and their children [144].

Although their richer and more widespread social contacts may provide women with health advantages, their more frequent empathy with and caring for others and greater chance for widowhood may cause stress and depression [146, 171]. This prediction only holds if these forms of social relationships have the same effects on men and women. This is not always the case, as exemplified in the differential beneficial effect of marital status on physical and mental health: Positive effects of marital status are almost always stronger for men than for women [166], although there has been some recent suggestion that the quality of the marital relationship is more important for women [172].

The advantages and disadvantages of the different forms of social relationship for the physical and mental health of older men and women need further explication [165]. A prerequisite for such investigations is more conceptually oriented assessments of various dimensions of social relationships than has been the case in research heretofore [159].

Data — Data on social relationships can be found in several studies. Common to almost all the studies are measures of the existence of a spouse and children. Measures of frequency of contact with family members, friends, or neighbors are also relatively frequently included in relevant studies. The *National Survey of the Aged*, the *National Senior Citizen Survey*, the *Myth and Reality of Aging*, the studies that use the *OARS* instrument, the *Aging Supplement* of the *National Health Interview Survey*, the *Quality of Life of Older Age Groups*, the *Massachusetts Health Care Panel Study*, and the *EPESE* studies are examples of surveys of the aged that contain such information. Such surveys of the entire adult population include the *Alameda County Study*, the *ECA* study at Duke University, the *General Social Survey*, and the *Quality of American Life*. Measures of participation in formal organizations are available in the *National Senior Citizen Survey*, in the *Quality of American Life, 1971*, in the *General Social Survey*, in the *Myth and Reality of Aging*, and in the *EPESE* studies. The availability of a particularly close relationship with a confidant — "somebody that you can talk to about things that really bother you" or "somebody that you can trust" — are available in the *Myth and Reality of Aging*, in the *National Senior Citizen Survey*, in some of the *EPESE* studies, and in the studies that use the *OARS* instrument. Other measures of the quality of a relationship (such as closeness and understanding) are included in some of the *EPESE* studies. Measures of geographic proximity can be found in the *National Senior Citizen Survey* and the *National Survey of the Aged*. Finally, measures of various forms of support received from others are assessed in the *National Survey of the Aged, 1975* and in some of the *EPESE* studies.

Stress

Stress and its physiological effects are implicated as links in the relationship between life conditions and illness. A recent review and assessment of this literature by the Institute of Medicine documents the association of disruptive life events such as job loss, bereavement, or relocation with increased risk for an impressive array of illnesses ranging from minor infections to arthritis, cancer, depression, and sudden cardiac death [151, p. 8]. This review also discusses measurement of the intervening psychological and physiological factors. Moreover, it stresses the importance of investigating other factors that may modify the relationship between stressful situations and illness. For example, personal resources such as intelligence, self-esteem, religiosity, and coping styles; and sociocultural resources such as social contacts and supports or financial asset, may help to weaken the impact of stressful situations.

Stress is an important concept to consider when attempting to explain differences in illness and mental health between men and women, since the life circumstances of men and women still differ considerably in modern societies, despite some well-documented changes in sex roles; and also since many moderating factors are different for the two sexes. Yet we do not know very much about the amount of stress that either women or men experience, how the amount of stress may change across the life span of either sex, and how the impact of stress on illness may differ for the sexes [151].

The gerontological literature typically concerns itself with one or another of a relatively small number of presumably stressful life events in the later part of life and asks whether these events do indeed have an impact on subjective well-being of older adults. Among these events are retirement, menopause, the empty nest, the loss of spouse or other close persons, illness, and a move to an institution or sheltered living situation. Some of these events are more likely to be experienced by older women than by older men. For example, older women have more health problems or illnesses; they are more likely to lose their spouses; and they are more likely to be institutionalized. Menopause, of course, is experienced uniquely by women. The only event that women are less likely to experience personally is retirement, although they are catching up with men even here.

As has been amply demonstrated by now, retirement, relocation, menopause, and the empty nest do not seem to have the universally negative impact on physical health and mental health that is predicted from a stress perspective. On the other hand, the loss of a spouse is often traumatic; for some, depression, death, and suicide follow [173-175]. Although it is sometimes said that the loss of a spouse is more devastating for husbands than for wives, several authors report no consistent sex differences in the effect of bereavement [173, 176, 177], and the effect may further differ for older and younger persons [8]. Likewise, health and physical disability are typically related to life satisfaction, morale, and depression among the aged [98, 114], but again, the impact may be no different for the two sexes [178, 179].

Such existing studies are unsatisfactory, however, in that they investigate a presumably stressful event in isolation from other stressors. It is quite possible that one stressful event can be coped with or even represents a challenge, while many stressful events in close proximity become overwhelming. For example, relocation may have an entirely different and less dramatic effect for a relatively young, healthy, and well-functioning older person with a spouse than for a frail, disoriented older person who just lost his or her spouse. In other words, we need to look at the accumulation of stress-related factors [151].

A standard way of measuring the total amount of stress is by measuring all major disruptive life events that have occurred in a specified time period, as exemplified in the Social Readjustment Rating Scale by Holmes and Rahe [180]. The negative relationship between the number of such life events and mental health has been amply demonstrated for a general population as well as for elderly persons [181, 182]. Some research suggests that this relationship may be due largely to what are generally considered *negative* events [183].

Stress measured by a summation of recent life events does not appear to show any sex difference [84, 184], although others have suggested that women suffer more stress or are more sensitive to the stresses they encounter [185, 186]. Researchers should not overlook the possibility that for many women it is not the occurrence of stressful events or situations but rather the absence of events that creates stress through boredom and lack of stimulation [151]. A similar argument may also be made for older persons, a hypothesis which is supported by the observation that the sum of recent life events does show a decline with increasing age [184, 187].

The measurement of stress by means of a summation of life events is considered outdated by many. There are at least three criticisms of particular relevance for research with the aged. First, the schedule of recent life events by Holmes and Rahe seems to contain more events for younger than for older age groups, more for men than for women: thus sex and age differences in numbers of stressful life events may be an artifact of the scale [188-189]. Second, and more generally, the amount of stress is defined by objective indices rather than by subjective perceptions of and reactions to one's own experience [190-192]. Third, stress conceptualized as discrete "stressful" events may be less relevant for the aged than chronic stresses caused, for example, by chronic illnesses, insufficient funds, or a lack of transportation [190, 192].

Chronic stress associated with the traditional female role in this society has been implicated by a fair amount of research explaining the higher rates of minor illness and depression among women. For example, Gove and Hughes have shown that women are less able to take care of themselves when ill than men, presumably because of competing responsibilities for the care of others [110]. These role responsibilities in combination with their lower self-reported mental health can account for the observed sex differences in physical health, according to these researchers. (But see critiques of their research by Mechanic and by Verbrugge [193, 194].) Similarly, Kessler and McLeod have shown that women's empathy with persons who are close to them and with what happens to these close people accounts for a good part of their higher depression rates [171]. A recent decline in sex differences on psychological distress has been attributed to sex roles becoming more similar in recent decades [195]. The fact that sex roles presumably become more similar in later parts of life might provide yet another explanation for the potential age-related decline in sex differences in depression.

Chronic stress has also been emphasized by Pearlin and Schooler, who focus on the stresses produced by major life roles such as spouse, parent, and worker. Unfortunately, their measurement approach at this point does not seem very suitable for use with elderly populations because it focuses on positions that many elderly no longer occupy [196].

We need to measure both objectively and subjectively defined stress. Although measures of the two are typically related, they represent different aspects of stress. For example, although the death of a spouse is probably one of the most stressful events [180], for some persons with a sick and disabled spouse it may actually represent a relief. Or, although full-time work may present a welcome challenge for some elderly persons, it probably is stressful for most.

Because of these measurement problems, we do not know how stress really changes across the life span. Clearly some major negative life events such as the death of a spouse, illness, retirement, and involuntary relocation become more frequent as people age. Yet, some recent reviews question the implied increase in overall stress level [146, 190, 197]. It is also possible that while the exposure to stressful situations does not increase with age, the vulnerability to stressful situations does. Or it may be that up to a certain age people become more experienced in dealing with stress, and thus fare increasingly better as they age. As people get even older, however, their vulnerability to stress may increase based on the decline in health, social support, and adaptive mechanisms [192, 197]. We also do not know how stress differs for the two sexes, and how such sex differences may change across the life span.

Data — Measures of "objective" stress in some form of major life events are available in the *Quality of Life in America, 1978*, in some of the *EPESE* studies, in the *Baltimore Longitudinal Study of Aging*, in the *Framingham Heart Study*, and in the *Longitudinal Study of Transitions in the Four Stages of Life*. Measures of "subjective" stress in form of self-reported problems and needs can be created from data in the *Myth and Reality of Aging*, the *National Survey of Black Americans*, the study *Coping with Stress and Challenge in Late Life*, and the *Massachusetts Health Care Panel Study*.

Coping

The general stress research tradition has not produced an overly strong relationship between stress and illness and, so far, has not provided a full explanation of the sex differences in depression and illness. Investigators have therefore turned increasingly to potential moderators of the relationship. The report by the Institute of Medicine lists person, process, and environmental factors that should be considered as potential moderators [151]. Pearlin and Schooler have proposed a useful distinction between coping resources and coping responses. According to Pearlin and Schooler, resources are whatever persons have available in developing their coping responses. These may be sociocultural (for example, personal networks and supports as well as financial and educational resources) or psychological (including personality characteristics such as mastery, self-esteem, or intelligence). Coping responses, on the other hand, refer to the behaviors, cognitions, and perceptions that persons use when they attempt to deal with their lives' stresses [196]. With regard to sex differences in mortality, illness, and mental health, it becomes particularly critical to examine coping responses and resources that differ in frequency or relative impact between men and women.

Research on coping responses so far has largely involved samples of young and middle-aged adults. Where sex differences within these age levels are reported, they are not always consistent, and are further complicated by the different types of stresses encountered and reported by women. Yet, some intriguing findings suggest the potential for further research. For example, three studies found that women were more likely to use coping responses having to do with the expression and control of emotions generated by stress [190, 198, 199]. The study by Quayhagen and Quayhagen, which included adults between forty and seventy years of age, further showed that this sex difference remained the same across age levels within the specified age range. If women do control and/or express their feelings about stressful situations more readily than do men, one might speculate that this in part accounts for their higher rates of self-reported depressive symptoms. One may wonder in turn whether emotion-focused coping may account for women's lower rates of heart condition by providing a sort of therapeutic outlet through expression instead of repression.

Other forms of coping responses that were shown in two studies to be more frequently used by women than by men are avoidance- or ignoring-type coping responses [196, 198]. What is particularly interesting about this finding is that these specific mechanisms of avoidance seem to be less effective in reducing the impact of stress-producing life events or situations than other coping responses [196]. Such a conclusion is also supported by Fiske's observation that, in the face of considerable stress, middle-aged women are less likely to cope success-fully than are men of the same age [145]. However, a third study suggests the opposite sex difference for these coping responses: women are more likely to do nothing or to undertake direct actions [83].

As suggested above, few studies have included older adults. In a cross-sectional study of adults McCrae measured a wide range of coping responses but found few age differences [200]. George and Siegler, using a retrospective design with older adults, also found few age-related differences in coping strategies that did not appear to be accountable for by differences in the types of stresses encountered at different life stages [190]. Veroff and his colleagues reported age differences in coping responses: older adults were less likely to use other people in solving their problems and more likely to use prayer [83]. The latter authors warn that their finding may represent a cohort effect rather than an effect of aging. Lazarus and Golden have speculated about denial-type coping responses –

which they want to be understood as separate from avoidance — and significance of denial in older age. They argue that denial responses may be beneficial in some ways, for example, for the elderly's management of negative emotions related to aging and its many stresses, which is almost like maintaining some illusions about life. But they also contend that denial can be maladaptive and potentially costly, for example, when it interferes with taking action to deal with an illness that can be cured if treated properly [201].

Further research on older men's and women's coping responses to different types of stressful situations and events would be most useful. Such research should control on the stressful situations, so as not to confound sex differences in coping with those in types of stressors encountered. Studies that focus on women's and men's coping with specific illnesses could be particularly useful. The research should further examine outcomes in terms of mental and physical health, preferably in a longitudinal design.

Many coping resources have been discussed in the literature. (For a review, see Elliott and Eisdorfer and Pearlin and Schooler [151, 196].) Let us consider just a few that show clear sex differences. Social relationships and supports, discussed elsewhere in this chapter as directly affecting health and mental health, can also act as an important moderating factor in the relationship between stress and illness [202-203] and are quite different for older men and older women.

Among other factors that may be critical in helping the individual cope with stressful life events and situations are religious beliefs, as suggested by the findings that the strength of those beliefs is related to subjective well-being [204, 205]. Some have argued that this relationship is explained by a religious ideology that provides a framework in which to understand pain and suffering [206]. However, much like denial, religiosity may not only aid but also interfere with effective coping, for example, when an older person puts his/her faith in God rather than seeking medical care. Although we do not know whether it reflects an aging or a cohort phenomenon, it is quite clear that religious feelings and attitudes are higher among older adults than among their younger counterparts [205] and that they report turning to faith more often when faced with adversities [83, 200]. Furthermore, within this age range women are more likely than men to attend church frequently [207]. Race differences are also notable, with older Blacks being more likely than older whites to resort to prayer in stressful situations [170].

Economic means are another important resource for coping with stress. For example, economic resources permit buying health care and home help if health problems and disability make daily life difficult. Or, if public transportation is difficult to use, economic resources may help to buy private transportation. Or, if loved ones live far away, long-distance telephone communication or air travel brings them closer. In sum, economic resources may be used to buffer the impact of stressful situations, yet older women are more likely to be poor or nearly poor than are older men.

Radloff and Monroe review the evidence for women's greater learned helplessness, a form of acquired lack of mastery, in this society [208]. Learned helplessness, in turn, is a contributing factor to depression [209]. Earlier the hypothesis has been noted that women become more assertive and oriented toward mastery as they get older [117]. Might this proposition imply that older women are less prone to depression than younger women? Interestingly, it has been argued by some that feelings of mastery and control may become maladaptive among older adults of both sexes, some of whom are forced by illness to adjust to a renewed dependence on others [206, 210].

Women's higher level of disability has also been interpreted as a lack of coping resources, although others have pointed to the increased health problems and disability among the aged as a factor contributing directly to higher levels of stress in older age [151, 197].

Data — Measures of coping responses are included in the study *Coping with Stress and Challenge in Late Life*, the *National Survey of Black Americans*, and in the *Baltimore Longitudinal Study of Aging*. Measures of various of the coping resources discussed above are included in many studies. While economic status and religiosity are measured in almost all major surveys, personality characteristics are less regularly included.

Health Behaviors

In recent years interest has developed in the health promotive or health damaging effects of certain common behaviors such as smoking, alcohol consumption, physical activity and exercise, Type A behavior, rest, and nutrition [24].

A life style with sufficient physical activities and exercise appears to have a beneficial effect in checking a range of potential health problems, such as high blood pressure, diabetes, cardiovascular dysfunction, weight gain, sleep problems, arthritis, osteoporosis, and early mortality [24, 211, 212]. Moreover, exercise programs have been implicated in relief from stress and in better morale and feelings about the self [213]. Physical exercise has traditionally been a man's domain. Data on physically active leisure activities such as, for example, from the *Tecumseh Community Health Study* show that women participate less in such activities but that if they do, the effects of physical activities on their health are similar to the effects on men's health [212]. We need to understand better why women participate in exercise less than men and what effects exercise might have on their physical and mental health.

It is estimated that a substantial part of the health problems experienced by the elderly are consequences of bad nutrition throughout their lives, although the nutritional needs of older persons are not well understood [214]. In older age, bad nutrition can take several forms. First, insufficient amounts of food may be available to the older person due to poverty or physical difficulty in shopping for and preparing food. Second, even with an adequate food supply, the older person may not eat, or may not eat enough to stay healthy. This may happen when a decreasing sense of smell, taste, or vision makes food appear less appetizing; when denture problems make chewing difficult; or when living alone means that the social stimuli for cooking and eating are lacking. Third, the older person may eat sufficient but nutritionally inadequate food. The elderly tend to make use of foods that involve little preparation, that require little chewing, and that are cheap. These foods include many prepackaged foods but exclude most meats and fresh vegetables. Fourth, as a consequence of an unbalanced diet, food consumption may be too high in calories, leading to overweight and obesity.

Poor nutrition in older age must be understood, therefore, in the context of the social, health, and economic conditions of the aged. Women are more likely than men to experience certain of those conditions, notably living alone, being poor, and being impaired by functional problems. Women's proper nutrition therefore may be in jeopardy. Studies that examine the food consumption of men and women and the social, health, and economic conditions that are associated with different forms of diets therefore are needed. Abraham et al. report that older women have poorer nutrition than do men [215]. Davis and her colleagues examined the effect of living arrangements on the adequacy of nutrition among older men and women, using the *NHANES* data. They found that living alone was associated with worse nutrition among men, while they found no such relationship for women [216].

Type A behavior, a hard-driving life style that expresses itself in competitiveness, aggressiveness, achievement orientation, a chronic sense of time urgency, and little patience, is related to increased risk of coronary heart disease among women and men [21, 217], although there are some indications that the relationship disappears among persons over the age of sixty-five [218]. Adult women and men in the United States differ in the prevalence of Type A behavior, with women exhibiting it less often [21], but this sex difference seems largely accountable for by sex differences in education, occupation, and socioeconomic status. When these factors are controlled for, women and men seem to show little difference in Type A behavior [217]. Among women certain age differences are further suggested. Type A behavior seems to be lower among very young and older women than among women in their thirties, but these findings are based on cross-sectional studies and thus may not represent real age changes [217].

Smoking and alcohol consumption represent behaviors that are damaging to health, as noted before, and both of them are less frequent among women than men, at least among today's older and middle-aged generations [219].

For all of these health behaviors we need to learn how they pattern themselves across the life-span, how these life-span patterns relate to illness conditions and mortality in later life, and how the patterns and their health effects differ for women and men.

Data — Information on reception of meal services is collected in the *Massachusetts Health Care Panel Study*, in the *National Senior Citizen Survey*, and in the *Aging Supplement* to the *NHIS*. Information on nutritional patterns is collected as part of the *NHANES* and the *Massachusetts Health Care Panel*. Information on physical activities and formal exercise is contained in some of the *EPESE* studies, in the *Aging Supplement* to the *NHIS*, and in the studies that use the *OARS* instrument. A measure of Type A behavior is included in the *Framingham Heart Study*. Measures of smoking behavior and/or of alcohol use are contained in the *EPESE* studies, in the *Massachusetts Health Care Panel Study*, in the *Alameda County Study*, and in the *General Social Survey*. Measures on sleep and rest patterns are included in the *EPESE* studies, in the *Massachusetts Health Care Panel Study*, in the *Ohio Longitudinal Study*, and in the *Alameda County Study*.

Biological Factors

As mentioned before, biological differences between men and women — related to genetic, hormonal, immunological, or metabolic factors — may account directly for some of the sex differences in mortality and physical and mental health, or they may differentially affect the susceptibility of the sexes to stress and other behavioral risk factors. For example, it has been suggested that X chromosome-linked genes contribute to women's lesser susceptibility to infectious disease mortality. Or, endogenous female sex hormones may reduce women's risk of coronary heart disease, potentially by way of affecting cholesterol metabolism. Male sex hormones may predispose men to higher levels of aggression and physical activity and thereby contribute to their higher death rates from accidents and homicides. Blood pressure and relative body weight are other potential explanatory factors for the sex difference in mortality. Some biological factors disadvantage women. For example, the female reproductive anatomy accounts for some of the major types of cancer — breast and genital cancer — among women. Despite these and other interesting leads, much about the contributions of biological factors to the sex differential remains to be firmly established and several contradictory findings have been reported in the literature. Recent reviews are provided by Hazzard [17, 220] and by Waldron [21, 221]. It is also worth repeating that several of the data sets referred to in this publication, including the *NHANES*, the *Framingham Heart Study*, the *Baltimore Longitudinal Study of Aging*, the *Tecumseh Community Health Study*, and the *Duke Second Longitudinal Survey*, contain physical examination and laboratory measures that might prove useful for investigations of biological mechanisms in explaining sex differences.

CONCLUSION

Health and illness show some remarkable differences between older women and men. Unfortunately, sex comparisons are not always adjusted for differences in age between the sexes. The average age of women is higher than that of men within each age group, and these age differences may account for some of the differences in health. This possibility needs to be attended to more consistently in future research. Although there are suggestions that some of these sex differences in health may weaken among older age groups, currently available evidence is not sufficient to confirm or refute the latter hypothesis. Moreover, if such a phenomenon of an "age by sex interaction" were confirmed, several general explanations such as selective survival, age changes, or cohort differences would have to be examined before more specific explanations are taken up. More descriptive work of sex differences by age levels and by cohorts would be very useful to help us assess the patterns of sex differences and their magnitude across the life span.

Much of the available information in the gerontological literature is based upon small samples of a somewhat limited nature that will not permit generalizations of findings. On the other hand, data from the large government-based health surveys that use large representative samples are often not reported in a form that would be most useful to gerontological researchers and do not readily find their way into the gerontological literature. A concise assessment is further complicated by the lack of conceptual clarity about major indicators of health and illness. As long as the significance of these indicators to a concept of health is not agreed upon, interpretations of sex differences in health remain ambiguous.

The specific explanations of the observed sex differences also remain unclear. Women differ from men in their biological makeup, their upbringing, their major life roles and life styles, their attitudes and behaviors. Many of these characteristics are related to the development of illness or the maintenance of health. Thus, it is likely that many of these factors contribute in complex ways to the observed sex differences. Understanding sex differences in health is almost like understanding health itself; it must take into account a major part of the explanations for health and illness.

Explanation of health and sex differences in health among the elderly are further complicated because health in older age must be understood as the outcome of a lifetime of relevant developments. This life-span approach, however, is largely lacking from health research among the elderly. Little is known about the long-term effects of symptoms and illness conditions, of work and family roles, of health behaviors such as nutrition or exercise. Instead, much of the existing knowledge about health among this age group consists of descriptions of current health status and of explanations in terms of immediately preceding causes. Life-span research is difficult to conduct because of the multitude of factors that come into play and the complex causal patterns between them and because of the data requirements.

Much work on the health of older women and men remains to be done in terms of both original research and secondary data analysis. It is hoped that this chapter will stimulate some of this needed research.

REFERENCES

1. U.S. Department of Health, Education, and Welfare, Public Health Service, *Current Estimates From the Health Interview Study, United States – 1977*, Vital and Health Statistics, Series 10, No. 126, 1978.
2. E. Shanas and G. L. Maddox, Aging, Health, and the Organization of Health Resources, in *Handbook of Aging and the Social Sciences*, R. H. Binstock and E. Shanas (eds.), Van Nostrand Reinhold, New York, 1976.
3. Louis Harris and Associates, *The Myth and Reality of Aging in America*, National Council on the Aging, Washington, D.C., 1975.
4. *Chartbook on Aging in America*, prepared for the 1981 White House Conference on Aging, 1981.
5. L. M. Verbrugge, A Health Profile of Older Women with Comparisons to Older Men, *Research on Aging, 6*, pp. 291–322, 1984.
6. U.S. Department of Health and Human Services, Public Health Service, *Sex Differences in Health and Use of Medical Care: United States, 1979*, Vital and Health Statistics, Series 3, No. 24, 1983.
7. J. K. Myers, M. M. Weissman, G. L. Tischler, C. E. Holzer III, P. J. Leaf, H. Orvaschel, J. C. Anthony, J. H. Boyd, J. D. Burke, M. Kramer, and R. Stoltzman, Six-Month Prevalence of Psychiatric Disorders in Three Communities, *Archives of General Psychiatry, 41*, pp. 959–967, 1984.
8. S. V. Kasl and L. F. Berkman, Some Psychosocial Influences on the Health Status of the Elderly: The Perspective of Social Epidemiology, in *Aging: Biology and Behavior*, J. L. McGaugh and S. B. Kiesler (eds.), Academic Press, New York, 1981.
9. J. Liang, The Structure of Self-Reported Physical Health Among Aged Adults, *Journal of Gerontology, 41*, pp. 248–260, 1986.
10. E. M. Brody and M. H. Kleban, Day-to-Day Mental and Physical Health Symptoms of Older People: A Report on Health Logs, *The Gerontologist, 23*, pp. 75–85, 1983.
11. World Health Organization, Text of the Constitution of World Health Organization, Official Records, World Health Organization, *2*, p. 100, 1948.
12. L. M. Verbrugge, Recent Trends in Sex Mortality Differentials in the United States, *Women and Health, 5*, pp. 17–37, 1980.
13. D. L. Wingard, The Sex Differential in Morbidity, Mortality, and Lifestyle, *Annual Review of Public Health*, Annual Reviews, Palo Alto, California, 1984.
14. L. M. Verbrugge, Women and Men: Mortality and Health of Older People, in *Aging in Society: Selected Reviews of Recent Research*, M. W. Riley,

B. B. Hess, and K. Bond (eds.), Lawrence Erlbaum, Hillsdale, New Jersey, 1983.

15. J. S. Siegel, Recent and Prospective Demographic Trends for the Elderly Population and Some Implications for Health Care, in *Second Conference on the Epidemiology of Aging*, S. G. Haynes and M. Feinleib (eds.), NIH Publication No. 80-969, U.S. Government Printing Office, Washington, D.C., 1980.

16. C. A. Nathanson, Sex Differences in Mortality, in *Annual Review of Sociology*, R. H. Turner and J. F. Short (eds.), Annual Reviews, Palo Alto, California, 1984.

17. W. R. Hazzard, The Sex Differential in Longevity, in *Principles of Geriatric Medicine*, R. Andres, E. L. Bierman, and W. R. Hazzard (eds.), McGraw-Hill, New York, 1985.

18. H. C. McGill, V. C. Anselmo, J. M. Buchanan, and P. J. Sheridan, The Heart is a Target Organ for Androgen, *Science, 207*, pp. 776-777, 1980.

19. U.S. Department of Health and Human Services, Public Health Service, *Sex Differences in Health and Use of Medical Care: United States, 1979*, Vital and Health Statistics, Series 3, No. 24, 1983.

20. D. T. Purtilo and J. L. Sullivan, Immunological Bases for Superior Survival of Females, *American Journal of Diseases of Children, 133*, pp. 1251-1253, 1979.

21. I. Waldron, An Analysis of Causes of Sex Differences in Mortality and Morbidity, in *The Fundamental Connection Between Nature and Nurture*, W. R. Gove and G. R. Carpenter (eds.), Lexington Books, Lexington, Massachusetts, 1982.

22. C. A. Nathanson, Sex Roles as Variables in Preventive Health Behavior, *Journal of Community Health, 3*, pp. 142-155, 1977.

23. D. L. Wingard, The Sex Differential in Mortality Rates, *American Journal of Epidemiology, 115*, pp. 205-216, 1982.

24. L. F. Berkman and L. Breslow, *Health and Ways of Living*, Oxford University Press, New York, 1983.

25. W. B. Kannel and T. Gordon, Cardiovascular Risk Factors in the Aged: The Framingham Study, *Second Conference on the Epidemiology of Aging*, S. G. Haynes and M. Feinleib (eds.), NIH Publication No. 80-969, U.S. Government Printing Office, Washington, D.C., 1980.

26. E. Palmore, The Relative Importance of Social Factors in Predicting Longevity, in *Prediction of Life Span*, E. Palmore and F. C. Jeffers (eds.), Lexington Books, Lexington, Massachusetts, 1971.

27. M. A. Okun, W. A. Stock, M. J. Haring, and R. A. Witter, Health and Subjective Well-Being: A Meta-Analysis, *International Journal of Aging and Human Development, 19*, pp. 111-132, 1984.

28. L. K. George and R. Landerman, Health and Subjective Well-Being: A Replicated Secondary Data Analysis, *International Journal of Aging and Human Development, 19*, pp. 133-156, 1984.

29. J. M. Mossey and E. Shapiro, Self-Rated Health: A Predictor of Mortality Among the Elderly, *American Journal of Public Health, 72*, pp. 800-808, 1982.

30. A. Zautra and A. Hempel, Subjective Well-Being and Physical Health: A Narrative Literature Review with Suggestions for Future Research, *International Journal of Aging and Human Development, 19,* pp. 95–110, 1984.
31. M. A. Okun and L. K. George, Physician- and Self-Ratings of Health, Neuroticism and Subjective Well-Being Among Men and Women, *Personality and Individual Differences, 5,* pp. 533–539, 1984.
32. M. P. Lawton, M. Ward, and S. Yaffee, Indices of Health in an Aging Population, *Journal of Gerontology, 22,* pp. 334–342, 1967.
33. K. F. Ferraro, Self-Ratings of Health Among the Old and the Old-Old, *Journal of Health and Social Behavior, 21,* pp. 377–383, 1980.
34. D. L. Wingard, personal communication, 1984.
35. S. Katz, A. B. Ford, R. W. Moskowitz, B. A. Jackson, and M. W. Jaffee, Studies of Illness in the Aged, The Index of ADL: A Standardized Measure of Biological and Psychosocial Function, *Journal of the American Medical Association, 185,* pp. 94–98, 1963.
36. Duke University Center for the Study of Aging and Human Development, *Multidimensional Functional Assessment: The OARS Methodology,* Duke University, Durham, North Carolina, 1978.
37. M. P. Lawton, Assessing the Competence of Older People, in *Research, Planning, and Action for the Elderly,* D. P. Kent, R. Kastenbaum, and S. Sherwood (eds.), Behavioral Publications, New York, 1972.
38. R. A. Kane and R. L. Kane, *Assessing the Elderly,* Lexington Books, Lexington, Massachusetts, 1981.
39. A. L. Stewart, J. E. Ware, R. H. Brook, and A. Davis-Avery, Conceptualization and Measurement of Health for Adults in the Health Insurance Study: Vol. II, Physical Health in Terms of Functioning, Rand, Santa Monica, California, July 1978.
40. A. M. Jette and L. G. Branch, The Framingham Disability Study: II. Physical Disability Among the Aging, *American Journal of Public Health, 71,* pp. 1211–1216, 1981.
41. E. Shanas, Self-Assessment of Physical Function: White and Black Elderly of the United States, in *Second Conference on the Epidemiology of Aging,* S. G. Haynes and M. Feinleib (eds.), NIH Publication No. 80-969, U.S. Government Printing Office, Washington, D.C., 1980.
42. N. L. Chappell, Measuring Functional Ability and Chronic Health Conditions Among the Elderly: A Research Note on the Adequacy of Three Instruments, *Journal of Health and Social Behavior, 22,* pp. 90–102, 1981.
43. M. Moss, personal communication, 1985.
44. C. A. Nathanson and G. Lorenz, Women and Health: The Social Dimensions of Biomedical Data, in *Women in the Middle Years,* J. Z. Giele (ed.), John Wiley and Sons, New York, 1982.
45. D. A. Hamburg, G. R. Elliott, and D. L. Parron, *Health and Behavior,* National Academy Press, Washington, D.C., 1982.
46. J. S. Kramer, E. H. Yelin, and W. V. Epstein, Social and Economic Impacts of Four Musculoskeletal Conditions, *Arthritis and Rheumatism, 26,* pp. 901–907, 1983.

47. G. E. Ehrlich, Social, Economic, Psychologic, and Sexual Outcomes in Rheumatoid Arthritis, *The American Journal of Medicine, 75,* pp. 27–34, 1983.
48. C. S. Kart, E. S. Metress, and J. F. Metress, *Aging and Health: Biologic and Social Perspectives,* Addison-Wesley, Menlo Park, California, 1978.
49. M. A. Davis, Sex Differences in Reporting Osteoarthritic Symptoms: A Sociomedical Approach, *Journal of Health and Social Behavior, 22,* pp. 298–310, 1981.
50. J. F. Fries, The Chronic Disease Data Bank: First Principles to Future Directions, *Journal of Medicine and Philosophy, 9,* pp. 161–180, 1984.
51. L. V. Avioli, Osteoporosis: Pathogenesis and Therapy, in *Metabolic Bone Disease, Vol. I,* L. V. Avioli and S. M. Krane (eds.), Academic Press, New York, 1977.
52. D. F. Giansiracusa and F. G. Kantrowitz, *Rheumatic and Metabolic Bone Diseases in the Elderly,* D.C. Heath, Lexington, Massachusetts, 1982.
53. J. L. Kelsey, H. Pastides, and G. E. Bisbee, Jr., *Musculo-Skeletal Disorders: Their Frequency of Occurrence and Their Impact on the Population of the United States,* Prodist, New York, 1978.
54. National Institutes of Health, *Osteoporosis,* Consensus Development Conference Statement, Vol. 5, No. 3, U.S. Government Printing Office, Washington, D.C., 1984.
55. J. W. G. Yarnell and A. S. St Leger, The Prevalence, Severity and Factors Associated with Urinary Incontinence in a Random Sample of the Elderly, *Age and Ageing, 8,* pp. 81–85, 1979.
56. S. S. Sutherland, The Psychology of Incontinence, in *Incontinence in the Elderly,* F. L. Willington (ed.), Academic Press, New York, 1976.
57. T. J. Wells, Social and Psychological Implications of Incontinence, in *Urology in Old Age,* J. C. Brocklehurst (ed.), Churchill Livingstone, New York, 1984.
58. N. J. Vetter, D. A. Jones, and C. R. Victor, Urinary Incontinence in the Elderly at Home, *The Lancet,* pp. 1275–1277, Dec. 5, 1981.
59. A. C. Diokno, B. M. Brock, M. B. Brown, and A. R. Herzog, Prevalence of Urinary Incontinence and Other Urologic Symptoms in the Noninstitutionalized Elderly, *Journal of Urology, 136,* pp. 1022–1025, 1986.
60. W. Rakowski, Health Psychology and Late Life: The Differentiation of Health and Illness for the Study of Health-Related Behaviors, *Research on Aging, 6,* pp. 593–620, 1984.
61. C. S. Kart, Experiencing Symptoms: Attribution and Misattribution of Illness Among the Aged, in *Elderly Patients and Their Doctors,* M. R. Haug (ed.), Springer, New York, 1981.
62. T. R. Prohaska, E. A. Leventhal, H. Leventhal, and M. L. Keller, Health Practices and Illness Cognition in Young, Middle Aged, and Elderly Adults, *Journal of Gerontology, 40,* pp. 569–578, 1985.
63. M. H. Becker (ed.), The Health Belief Model and Personal Health Behavior, *Health Education Monographs, 2,* pp. 324–511, 1974.
64. N. K. Janz and M. H. Becker, The Health Belief Model: A Decade Later, *Health Education Quarterly, 11,* pp. 1–47, 1984.

65. H. Leventhal, D. Meyer, and D. Nerenz, The Commonsense Representation of Illness Danger, in *Medical Psychology, Vol. 2,* S. Rachman (ed.), Pergamon, New York, 1980.

66. R. D. Koeske, Toward a Biosocial Paradigm for Menopause Research: Lessons and Contributions from the Behavioral Sciences, in *Changing Perspectives on Menopause,* A. M. Voda, M. Dinnerstein, and S. R. O'Donnell (eds.), University of Texas Press, Austin, 1982.

67. E. Shanas, *The Health of Older People,* Harvard University Press, Cambridge, Massachusetts, 1962.

68. J. Griffen, Cultural Models for Coping with Menopause, in *Changing Perspectives on Menopause,* A. M. Voda, M. Dinnerstein, and S. R. O'Donnell (eds.), University of Texas Press, Austin, 1982.

69. M. Flint, Male and Female Menopause: A Cultural Put-on, in *Changing Perspectives on Menopause,* A. M. Voda, M. Dinnerstein, and S. R. O'Donnell (eds.), University of Texas Press, Austin, 1982.

70. S. M. McKinley and J. B. McKinlay, Selected Studies of the Menopause, *Journal of Biosocial Science, 5,* pp. 533–555, 1973.

71. N. F. Woods, Menopausal Distress: A Model for Epidemiologic Investigation, in *Changing Perspectives on Menopause,* A. M. Voda, M. Dinnerstein, and S. R. O'Donnell (eds.), University of Texas Press, Austin, 1982.

72. B. Gastel, J. Cornoni-Huntley, and J. A. Brody, Estrogen Use and Postmenopausal Women: A Basis for Informed Decisions, *Journal of Family Practice, 11,* pp. 851–860, 1980.

73. R. D. Gambrell, Jr., Estrogen-Progestogen Therapy During Menopause, *Postgraduate Medicine, 80,* pp. 261–267, 1986.

74. H. L. Judd, R. E. Cleary, W. T. Creasman, D. C. Figge, N. Kase, Z. Rosenwaks, and G. E. Tagatz, Estrogen Replacement Therapy, *Obstetrics and Gynecology, 58,* pp. 267–275, 1981.

75. E. Pfeiffer, Psychopathology and Social Pathology, in *Handbook of the Psychology of Aging,* J. E. Birren and K. W. Schaie (eds.), Van Nostrand Reinhold, New York, 1977.

76. D. G. Blazer, *Depression in Late Life,* C. V. Mosby, St. Louis, Missouri, 1982.

77. B. J. Gurland, The Comparative Frequency of Depression in Various Adult Age Groups, *Journal of Gerontology, 31,* pp. 283–292, 1976.

78. B. J. Gurland and J. A. Toner, Depression in the Elderly: A Review of Recently Published Studies, in *Annual Review of Gerontology and Geriatrics,* Vol. 3, C. Eisdorfer (ed.), Springer, New York, 1982.

79. G. L. Klerman, Problems in the Definition and Diagnosis of Depression in the Elderly, in *Depression and Aging,* L. D. Breslau and M. R. Haug (eds.), Springer, New York, 1983.

80. D. A. Regier, J. K. Myers, M. Kramer, L. N. Robins, D. G. Blazer, R. L. Hough, W. W. Eaton, and B. Z. Locke, The NIMH Epidemiologic Catchment Area Program: Historical Context, Major Objectives, and Study Population Characteristics, *Archives of General Psychiatry, 41,* pp. 934–941, 1984.

81. B. P. Dohrenwend and B. S. Dohrenwend, Sex Differences and Psychiatric Disorders, *American Journal of Sociology, 81,* pp. 1447–1454, 1976.

82. U.S. Department of Health, Education, and Welfare, Public Health Service, *Basic Data on Depressive Symptomatology,* Vital and Health Statistics, Series 11, No. 216, 1980.

83. J. Veroff, E. Douvan, and R. A. Kulka, *The Inner American: A Self-Portrait from 1957 to 1976,* Basic Books, New York, 1981.

84. M. M. Weissman and G. L. Klerman, Sex Differences and the Epidemiology of Depression, *Archives of General Psychiatry, 34,* pp. 98–111, 1977.

85. R. R. Frerichs, C. S. Aneshensel, and V. A. Clark, Prevalence of Depression in Los Angeles County, *American Journal of Epidemiology, 113,* pp. 691–699, 1981.

86. B. Gurland, L. Dean, P. Cross, and R. Golden, The Epidemiology of Depression and Dementia in the Elderly: The Use of Multiple Indicators of These Conditions, in *Psychopathology in the Aged,* J. O. Cole and J. E. Barett (eds.), Raven, New York, 1980.

87. A. Stenback, Depression and Suicidal Behavior in Old Age, in *Handbook of Mental Health and Aging,* J. E. Birren and R. B. Sloane (eds.), Prentice-Hall, Englewood Cliffs, New Jersey, 1980.

88. R. C. Atchley, Aging and Suicide: Reflection of the Quality of Life?, in *Second Conference on the Epidemiology of Aging,* S. G. Haynes and M. Feinleib (eds.), NIH Publication No. 80-969, U.S. Government Printing Office, Washington, D.C., 1980.

89. M. Miller, *Suicide After Sixty,* Springer, New York, 1979.

90. K. Shulman, Suicide and Parasuicide in Old Age: A Review, *Age and Ageing, 7,* pp. 201–209, 1978.

91. J. Cohen, Comment, in *Second Conference on the Epidemiology of Aging,* S. G. Haynes and M. Feinleib (eds.), NIH Publication No. 80-969, U.S. Government Printing Office, Washington, D.C., 1980.

92. R. H. Steffensmeier, Suicide and the Contemporary Woman: Are Male and Female Suicide Rates Converging?, *Sex Roles, 10,* pp. 613–631, 1984.

93. R. W. Maris, *Pathways to Suicide: A Survey of Self-Destructive Behaviors,* Johns Hopkins University Press, Baltimore, 1981.

94. F. M. Andrews and S. B. Withey, *Social Indicators of Well-Being: Americans' Perceptions of Life Quality,* Plenum, New York, 1976.

95. A. Campbell, P. E. Converse, and W. L. Rodgers, *The Quality of American Life: Perceptions, Evaluations, and Satisfactions,* Russell Sage Foundation, New York, 1976.

96. A. R. Herzog, W. L. Rodgers, and J. Woodworth, Subjective Well-Being Among Different Age Groups, Research Report No. 9017, Institute for Social Research, Ann Arbor, Michigan, 1982.

97. E. Spreitzer and E. E. Snyder, Correlates of Life Satisfaction Among the Aged, *Journal of Gerontology, 29,* pp. 454–458, 1974.

98. R. Larson, Thirty Years of Research on the Subjective Well-Being of Older Americans, *Journal of Gerontology, 33,* pp. 109–125, 1978.

99. J. Liang, Sex Differences in Life Satisfaction Among the Elderly, *Journal of Gerontology, 37,* pp. 100–108, 1982.

100. N. M. Bradburn, *The Structure of Psychological Well-Being,* Aldine, Chicago, 1969.

101. L. K. George, The Impact of Personality and Social Status Factors Upon Levels of Activity and Psychological Well-Being, *Journal of Gerontology, 33,* pp. 840–847, 1978.

102. E. Pfeiffer, A Short Portable Mental Status Questionnaire for the Assessment of Organic Brain Deficit in Elderly Patients, *Journal of the American Geriatrics Society, 23,* pp. 433–441, 1975.

103. M. F. Folstein, S. Folstein, and P. R. McHugh, Mini-Mental State: A Practical Method for Grading the Cognitive State of Patients for the Clinician, *Journal of Psychiatric Research, 12,* pp. 189–198, 1975.

104. Secretary's Task Force on Alzheimer's Disease, *Alzheimer's Disease,* DHHS Publication No. (ADM)84-1323, U.S. Government Printing Office, Washington, D.C., 1984.

105. E. Miller, Cognitive Assessment of the Older Adult, in *Handbook of Mental Health and Aging,* J. E. Birren and R. B. Sloane (eds.), Prentice-Hall, Englewood Cliffs, New Jersey, 1980.

106. D. W. K. Kay and K. Bergmann, Epidemiology of Mental Disorders Among the Aged in the Community, in *Handbook of Mental Health and Aging,* J. E. Birren and R. B. Sloane (eds.), Prentice-Hall, Englewood Cliffs, New Jersey, 1980.

107. R. Neugebauer, Formulation of Hypotheses About the True Prevalence of Functional and Organic Psychiatric Disorders Among the Elderly in the United States, in *Mental Illness in the United States,* B. P. Dohrenwend, B. S. Dohrenwend, M. Gould, B. Link, R. Neugebauer, and R. Wunsch-Hitzig (eds.), Praeger, New York, 1980.

108. D. Blazer, The Epidemiology of Mental Illness in Late Life, in *Handbook of Geriatric Psychiatry,* E. Busse and D. Blazer (eds.), Van Nostrand Reinhold, New York, 1980.

109. B. Gurland, J. Copeland, J. Kuriansky, M. Kelleher, L. Sharpe, and L. L. Dean, *The Mind and Mood of Aging,* Haworth, New York, 1983.

110. W. R. Gove and M. Hughes, Possible Causes of the Apparent Sex Differences in Physical Health: An Empirical Investigation, *American Sociological Review, 44,* pp. 126–146, 1979.

111. E. B. Palmore, Predictors of the Longevity Difference: A 25-Year Follow-Up, *The Gerontologist, 22,* pp. 513–518, 1982.

112. M. Romaniuk, W. J. McAuley, and G. Arling, An Examination of the Prevalence of Mental Disorders Among the Elderly in the Community, *Journal of Abnormal Psychology, 92,* pp. 458–467, 1983.

113. C. S. Aneshensel, R. R. Frerichs, and G. J. Huba, Depression and Physical Illness: A Multiwave, Nonrecursive Causal Model, *Journal of Health and Social Behavior, 25,* pp. 350–371, 1984.

114. B. Gurland, D. Wilder, R. Golden, J. Teresi, R. Gurland, and J. Copeland, The Relationship between Depression and Disability in the Elderly: Data from the Comprehensive Assessment and Referral Evaluation (CARE), in Wattis (eds.), Churchill Livingstone, London (in press).

115. M. Haug, L. L. Belgrave, and B. Gratton, Mental Health and the Elderly: Factors in Stability and Change Over Time, *Journal of Health and Social Behavior, 25,* pp. 100–115, 1984.

116. Z. J. Lipowski, Psychiatry of Somatic Diseases: Epidemiology, Pathogenesis, Classification, *Comprehensive Psychiatry, 16,* pp. 105–124, 1975.

117. B. L. Neugarten and D. Gutmann, Age-Sex Roles and Personality in Middle Age: A Thematic Apperception Study, *Psychological Monographs: General and Applied, 72,* No. 470, 1958.

118. D. Gutmann, Parenthood: A Key to the Comparative Study of the Life Cycle, in *Life-Span Developmental Psychology,* N. Datan and L. Ginsburg (eds.), Academic Press, New York, 1975.

119. D. Gutmann, The Cross-Cultural Perspective: Notes Toward a Comparative Psychology of Aging, in *Handbook of the Psychology of Aging,* J. E. Birren and K. W. Schaie (eds.), Van Nostrand Reinhold, New York, 1977.

120. L. E. Troll and E. M. Parron, Age Changes in Sex Roles Amid Changing Sex Roles: The Double Shift, in *Annual Review of Gerontology and Geriatrics,* Vol. 2, C. Eisdorfer (ed.), Springer, New York, 1981.

121. R. Andersen and J. F. Newman, Societal and Individual Determinants of Medical Care Utilization in the United States, *Milbank Memorial Fund Quarterly, 51,* pp. 95–124, 1973.

122. R. Andersen, A Behavioral Model of Families' Use of Health Services, Research Series No. 25, Center for Health Administration Studies, University of Chicago, Chicago, 1968.

123. C. Coulton and A. K. Frost, Use of Social and Health Services by the Elderly, *Journal of Health and Social Behavior, 23,* pp. 330–339, 1982.

124. M. R. Haug, Age and Medical Care Utilization Patterns, *Journal of Gerontology, 36,* pp. 103–111, 1981.

125. C. M. Wylie, Contrasts in the Health of Elderly Men and Women: An Analysis of Recent Data for Whites in the United States, *Journal of the American Geriatrics Society, 39,* pp. 670–675, 1984.

126. F. D. Wolinsky, R. M. Coe, D. K. Miller, J. M. Prendergast, M. J. Creel, and M. N. Chavez, Health Services Utilization Among the Noninstitutionalized Elderly, *Journal of Health and Social Behavior, 24,* pp. 325–337, 1983.

127. M. G. Kovar, Health of the Elderly and Use of Health Services, *Public Health Reports, 92,* pp. 9–19, 1977.

128. L. G. Branch and A. M. Jette, A Prospective Study of Long-Term Care Institutionalization Among the Aged, *American Journal of Public Health, 72,* pp. 1373–1379, 1982.

129. T. T. H. Wan and W. Weissert, Social Support Networks, Patient Status, and Institutionalization, *Research on Aging, 3,* pp. 240–256, 1981.

130. W. Weissert and W. Scanlon, Determinants of Institutionalization of the Aged, Working Paper No. 1466-21, The Urban Institute, Washington, D.C., 1982.
131. R. W. Redick and C. A. Taube, Demography and Mental Health Care of the Aged, in *Handbook of Mental Health and Aging*, J. E. Birren and R. B. Sloane (eds.), Prentice-Hall, Englewood Cliffs, New Jersey, 1980.
132. S. Shapiro, E. A. Skinner, L. G. Kessler, M. Von Korff, P. S. German, G. L. Tischler, P. J. Leaf, L. Benham, L. Cottler, and D. A. Regier, Utilization of Health and Mental Health Services, *Archives of General Psychiatry, 41*, pp. 971–978, 1984.
133. M. Pernick, personal communication, 1984.
134. L. M. Verbrugge and R. P. Steiner, Physician Treatment of Men and Women Patients: Sex Bias or Appropriate Care?, *Medical Care, 19*, pp. 609–632, 1981.
135. E. M. Brody, M. H. Kleban, and E. Moles, What Older People Do About Their Day-to-Day Mental and Physical Health Symptoms, *Journal of the American Geriatrics Society, 31*, pp. 489–498, 1983.
136. E. Cumming, C. Lazar, and L. Chisholm, Suicide as an Index of Role Strain Among Employed and Not Employed Married Women in British Columbia, *Canadian Review of Sociology and Anthropology, 12*, pp. 462–470, 1975.
137. L. S. Hauenstein, S. V. Kasl, and E. Harburg, Work Status, Work Satisfaction, and Blood Pressure Among Married Black and White Women, *Psychology of Women Quarterly, 1*, pp. 334–349, 1977.
138. M. A. Haw, Women, Work and Stress: A Review and Agenda for the Future, *Journal of Health and Social Behavior, 23*, pp. 132–144, 1982.
139. S. G. Haynes and M. Feinleib, Women, Work and Coronary Heart Disease: Prospective Findings From the Framingham Heart Study, *American Journal of Public Health, 70*, pp. 133–141, 1980.
140. E. Shanas, Older Women: Retired Workers and Housewives, Final Report to the Social Security Administration, June 1981.
141. L. M. Verbrugge, Multiple Roles and Physical Health of Women and Men, *Journal of Health and Social Behavior, 24*, pp. 16–30, 1983.
142. G. Sorensen and J. T. Mortimer, Women, Work, and Health, in *Work and Family*, H. Gross and N. Gerstel (eds.), Guilford, New York, 1984.
143. C. Hollenshead, Older Women at Work, *Educational Horizons, 60*, pp. 137–146, 1982.
144. E. M. Brody, "Women in the Middle" and Family Help to Older People, *The Gerontologist, 21*, pp. 471–480, 1981.
145. M. Fiske, Tasks and Crises of the Second Half of Life: The Interrelationship of Commitment, Coping, and Adaptation, in *Handbook of Mental Health and Aging*, J. E. Birren and R. B. Sloane (eds.), Prentice-Hall, Englewood Cliffs, New Jersey, 1980.
146. L. E. Troll and B. F. Turner, Sex Differences in Problems of Aging, in *Gender and Disordered Behavior*, E. S. Gomberg and V. Franks (eds.), Brunner/Mazel, New York, 1979.
147. B. Gratton and M. R. Haug, Decision and Adaptation: Research on Female Retirement, *Research on Aging, 5*, pp. 59–76, 1983.

148. M. Minkler, Research on the Health Effects of Retirement: An Uncertain Legacy, *Journal of Health and Social Behavior, 22,* pp. 117–130, 1981.
149. R. L. Kahn, *Work and Health,* Wiley, New York, 1981.
150. J. S. House, Occupational Stress and Coronary Heart Disease: A Review and Theoretical Integration, *Journal of Health and Social Behavior, 15,* pp. 12–27, 1974.
151. G. R. Elliott and C. Eisdorfer, *Stress and Human Health,* Springer, New York, 1982.
152. J. Miller, C. Schooler, M. L. Kohn, and K. A. Miller, Women and Work: The Psychological Effects of Occupational Conditions, *American Journal of Sociology, 85,* pp. 66–94, 1979.
153. G. Sorensen, P. Pirie, A. Folsom, R. Luepker, D. Jacobs, and R. Gillum, Gender Differences in the Relationship Between Work and Health, paper presented at the Annual Meeting of the American Sociological Association, Detroit, September 1983.
154. V. K. Oppenheimer, The Female Labor Force in the United States: Demographic and Economic Factors Governing its Growth and Changing Composition, Population Monograph Series No. 5, Institute of International Studies, University of California, Berkeley, California, 1970.
155. B. R. Bergman, Occupational Segregation, Wages and Profits When Employers Discriminate by Race or Sex, *Eastern Economic Journal, 1,* pp. 103–110, 1974.
156. J. M. Stellman, Occupational Health Hazards of Women: An Overview, *Preventive Medicine 7,* pp. 281–293, 1978.
157. B. G. F. Cohen, Organizational Factors Affecting Stress in the Clerical Worker, *Occupational Health Nursing, 31,* pp. 30–34, 1983.
158. J. Z. Giele, Women's Work and Family Roles, in *Women in the Middle Years,* J. Z. Giele (ed.), John Wiley, New York, 1982.
159. L. F. Berkman, Assessing the Physical Health Effects of Social Networks and Social Support, in *Annual Review of Public Health,* Vol. 5, L. Breslow, J. E. Fielding and L. B. Lave (eds.), Annual Reviews, Palo Alto, California, 1984.
160. L. F. Berkman and S. L. Syme, Social Networks, Host Resistance, and Mortality: A Nine-Year Follow-Up Study of Alameda County Residents, *American Journal of Epidemiology, 109,* pp. 186–204, 1979.
161. D. G. Blazer, Social Support and Mortality in an Elderly Community Population, *American Journal of Epidemiology, 115,* pp. 684–694, 1982.
162. S. Cobb, Social Support and Health Through the Life Course, in *Aging From Birth to Death,* M. W. Riley (ed.), Westview Press, Boulder, Colorado, 1979.
163. J. S. House, C. Robbins, and H. L. Metzner, The Association of Social Relationships and Activities with Mortality: Prospective Evidence from the Tecumseh Community Health Study, *American Journal of Epidemiology, 116,* pp. 123–140, 1982.
164. M. F. Lowenthal and C. Haven, Interaction and Adaptation: Intimacy as a Critical Variable, *American Sociological Review, 33,* pp. 20–30, 1968.

165. T. C. Antonucci, Personal Characteristics, Social Support, and Social Behavior, in *Handbook of Aging and the Social Sciences*, 2nd edition, R. H. Binstock and E. Shanas (eds.), Van Nostrand Reinhold, New York, 1985.
166. J. S. House and R. L. Kahn, Measures and Concepts of Social Support, in *Social Support and Health*, S. Cohen and L. Syme (eds.), Academic Press, New York, 1985.
167. E. A. Powers and G. L. Bultena, Sex Differences in Intimate Friendships of Old Age, *Journal of Marriage and the Family, 38*, pp. 739–747, 1976.
168. L. A. Strain and N. L. Chappell, Confidants, *Research on Aging, 4*, pp. 479–502, 1982.
169. R. C. Atchley and S. J. Miller, Older People and Their Families, in *Annual Review of Gerontology and Geriatrics*, Vol. 1, C. Eisdorfer (ed.), Springer, New York, 1980.
170. R. C. Gibson, Blacks at Middle and Late Life: Resources and Coping, *Annals of the American Academy of Political and Social Science, 464*, pp. 79–90, 1982.
171. R. C. Kessler and J. D. McLeod, Sex Differences in Vulnerability to Undesirable Life Events, *American Sociological Review, 49*, pp. 620–631, 1984.
172. W. R. Gove, M. Hughes, and C. B. Style, Does Marriage Have Positive Effects on the Psychological Well-Being of the Individual?, *Journal of Health and Social Behavior, 24*, pp. 122–131, 1983.
173. D. E. Gallagher, J. N. Breckenridge, L. W. Thompson, and J. A. Peterson, Effects of Bereavement on Indicators of Mental Health in Elderly Widows and Widowers, *Journal of Gerontology, 38*, pp. 565–571, 1983.
174. P. J. Clayton, Mortality and Morbidity in the First Year of Widowhood, *Archives of General Psychiatry, 30*, pp. 747–750, 1974.
175. K. F. Rowland, Environmental Events Predicting Death for the Elderly, *Psychological Bulletin, 84*, pp. 349–372, 1977.
176. S. K. Bettis and F. G. Scott, Bereavement and Grief, in *Annual Review of Gerontology and Geriatrics*, Vol. 2, C. Eisdorfer (ed.), Springer, New York, 1981.
177. D. K. Heyman and D. T. Gianturco, Long-Term Adaptation by the Elderly to Bereavement, *Journal of Gerontology, 28*, pp. 359–362, 1973.
178. M. L. Medley, Satisfaction with Life Among Persons Sixty-Five Years and Older, *Journal of Gerontology, 31*, pp. 448–455, 1976.
179. E. Palmore and C. Luikart, Health and Social Factors Related to Life Satisfaction, *Journal of Health and Social Behavior, 13*, pp. 68–80, 1972.
180. T. H. Holmes and R. H. Rahe, The Social Readjustment Rating Scale, *Journal of Psychosomatic Research, 11*, pp. 213–218, 1967.
181. B. S. Dohrenwend and B. P. Dohrenwend, *Stressful Life Events and Their Contexts*, Prodist, New York, 1981.
182. E. Palmore, W. P. Cleveland, J. B. Nowlin, D. Ramm, and I. C. Siegler, Stress and Adaptation in Later Life, *Journal of Gerontology, 34*, pp. 841–851, 1979.

183. A. Vinokur and M. L. Selzer, Desirable Versus Undesirable Life Events: Their Relationship to Stress and Mental Distress, *Journal of Personality and Social Psychology, 32,* pp. 329–337, 1975.

184. E. H. Uhlenhuth, R. S. Lipman, M. B. Balter, and M. Stern, Symptom Intensity and Life Stress in the City, *Archives of General Psychiatry, 31,* pp. 759–764, 1974.

185. B. S. Dohrenwend, Social Status and Stressful Life Events, *Journal of Personality and Social Psychology, 28,* pp. 225–235, 1973.

186. R. C. Kessler, A Strategy for Studying Differential Vulnerability to the Psychological Consequences of Stress, *Journal of Health and Social Behavior, 20,* pp. 100–108, 1979.

187. D. J. Dekker and J. T. Webb, Relationships of the Social Readjustment Rating Scale to Psychiatric Patient Status, Anxiety, and Social Desirability, *Journal of Psychosomatic Research, 18,* pp. 125–130, 1974.

188. D. Belle, The Stress of Caring: Women as Providers of Social Support, in *Handbook of Stress: Theoretical and Clinical Aspects,* L. Goldberger and S. Breznitz (eds.), Free Press, New York, 1982.

189. J. G. Rabkin and E. L. Struenig, Life Events, Stress, and Illness, *Science, 194,* pp. 1013–1020, 1976.

190. L. K. George and I. C. Siegler, Coping With Stress and Challenge in Later Life, Final Report to the AARP Andrus Foundation, Duke University Center for the Study of Aging and Human Development, Durham, North Carolina, 1981.

191. M. F. Lowenthal and D. Chiriboga, Social Stress and Adaptation: Toward a Life-Course Perspective, in *The Psychology of Adult Development and Aging,* C. Eisdorfer and M. P. Lawton (eds.), American Psychological Association, Washington, D.C., 1973.

192. V. J. Renner and J. E. Birren, Stress: Physiological and Psychological Mechanisms, in *Handbook of Mental Health and Aging,* J. E. Birren and R. B. Sloane (eds.), Prentice-Hall, Englewood Cliffs, New Jersey, 1980.

193. D. Mechanic, Comment on Gove and Hughes, 1979, *American Sociological Review, 45,* pp. 513–514, 1980.

194. L. M. Verbrugge, Comment on Gove and Hughes, 1979, *American Sociological Review, 45,* pp. 507–513, 1980.

195. R. C. Kessler and J. A. McRae, Jr., Trends in the Relationship Between Sex and Psychological Distress: 1957–1976, *American Sociological Review, 46,* pp. 443–452, 1981.

196. L. I. Pearlin and C. Schooler, The Structure of Coping, *Journal of Health and Social Behavior, 19,* pp. 2–21, 1978.

197. J. S. House and C. Robbins, Age, Psychosocial Stress, and Health, in *Aging in Society: Selected Reviews of Recent Research,* M. W. Riley, B. B. Hess, and K. Bond (eds.), Lawrence Erlbaum, Hillsdale, New Jersey, 1983.

198. A. G. Billings and R. H. Moos, The Role of Coping Responses and Social Resources in Attenuating the Stress of Life Events, *Journal of Behavioral Medicine, 4,* pp. 139–157, 1981.

199. M. P. Quayhagen and M. Quayhagen, Coping with Conflict, *Research on Aging, 4,* pp. 364–377, 1982.

200. R. R. McCrae, Age Differences in the Use of Coping Mechanisms, *Journal of Gerontology, 37,* pp. 454–460, 1982.

201. R. S. Lazarus and G. Y. Golden, The Function of Denial in Stress, Coping, and Aging, in *Aging: Biology and Behavior,* J. L. McGaugh and S. B. Kiesler (eds.), Academic Press, New York, 1981.

202. S. Gore, The Effect of Social Support in Moderating the Health Consequences of Unemployment, *Journal of Health and Social Behavior, 19,* pp. 157–165, 1978.

203. S. Cobb, Social Support as a Moderator of Life Stress, *Psychosomatic Medicine, 38,* pp. 300–314, 1976.

204. C. K. Hadaway, Life Satisfaction and Religion: A Reanalysis, *Social Forces, 57,* pp. 636–643, 1978.

205. D. O. Moberg, Religiosity in Old Age, *The Gerontologist, 5,* pp. 78–87, 1965.

206. G. E. West and R. L. Simons, Sex Differences in Stress, Coping Resources, and Illness Among the Elderly, *Research on Aging, 5,* pp. 235–268, 1983.

207. R. C. Atchley, *The Social Forces in Later Life,* 2nd Edition, Wadsworth, Belmont, California, 1977.

208. L. S. Radloff and M. K. Monroe, Sex Differences in Helplessness – With Implications for Depression, in *Career Development and Counseling of Women,* L. S. Hansen and R. S. Rapoza (eds.), Charles Thomas, Springfield, Illinois, 1978.

209. M. E. P. Seligman, *Helplessness: On Depression, Development and Death,* W. H. Freeman, San Francisco, 1975.

210. L. F. Jarvik, The Impact of Immediate Life Situations on Depression: Illnesses and Losses, in *Depression and Aging: Causes, Care, and Consequences,* L. D. Breslau and M. R. Haug (eds.), Springer, New York, 1983.

211. R. S. Paffenbarger and W. E. Hale, Work Activity and Coronary Heart Mortality, *New England Journal of Medicine, 292,* pp. 545–550, 1975.

212. H. L. Metzner, W. J. Carman, and J. House, Health Practices, Risk Factors, and Chronic Disease in Tecumseh, *Preventive Medicine, 12,* pp. 491–507, 1983.

213. C. H. Folkins and W. E. Sime, Physical Fitness Training and Mental Health, *American Psychologist, 36,* pp. 373–389, 1981.

214. M. Rookstein and M. L. Sussman, *Nutrition, Longevity, and Aging,* Academic Press, New York, 1976.

215. S. Abraham, M. D. Carroll, C. M. Dresser, and C. L. Johnson, *Dietary Intake Findings, United States, 1971–74,* Vital and Health Statistics, Series 11, No. 202, National Center for Health Statistics, Hyattsville, Maryland, 1977.

216. M. A. Davis, E. Randall, R. N. Forthofer, E. S. Lee, and S. Margen, Living Arrangements and Dietary Patterns of Older Adults in the United States, *Journal of Gerontology, 40,* pp. 434–442, 1985.

217. L. J. Baker, M. Dearborn, J. E. Hastings, and K. Hamberger, Type A Behavior in Women: A Review, *Health Psychology, 3,* pp. 477–497, 1984.

218. S. G. Haynes, M. Feinleib, S. Levine, N. Scotch, and W. B. Kannel, The Relationship of Psychosocial Factors to Coronary Heart Disease in the Framingham Study, II, Prevalence of Coronary Heart Disease, *American Journal of Epidemiology, 107,* pp. 384–402, 1978.

219. E. F. Borgatta, R. J. V. Montgomery, and M. L. Borgatta, Alcohol Use and Abuse, Life Crisis Events, and the Elderly, *Research on Aging, 4,* pp. 378–408, 1982.

220. W. R. Hazzard, Biological Basis of the Sex Differential in Longevity, *Journal of the American Geriatrics Society, 34,* pp. 455–471, 1986.

221. I. Waldron, What Do We Know About Causes of Sex Differences in Mortality? − A Review of the Literature, *Population Bulletin of the United Nations, 18,* pp. 59–76, 1985.

CHAPTER
5

Economic Status of Older Women: A Summary of Selected Research Issues

Karen C. Holden

INTRODUCTION

Social policy over the past fifty years has altered the role of government and the family in providing income to the elderly. Once considered the responsibility primarily of the individual, it has become one increasingly shared with the federal government through direct income and in-kind transfers and the federal regulation of private pensions. The result has been a marked and rapid improvement in both the absolute and relative levels of well-being of the elderly. In 1959, 35 percent of the population sixty-five years of age or older were below the poverty threshold; in 1984 only 12.4 percent were poor. Despite this success, differences in economic well-being between elderly women and men persist. Indeed, by some measures the gap may have grown, sparking a debate over the adequacy and equity of government efforts in this area.

Elderly women living alone are at a disproportionate risk of being poor. While only one-quarter of the population sixty-five and older in 1984 were unrelated women (i.e., women living alone or with nonrelatives only), the 25 percent of this group that were poor accounted for over one-half of the elderly poor. This is a result not of overtly different treatment of women and men by government and private income support programs, but of the dependence of benefits from these programs on past work records and current marital status.[1]

---

[1] In general government and private pension programs must treat women and men in the same way and cannot provide different benefits based on sex alone. Nevertheless, men and women will fare differently when benefits are based on work patterns and earnings. Thus, these programs perpetuate the effects of earning inequities among women and men into retirement.

For this reason, the economic status of elderly women can be understood only by tracing how their life-time work histories and how their past and current marital status influence the benefits received from public and private income programs.

This chapter reviews the empirical literature in two major areas: the determinants of poverty status and the receipt of pension income by older women. While poverty rates are affected by the definition of the poverty threshold, research on poverty illuminates the more general issue of why women's economic status in old age is less favorable than that of elderly men, of younger men, and of women themselves when younger. Measures of economic well-being used in the gerontological literature are most often based on annual income alone. Nevertheless, more inclusive measures of economic well-being are and should be used, an issue we discuss later in this chapter. The discussion of pensions focuses on women at the other end of the income distribution — those who were relatively well off when married or working and when retired.

Any discussion of the economic status of women cannot ignore that of men. Most older women are, or once were, wives and share the consequences of earlier choices made jointly with or solely by their husbands. We mention these decisions of husbands and their impact on the economic status of their widows, but because our focus here is on women, we pose issues and problems of data analysis in terms of women only.

This chapter is organized as follows. We first present an overview of the economic status of elderly women and how it has changed in the recent past. Next we discuss the literature that has looked at life-time patterns of income and the transitions that lead women into poverty in later life. The following section focuses on pension issues, particularly the determinants of differences between women and men in pension coverage and benefit receipt. We next turn to a discussion of the reasons why a more comprehensive definition of economic status than the most typically used annual income measure can increase our understanding of the economic position and problems of older women. The final section describes some large, national sample data sets that might be used to address the research issues raised here.

INCOMES OF OLDER WOMEN: A BACKGROUND SUMMARY

Over the last two decades the relative economic status of the elderly has risen dramatically, due both to the introduction and expansion of public programs designed to reduce the risk of poverty among the aged and to general economic growth. Public policy changes included above-inflation increases in Social Security payments,[2] improvements in survivor benefits, the introduction in

---

[2] We use the term Social Security to refer to the Old Age and Survivor Insurance program (OASI). Although many of the attributes and changes mentioned may also apply to the Disability Insurance portion of the program, this program is sufficiently different in the characteristics of its beneficiary population that we do not include it in our discussion here. The Health Insurance program is mentioned separately when appropriate.

1974 of the Supplemental Security Income program for the aged, blind, and permanently and totally disabled, the 1974 Employee Retirement Income Security Act (ERISA), the passage and expanded coverage of Medicare and Medicaid, and changes in the tax laws such that some incomes of older persons were treated preferentially. More recently, expanded retirement income options under ERISA (e.g., Keough plans and Individual Retirement Accounts (IRAs)) for workers and nonworking spouses, the elimination in 1986 of mandatory retirement for all but a few groups of workers, and the 1984 Retirement Equity Act are expected to further improve the income position of elderly persons.

The aged no longer face a disproportionate risk of being poor compared to other demographic groups. Between 1966 and 1981, the median income of families headed by a person sixty-five or older rose from 49 percent to 64 percent of that of all families. When adjustments are made for family size, elderly households on average are no worse off than those headed by a non-elderly individual [1]. Although in 1966 elderly individuals were more than twice as likely to be poor as were all persons, in 1984 the poverty rate for those sixty-five or older was only slightly above that of the total population. Despite the increase in the population sixty-five years or older from 9.9 percent of the population in 1970 to 11.4 percent in 1983 [2], the percent of all poor who were in this age group fell from 18 percent in 1966 to 10 percent in 1982 [3].

Economic growth, by increasing preretirement wage earnings, has almost certainly played an important role in raising the earnings-related benefits paid to older persons by Social Security and employer pensions [4, 5]. Nevertheless, the most important cause of the relatively rapid growth in the income of the elderly can be attributed to legislated increases in Social Security benefits which awarded to retirees benefits far above those that would be payable based on their own past contributions and earned interest alone. These income transfers through Social Security have fundamentally altered the relative risks of sustaining income losses over the life cycle. Social Security retired-workers benefits are paid without regard to nonearned income and assets, while younger households face strict asset and income limits in the government programs for which they may be eligible. It is for this reason that elderly families who would be poor without Social Security transfers are on average more likely to be raised out of poverty than are younger households with identical pretransfer incomes [6].

It is not only the poor elderly whose relative economic status (compared to younger persons) has been raised by Social Security. Relatively high income elderly also gained from across-the-board increases in benefits. In addition, when rapid inflation during the 1970s eroded the real incomes of working families, the elderly were better protected through inflation-adjusted government transfers and the prevalence of partial inflation adjustments in private pension plans [7-9]. In-kind transfer programs, designed specifically to reduce the need of poor households to use scarce cash resources, also improved the relative level of economic well-being of households headed by older persons [10, 11].

These gains in income, however, have not been uniformly shared by all elderly groups. Even during periods of relative prosperity, a large minority of older persons face higher risks of becoming poor because of low lifetime earnings, poor health, and sporadic work patterns that reduce their ability or willingness to accumulate resources for retirement.

Income data consistently show that unmarried older women are, on average, worse off than are couples and unmarried men. In 1982 the median income of widows sixty-five and older was $5,733 compared to $7,547 and $9,792 for widowed men and married men. Poverty rates for these groups were 22.8, 17.7, and 8.0, respectively [3, 12]. Although the 17.5 percent poverty rate for all women sixty-five and older was lower in 1982 than in 1970 when 28.5 percent were poor, women — and especially black women — were less likely than men to receive income transfers sufficient to raise them out of poverty. In 1982, 42.4 percent of all black women sixty-five and older were poor as were 31.3 percent of women of Hispanic origin. Although women account for only 59 percent of the population over sixty-five, the more rapid decline in poverty among males and couples raised the share of the elderly poor who were unmarried women to 71 percent in 1982 [13]. Poverty in old age is increasingly likely to be a characteristic of women [14].

The association found in cross-sectional data between the marital status of women and their income is often taken as evidence that widowhood causes precipitous declines in economic status. The relatively low income status of widowed, divorced, and separated women and their greater dependence compared to married women on Social Security and public assistance for 90 percent or more of their income [15-18] is consistent with the hypothesis that for most women, pensions cease and income from other sources falls sharply with their husbands' deaths. However, cross-sectional data may overstate the causal relationship between widowhood and income. Widows are on average older than married women. Even when married their own and their husbands' retirement income on average will have been lower than those of younger cohorts. For example, in any single year, Social Security retired-worker benefits paid to men fall sharply with increasing age. This is an expected result in an earnings-related retirement income program when real earnings of workers increase over time. Because older retired men would not have shared in the growth of real wages since their own retirement, their widows, even if their husbands had not died, would have been worse off than more recently retired couples.

The income of elderly women is directly related to their own current and past labor market earnings and occupational choices [19, 20]. Widows who work for pay are better off than those who do not. Women with income from a pension other than Social Security have higher incomes than women without. Couples in which the woman is entitled to her own retired-worker benefits tend to be better off than couples in which the woman is entitled to a spousal benefit only [21].

Transfer programs may also favor married couples, thus exacerbating the low relative incomes of elderly widows. As wives of retired men, married women are eligible for a payment supplement from Social Security. Warlick notes that the Social Security program biases payments toward married couples by awarding a 50 percent income supplement to single-earner couples although the poverty threshold for couples assumes an increase in needs for a two-person household of only 25 percent over individuals living alone [22]. In part because of the more generous payment schedule for couples than widows, less than one-third of otherwise poor widowed women were raised out of poverty by the receipt of supplemental survivor benefits (i.e., that benefit for which they were eligible over and above their own retired workers' benefit). The payment of supplemental spouse benefits raised 41 percent of otherwise poor couples out of poverty [23].

Research Issues: Cross-Sectional Analysis

Published research on the income characteristics of the aged that use cross-sectional data is good and provides a clear and consistent picture of who is poor and of their income sources, family status, and living-arrangements. Women are not neglected in these descriptive studies. In addition, fairly comparable data over time from the decennial censuses and the *Current Population Survey* allow investigation of how the composition and economic characteristics of the aged have changed over time. We need not duplicate reviews of this literature which can be found in Espenshade and Braun, Clark et al., and Schulz [24–26]. These reviews indicate the more limited data that can be obtained from cross-sectional surveys on the dynamics of income change, patterns of poverty as individuals age over time, and, most important, the life-cycle causes and consequences of the relatively low income status of older women.

There are some remaining deficiencies in descriptive studies of the distribution of income among older women and of the characteristics of the poor aged. In addition, there is a continuing need to update information on income levels and income sources in order to track changes in the absolute and relative incomes of older women over time and in response to economic and policy changes. There have been few studies of the level and distribution of income among nonwhite population groups. This may not reflect disinterest in analyzing minority groups as much as it does the small numbers of nonwhite respondents when populations are sampled randomly. It may be, however, that the sparsity of research on nonwhite women reflects unsubstantiated stereotypes about similarities in earnings and retirement behavior across social groups [27].

By combining divorced, separated, and never-married women into a single unmarried category, as is typically done, information is lost on the effect of these different marital statuses on economic well-being in retirement. This distinction is likely to become increasingly important as the percentage of older women who are divorced or never-married increases over time. Studies that identify these separate marital status groups indicate differences in economic status for white women [28] but not for nonwhite women [14]. The greater uniformity by marital status among nonwhite women probably reflects the across-the-board disadvantaged economic position of nonwhites. Whether this relative uniformity in income among nonwhite women is changing among more recent cohorts of older nonwhite women should be investigated.

Cross-sectional data compared over time show that higher lifetime earnings and improvements in earnings-related benefit programs have raised retirement incomes of males and unmarried women unevenly. The result has been a feminization of poverty in old age, not because the economic status of older women has not improved over time, but because that of couples and men has improved more. We know from cross-sectional studies that older unmarried women, particularly those in minority groups, face a higher risk of being poor in old age than do men and their wives, and that this can be attributed in part to their own lower lifetime earnings and those of their deceased or divorced husbands. But we do not yet have a good explanation of why, in periods of rapid economic growth and slowly rising ratios of female to male earnings, similar economic gains have not accrued to older women as to men.

Widowhood is an experience primarily of women, as they are far more likely to be widowed and less likely to remarry than are men. The role of widowhood in lowering incomes of women is not well-understood. Moon suggests that being widowed, not the age at widowhood or the length of the widowhood period, may be the problem since older widows are no more likely to be poor than are younger widows [14]. On the other hand, Tissue's finding that the risk of being poor is no different among widowed, divorced, and never-married women suggests that factors more generally shared by women who are not married rather than the death of a spouse may cause relatively low income [28]. Both of these conclusions, drawn from cross-sectional data, are contradicted by Holden, Burkhauser, and Feaster who use longitudinal data to follow married women as they become widowed [29]. They conclude that younger widows are at a distinctly greater risk of entering poverty upon widowhood and that widowhood itself presents a major economic threat to the well-being of elderly women.

In summary, cross-sectional surveys provide a single snapshot view of the economic status of older women. These single-year data reflect the rich variation in marital, fertility, savings, and work histories among older women, but the patterns of those histories cannot be ascertained directly from these data. Comparisons across women of different ages are often used to infer the life-cycle histories of older women. When marriage patterns, labor force participation, and fertility have changed as markedly as they have over the past decades, such comparisons probably do not give us very accurate information about the work and family histories of older women today. Even among the current elderly, few women have remained out of the paid workforce throughout their lives, and the percent who spent the majority of their child-raising years at home has steadily fallen. Longitudinal surveys that follow individual women over time are necessary to accurately assess how marriage, work, and family patterns determine the economic status of women as they age and enter the retirement period. It is likely that the relationships observed in cross-sectional data among women of different ages and marital statuses will not be entirely duplicated as individual women pass through these different demographic states.

LONGITUDINAL PATTERNS OF INCOME CHANGE

The effects of age, widowhood, and preretirement socioeconomic status on the relative economic status of older women can be disentangled using longitudinal data. A study by Burkhauser and Wilkinson and another by Moon suggest that poverty among elderly couples, women, and nonwhites in general can be attributed largely to their relatively unfavorable labor market experiences throughout their lifetimes [14, 30]. Moon points out, however, that because most poor widows were not members of poor couples when their husbands were alive, the reasons for the relatively low economic status of unmarried women may be more complex [14]. In addition, Holden, Burkhauser and Myers conclude that poverty is not a permanent state for the majority of poor older couples and widows [31]. They find considerable movement into and out of poverty among the elderly, suggesting that cross-sectional measures of economic status may be misleading indicators of both the total risk of ever being poor and the pattern of age-associated income changes.

Only a few of the factors that appear to affect the relationship between sex and income have been satisfactorily investigated using a dynamic framework. The timing of retirement among women affects Social Security and pension amounts; inflation during retirement may reduce the real value of incomes of widows many years after their spouses' deaths; the consumption choices of couples and widows will affect the rate at which assets are spent-down or accumulated; and the decisions made by husbands about insurance against their deaths will affect the income streams and assets of their widows. All of these factors play an important role in determining the economic position of women at retirement, upon widowhood, and throughout their remaining years of life. Each of these factors requires further research using methodologies that are suited to the analysis of the dynamics of change. In the remainder of this section each will be discussed in turn, highlighting gaps in the literature.

The Relationship Between Earnings and Retirement Income

Preretirement labor market earnings are an important means by which women (and men) can reduce the risk of poverty in old age. This is because higher earned income allows workers, through savings, to maintain consumption in retirement. In addition, earnings-related Social Security and pension programs reward higher paid workers with larger retirement benefits. Intuitively, it might appear that higher earnings of women would indeed increase old age incomes and provide additional insurance against poverty in old age. Preretirement work does not, however, guarantee higher retirement incomes. Earners may not save out of current earnings either because of above average expenses prior to retirement (e.g., college expenses, larger families, higher health care costs), lack of information on savings opportunities, marital disruption, or their own preferences for higher current consumption. Pension income (discussed below) in old age may not increase if women workers are unable to meet participation requirements or become vested, or if benefit formulae and break-in-service rules reduce payments for long-service workers who exit and return to work. The gradual increase in the income averaging period under Social Security reduces the degree to which higher earnings of successive cohorts of women will be reflected in increases over time in Social Security benefits paid to older women.[3] For those women whose own retired worker benefits remain below their spouse and widows benefits, there will be no gain in terms of Social Security benefits from their wage earnings.[4]

Some of the reduction in poverty among older widows over the past two decades is undoubtedly due to the long run increase in paid work by women. Labor force participation increased from 43.8 percent in 1955 to 61.6 percent in 1982 among women forty-five to fifty-four years of age. In 1980, the first cohort of women was seventy to seventy-nine and the second on the brink of retirement, but with longer work histories and higher lifetime earnings than the first [32]. Despite these gains, the interruptions in work due to childbearing [29, 33], occupational segregation [19, 34], and lower pension coverage [35, 36]

[3] For most workers benefits are calculated from average indexed monthly earnings over a number of years equal to the number of years between 1955 or age twenty-six, if later, and the year before they become sixty-two. Workers reaching sixty-two in 1984, for example, will have twenty-eight years of earnings included in this calculation while those reaching age sixty-two one year later will have earnings averaged over an additional year (i.e., twenty-nine years). An extra year of higher earnings will always be important for women receiving retired workers benefits. However, the extra year of earnings for the younger woman in this example will not necessarily raise her benefits compared to the woman one year older. For workers reaching age sixty-two in 1990 or later, indexed earnings will be averaged over thirty-five years. Workers whose coverage is solely due to the compulsory coverage of federal workers, a provision of the 1983 Amendments to the Social Security Act, and employees of nonprofit firms similarly affected by that act are subject to a special phase-in schedule.

[4] Wives and husbands are eligible for a benefit equal to one-half the benefit paid to the primary beneficiary. Widows and widowers are eligible for a benefit equal to the full benefit that would have been payable to the deceased worker. To gain in terms of Social Security benefits, wives' retired worker benefits must be equal to more than half of their husbands' and widows' must be equal to more than those of their deceased husbands. Note that there is some gain to wives from their work in Social Security covered jobs in that they are covered by the Disability Insurance portion of the OASDI program, their survivors are eligible for benefits if they themselves should die, and they are entitled to receive Social Security benefits when sixty-two even if their husbands do not retire.

reduce benefit levels to women from earnings-related retirement benefits. Thus the persistence of occupational segregation by sex will continue to be associated with lower wages and fewer pension opportunities for women [37-39].

The effect of preretirement earnings of women on their subsequent economic status is also determined by the degree to which women workers and their families save in anticipation of retirement needs. There has been some research on the role of wives' earnings on raising and maintaining the economic status of two-earner families over time [40] but whether two-earner families have different patterns of saving from single-earner families with the same incomes and whether the gains in earnings are carried over into the later years of life has not been investigated. If retirement needs are one reason why women work and families save, more market work and higher earnings among wives will lead to higher retirement income over time. Few studies have been done on the role of retirement needs in the work behavior of women. Indirect evidence from studies of the effect of public pension programs on savings gives conflicting results [41]. Lopata finds that few women alter earnings behavior on the basis of expected retirement income [42]. Whether this may also be true of savings − i.e., that retirement income goals have little impact on savings of two-earner households − needs to be investigated.

There is evidence that the value of nonpension assets with which retirees enter retirement has been growing. In 1982, income from nonpension assets was received by 84 percent of couples and 73 percent of unmarried women interviewed in the *New Beneficiary Survey* [21]. In 1967 only 60 percent of all married couples sixty-five years of age and older and only 45 percent of unmarried women had income from assets [43]. It is clear from these and other data that a higher percentage of more recent retirees have nonpension wealth; whether the earnings of married women have played a role in this accumulation remains an under-studied research issue.

In summary, future improvements in retirement incomes of women will depend on how higher preretirement earnings of successive cohorts of women are translated over their lifetimes into higher retirement incomes. The positive relationship between work experience and retirement income has led to predictions that retirement incomes of women will continue to rise as women work more over their lifetime and as occupational segregation declines [44, 45]. However, white never-married women and all nonwhite women, despite their relatively long labor market histories (compared to married women), have always had relatively low incomes in retirement. This has led Reno and Rader to suggest that improvements in the economic position of women in old age will occur primarily for married (and, presumably, later for widowed) women and less so for unmarried women [46]. Even among married women, however, we do not know whether, as their earnings rise, income in retirement from sources other than Social Security and pensions change as well. Higher earnings may increase a couple's ability to save; on the other hand preretirement consumption may rise with neither the total amount or pattern of savings changing. We know little about how higher earnings of women influence their own and their husbands' (if married) total savings, about the distribution of ownership of assets between husband and wife (e.g., higher earnings of the wife could permit either more contributions by the husband to his pension, higher contributions by the wife to hers, or the accumulation of jointly held assets), or about the type of assets held given a distribution of ownership.

Finally, predictions about preretirement earnings of future cohorts of older women depend on how family roles shape earnings behavior of women. There is a serious lack of data on nontraditional families. High rates of marital dissolution, the growing number of single parent and "blended" families, and the rise in nonmarried heterosexual and homosexual couples make research on the work behavior, retirement, and retirement incomes of women in these nontraditional families imperative. Although it is clear that family responsibilities do play a role in work and savings decisions of women, few studies directly consider the relative importance of family responsibilities versus other market phenomena in shaping those choices. One body of literature in which this issue is a major area of debate is that on occupational segregation [38, 47]. Whether women concentrate in particular occupations because of limited work options, labor market discrimination, or because some wives and mothers choose those jobs that are most compatible with their need for flexible hours of work are the questions addressed. We do not fully understand how employed women make choices among their multiple responsibilities and the importance of retirement income security in their work decisions. While the relatively low average post-retirement income of women is firmly established, we do not know whether this results in part from the conscious choices women must make as young workers between family responsibilities and their own future economic security. For this reason it is difficult to predict with any degree of certainty whether family structure will continue to shape the employment choices of women in the future and their own economic security in retirement. Women are likely to continue paying an economic price for their role as primary caregivers within the family. O'Rand and Landerman find that family roles have an independent effect on retirement incomes of women [20], suggesting that even as the earnings histories of women improve, their dual roles as mothers and workers will exact an economic price in terms of lifetime earnings and retirement benefits that is not imposed on men.

Timing of Retirement Among Women

The point at which retirement actually occurs for women or men is not easy to identify. Retirement has been defined in many ways, but is generally assumed to mark an abrupt change in labor force participation and wage earnings. Because women exhibit less uniform patterns of work over their lifetimes than do men it is more difficult to identify a single work transition for them that can be termed "retirement." For this reason the retirement transitions of women have been studied less often than those of men. More needs to be done.

Each of the most frequently used definitions of retirement presents particular problems in its application to women. Retirement has alternatively been defined as 1) acceptance of Social Security or pension benefits, 2) not in the labor force (either as a worker or looking for work) during a calendar reference period, 3) a sharp, well-defined change from full-time work to either no work or to a different job at fewer hours, 4) work below a specified number of hours during the week or of weeks during the past year, or 5) a person's own identification of himself or herself as being retired.

That the choice of definition makes a difference has been shown by Palmore, Fillenbaum, and George who find that, for men, the predictors and the consequences of retirement vary considerably depending on the retirement definition used [48, 49]. The degree to which patterns of work and retirement for women are affected by alternative definitions of retirement has not been studied. That traditional definitions of retirement may not be measuring the same type of transitions for women as they do for men can be illustrated with the one frequently used measure of retirement: the acceptance of Social Security benefits.

Social Security Administration data indicate that women are more likely to "retire" early when that event is defined as the timing of benefit acceptance. This is an appealing and, therefore, often used measure of retirement since Social Security benefits are payable to virtually all elderly men and women (and thus all are eligible for retirement by this definition), the timing of initial receipt is easily identified, and the earnings test prohibits substantial labor market work among new recipients below the age of seventy. If full-time, full-year work is the assumed alternative to "retirement," first receipt of retired-worker benefits from Social Security is a reasonably accurate measure of having made a recent work transition.

For female beneficiaries, however, total cessation of labor force work may have occurred many years prior to receipt, or work may continue without any change if earnings prior to benefit acceptance were below the earnings limit. Of respondents to the *New Beneficiary Survey*, a survey of persons first receiving Social Security benefits in a one-year period, 14 percent of unmarried women and 35 percent of married women had ceased work three or more years prior to first receipt, compared to only 8 percent of married men [50]. In contrast to the observed case for men, retirement benefit acceptance by women is less likely to coincide with a change in labor market activity.

The difficulty in using standard objective measures of retirement in identifying that labor force status among women is evident. Subjective measures of retirement also share this difficulty. These have been used on the assumption that, because all types of job changes near the end of workers' careers are difficult to specify in a survey, a job change associated with retirement is best identified by the worker's own statement of his or her retirement status. Because many long-time homemakers prefer to call themselves retired when their husbands move into that status or when family change alters their homemaking responsibilities, a subjective measure of retirement may not coincide with changes for women in paid employment [51].

There needs to be more comparative work on the meaning of standard retirement definitions when applied to women, on developing alternatives that may better capture job transitions that occur near the end of a woman's work life, and on the difference in results that are obtained when different retirement measures are used. This is not to say that traditional measures of retirement are entirely inappropriate in the study of older women, only that their interpretation may be affected by the gender of the respondent. Until we know how gender affects the pattern or shape of retirement, it is more difficult in the case of women than of men to draw conclusions about the causal relationship between the retirement decision and subsequent economic status.

The relatively few studies of the retirement decisions of women typically define retirement as a status characterized by complete labor market inactivity and/or the receipt of a private or public retirement benefit. Masters and Garfinkel examine the labor supply behavior of women aged fifty-five to sixty-one and of women seventy-three or older and find that Social Security and pension eligibility reduces the probability of work at these ages [52]. Henretta and O'Rand examine the rate at which wives of men in the *Retirement History Study (RHS)* left the labor force between 1969 and 1973. They find that support of family members, husband's pension coverage, previous work and pension coverage by the wife, and husband's health had significant effects on retirement timing, though the effects varied according to the wife's age [53].

Clark et al. provide one of the few analyses of the joint retirement decisions of husbands and wives, defined, again, as the choice between work and total labor force withdrawal [54]. Following intact couples in the *RHS* over the 1969 to 1973 period, they conclude that the retirement decision of a two-worker couple is, indeed, a joint one but that the effects of the independent variables change as the couple ages. Although for a wife, the wealth value of the husband's Social Security benefits had a significant and negative influence on her participation in the labor force in all years, the effect of her own benefits, initially positive, became negative as the sample aged over time. This change with aging in the effect of some variables is also noted by Henretta and O'Rand [53].

Studies that find differences in behavior as women age may in fact be measuring differences in behavior between women with long labor force attachment and women with less labor market commitment and the effect on retirement patterns as the composition of women who work changes with age. That is, as a cohort of women age, those who work are more likely to be those who have earlier ignored the disincentive effects on work of husband's income and family assets because of their own career goals. Szinovacz argues that women who delay retirement may be those who after their "return to work may not be able to accomplish occupational goals by the [traditional] time of retirement . . ." [51, p. 97]. Women who delay retirement are different from those who retire earlier. Those who delay Social Security receipt past age sixty-five are significantly more likely to have longer work histories; to be in executive, administrative, management, or professional jobs; and to be covered by pension plans from which they expect to receive benefits. At the time they first receive Social Security benefits, they are far less likely than were younger recipients to have left their last job three or more years earlier [50, 55]. Clearly, prior work histories, job commitment, and pension gains have an effect on retirement timing. Unfortunately, few data sources have information sufficient to study the effects of these life cycle variables on current employment status.

In conclusion, studies of the timing of retirement for women suggest that, as for men, economic variables are key determinants of labor force withdrawal. Studies indicate a joint decision by wives and husbands that may result in delayed retirement by either spouse depending on the relative earnings, ages, and pension eligibility and income of each. All of these studies suggest a pattern of retirement and decision making that requires a far more complex modeling of retirement timing decisions than has generally been assumed. Only a limited number of studies of the retirement decision of women reflect the complexity of their labor force histories and explicitly allow for joint decision making by couples.

Effect of Retirement on Economic Status

Because retired workers have lower incomes than do their counterparts who remain in the labor force, it is generally assumed that the cessation of work causes a decline in the economic status and is itself a major contributor to the economic problems faced by households as they age [51]. This assumption is supported by the correlation between earnings and income; households receiving labor market earnings are better off than those that do not. In addition, average incomes of workers fall at the time of retirement when pension and Social Security benefits only partially replace prior earnings.

Despite these cross-sectional findings, the role that changes in older women's own work status (versus that of their husbands) play in explaining their lower income is not completely understood. As mentioned earlier, cross-sectional data do not always provide an accurate picture of changes that have taken place as individual cohorts of women age. Then too, retirement may be a more complex phenomenon among women than men. One problem with drawing conclusions about effects of retirement on income from cross-sectional data is that at a given point earners will be different from nonearners both in current characteristics and past histories and this difference may increase with age. For example, the lower incomes of women who do not work is explained only in part by the absence of wage income. These women are also less likely to have ever worked and thus are likely to receive the lower pension and Social Security incomes reflective to that fact. In short, what matters most in explaining the relatively low economic status of nonworking women is not their current retirement status per se, but the lifetime work history and relatively low earnings of these women. Even if they were to continue to work, these women, though somewhat better off than they would be otherwise, would not be as well off as those who in fact postpone retirement and remain in the labor force.

The causal relationship between economic status and retirement can be closely examined with panel data that include the period during which the transition to retirement takes place. Palmore, Fillenbaum, and George found that when they controlled for preretirement characteristics, the effect of retirement on postretirement income differences for couples and men is substantially reduced [48]. Burkhauser and Wilkinson found that couples in the *Retirement History Study* who are poor later in life tended to be of lower economic status throughout their lifetimes [30]. Clark and McDermed also found retirement per se has a smaller effect on postretirement income differences among men than cross-sectional data might suggest [56]. We have already discussed studies showing women who delay retirement have more favorable work histories compared to women who retire early [50, 55]. Thus, the correlation at a given time between work status and income for women (and couples) may be due, not so much to the effect of retirement income, as to the fact that women with past low earnings, and therefore lower retirement income, are more likely to be retired. To confirm this, more research needs to be done on preretirement determinants of economic status and on gains to groups of women from continued work.

The Effects of Widowhood, Longevity, and Inflation

There is no doubt that widows face a greater risk of becoming poor than do married women, although poverty in the period immediately after their husbands' death may be somewhat exaggerated by income survey procedures [57]. The magnitude of the increase in poverty among widows is not well-understood, especially in the U.S. where insurance should enable many couples to smooth income over their joint lifetime and that of the widow [58, 59]. Differences in death rates among males by income group, inappropriate insurance decisions by couples, lack of information on the risk of widowhood, and unexpected health and real income changes during retirement may provide partial explanations.

Only a few studies have looked at how the well-being of the surviving partner is affected by decisions made by couples about the accumulation of financial instruments and the distribution after one dies. Consumption when both members are living will determine the rate at which wealth is depleted prior to the husband's death and the ability of the widow to maintain that level of consumption. The timing of retirement will determine not only the retirement income of the worker, but the absolute level of work-related benefits available to his or her survivor. Insurance against uncertain death may require a reduction during a person's lifetime, but in return for a larger income to the survivor.

Hamermesch argues that the consumption decisions of couples may be biased towards consumption (and wealth decumulation) during the immediate post-retirement period [60]. Using data on consumption and wealth for white couples in the *Retirement History Study*, he finds the level of consumption immediately after retirement is at a level that could not be maintained during the expected lifetime of the household, given reported physical and financial assets and Social Security and pension wealth. He finds that consumption is adjusted as couples age despite (or because of) this initial overconsumption. Because his sample excludes respondents who died, there is no direct evidence of how the initial high rates of consumption among retired couples affect the consumption and wealth of widows.

Wolfe finds that men who elect early, actuarially reduced, Social Security benefits are those with higher probabilities of death [61]. For these individuals, the early acceptance of Social Security benefits yields higher lifetime wealth while persons with longer expected lifetimes gain more by postponing entitlement. Wolfe concludes that in choosing when to take Social Security benefits men generally appear to estimate correctly and take into account their expected remaining years of life. The data he uses do not allow him to calculate expected Social Security benefits payable over the lifetime of men and their wives. Whether men who die early also have wives with relatively short lifetimes (and who, therefore, would also gain from their husbands' early and reduced Social Security benefits) is not investigated. Yet, if this is not the case, widows may be poorer in part because their husbands based retirement timing only on their own expected life-times rather than considering as well the future needs of their widows.

Finally, there has been very little research on the effect of life insurance protection and the pension-option choice made by their husbands on economic well-being on women after their death. Husbands with pensions who chose a single-life pension (i.e., one that ceases upon his death) leave widows who have lower incomes than do widows whose husbands chose a plan paying some fraction of his pension to his widow [59]. The decline in income upon widowhood, however, was the same for both groups. Thus the first group of husbands may be no less concerned about the well-being of their widows than the other; the relative income of women when widowed compared to their income when married is the same. Better data on pension and insurance choices of couples combined with necessary demographic and economic data on individuals are needed to obtain more definitive results on this issue.

Other factors may deplete the resources of some couples such that they are both more likely to be poor prior to the death of the husband, and more likely to experience a spousal death. Prior health problems of husbands prompting low life-time earnings may worsen with age and deplete already strained resources. Widows may also be poor because of the costs of caring for a terminally ill spouse. Taubman and Rosen found that the health of older men declines more rapidly with age among the less educated (and presumably lower income), but that married men are more likely to remain alive in worse condition than are men without wives [62]. This suggests that some couples, prior to the death of the husband, may have to spend down financial and physical assets to pay for his substantial health care costs. The effects on both the financial and physical condition of the surviving widow may be later observed in the relatively low economic status of widows and their reported poor health immediately after the death of a spouse [63].

"Living too long" — in the sense that older men and women underestimated longevity when planning for retirement — is sometimes asserted to be a cause of low economic status in old age for women [53]. This would be the case if economic resources available at the time of widowhood are depleted over time and if inflation in general or rising prices of specific goods purchased by the elderly erode the real value of their income. There is, however, little empirical evidence that length of widowhood matters.

Studies of the effect of inflation on the elderly consistently report that price changes do not disproportionately erode their incomes. Marsh reports that real incomes of the aged were maintained between 1966 and 1978 (a period of rapid price increases) with the exception of the small percentage of non-Social Security beneficiaries among the aged and of unmarried males and unmarried Blacks whose income gains lagged behind price changes [18]. Clark and Sumner surveyed price adjustments in pensions and Social Security and found real incomes of retirees decline less during inflationary periods than do incomes of other age groups [9]. Burkhauser, Holden, and Feaster find that during the 1970s when inflation reached 10 percent per year only a small proportion of elderly couples and widows who became poor did so due to inflation alone [64]. Ironically, because of their greater dependence on Social Security, and its built-in cost of living adjustments, older women are even more likely than other groups of retirees to maintain real incomes over periods of price increases. Price changes over their longer lifetimes do not seem to be a major factor in explaining the relatively low incomes of older widows.

Though cross-sectional findings suggest younger retirees have more assets than do older retirees, studies of asset accumulation by elderly households indicate that this association does not arise from the consumption of assets as persons age [65, 66]. Mirer argues that the negative association between age and asset value among the elderly is due to the higher asset accumulation of the more highly educated, younger cohorts entering retirement. Adjusting for the effect of initial conditions, he estimates a positive association between asset levels and age. McConnel and Deljaven found that, though consumption patterns might change upon retirement, there is no evidence when retired and working households are compared "that the average (retired) household was required to draw on previously accumulated savings in order to attain a desired level of consumption" [67, p. 489]. This pattern was found among all racial groups. Davies argues that uncertain lifetimes are sufficient to explain the increase in the real value of assets over time among the elderly [68]. On the other hand, if the desire to leave bequests to children is a major motivation for accumulating assets [69], asset accumulation may coincide with (or even require) sharp reductions in consumption as elderly individuals age. The level of well-being of the elderly — measured by consumption — may be well below attainable levels.

The strong association between widowhood and economic status is not fully explained by empirical work on this issue. Cross-sectional data do not measure those factors that, over the lifetime of couples, may determine the subsequent economic status of the widow. The traditional explanations of poverty among widows — inflation, consumption of assets, lack of insurance — have either been contradicted by the evidence or not sufficiently studied to lead to any firm conclusion on their importance. As in other areas of research on women, it is probably a complex process, one in which the intuitive explanations apply to some but not to other women. Surely it is a dynamic process; one which must be studied accordingly.

PENSIONS: EFFECT ON THE ECONOMIC STATUS OF OLDER WOMEN

Increase in pension coverage and the growing percentage of retired workers receiving benefits from non-Social Security pensions has played an important role in raising the retirement incomes of persons. These changes have increased income security in old age, altered retirement patterns, and changed savings behavior [4, 70, 71]. Differences between men and women in coverage, receipt, and benefit amounts from pensions have been identified as one reason for the relatively low incomes of women in old age [70, 72]. The literature cited in the previous section shows that women with pension income have higher total incomes than those who do not. This is also true for men and couples. On the other hand, persons with pensions are also likely to have higher nonpension incomes than do those who must do without [73]. Clearly pension receipts are correlated with attributes that lead to higher incomes in retirement both from pensions and other sources as well.

A pension is only one way to insure against earnings loss; it is different from other income sources in that there is only limited personal control over the accrual of pension rights. Although workers may alter the rate at which pension wealth is accumulated through job choice and earnings behavior, on any given job, pension contributions and benefits are generally determined through collective, not individual, action. Because the accumulation of pension rights represents a reallocation of income from current consumption to the retirement years, the present value of pension coverage to individual workers depends on whether they prefer future income (the real value of which may be reduced by inflation, uncertain receipt and their death but increased by earnings) over current consumption.

The broad question addressed by all studies of the relationship between pensions and the economic status of women in retirement is: How do different earnings patterns of women affect the probability of their receiving pension income in retirement and the absolute size of those benefits? We list below some of the more specific issues on which further research was suggested at the conference and then briefly discuss each in turn.

1. What has been the historical pace of coverage, receipt, and benefit amount for women? Have these trends differed from those for male workers?
2. Do women differ from men in the types of plans and particular provisions of those plans by which they are covered? What are the effects of these differences on lifetime well-being?
3. What are the relative gains to women from pension coverage compared to the receipt of higher current income or coverage by other fringe benefits?
4. What are the characteristics of women (and their husbands) who are not covered by pensions?
5. What are the determinants of the decisions made by couples about the form in which to take their retirement pension and the timing of pension receipt? To what extent does the form of benefits confound the data on pension amounts?
6. What is the position of women after the occurrence of an unexpected event such as a divorce or the death of their working husbands with respect to the probability of pension income receipt based on their husbands' pension?
7. To what degree does the integration of employer pensions with Social Security reduce the lifetime gains to women from pension coverage?

Pension Characteristics of Women

A compendium of statistics on pensions provide data on trends over time in coverage, receipt, and benefit payments for women and men [74]. Women have shared in the growth in pension coverage and receipt over time [20, 75], although Ross shows that, on average, the contribution of pensions to increases in economic well-being has been less important for older women than it has for men [76]. On the other hand, when males and females follow similar career patterns, there is little difference in final pension outcomes. For example, the percent of females receiving pension benefits rises with educational level, as is true for men, and women with seventeen or more years of education have pension receipts comparable to similar men [74].

Although there are data on pension coverage and vested status by gender and race, it is more difficult to find data with which to follow the pension coverage and vesting histories of individual workers. Data show that a smaller proportion of covered women than men are vested and that fewer nonwhites than whites are vested. These sex and race differences are found at all ages, although the percent vested increases with age for all groups. For workers aged fifty-six to sixty who are covered by a pension, 72 percent of white men, 69 percent of nonwhite men, 64 percent of white women, and 59 percent of nonwhite women are vested. A major problem in the interpretation of these numbers is the large number of persons who do not know what their vested status is — 11, 18, 13, and 27 percent, respectively [74].

Pension coverage, vesting, and pension receipt are determined by the types of occupations and industries in which workers are employed, the length of continuous years of employment, and earnings. At relatively high earning levels the percent of women workers covered by a pension plan is equal to or higher than male workers with similar earnings. Nonwhites have lower rates of coverage than whites, a difference that may be a product of racial differences in employment patterns. At younger ages, however, nonwhites are more likely to be covered by a pension than are white workers. Cross-sectional analysis indicates that for all workers coverage rates are tied to firm size, union status, education of the workers, and earnings. All these factors produce lower coverage rates for female workers. Women are less likely to be employed in manufacturing and unionized industries in which pension coverage is high and are more likely to work in smaller firms where pension coverage is less likely to be available.

A major barrier to the study of pensions and the economic well-being of older women is the lack of data on prior patterns of pension coverage for current retirees. Because we know that even current workers do not always know if they are covered by a pension on their job, the validity of retrospective questions asked of current retirees on their prior pension coverage is questionable. Because retrospective data, however, are the only means of obtaining the information necessary to study the lifetime determinants of the current economic status of older women, it is important to test the accuracy of these data. One way to do so would be to match information given by individuals with that from employers.

Inferring causal relationships from data on current pension benefits of retired women is further complicated by the difficulty of separating benefits received from the deceased spouse's retirement plan from those attributed to the pensions drawn from past jobs. This can be achieved in part with proper questioning of respondents or by using data reported by pension plans or employers on the characteristics of beneficiaries. The second approach, while giving the best data on pension amounts paid to individuals, cannot easily identify multiple pension recipients. These data will, for this reason, underestimate average pension incomes received by individuals if some are eligible for a pension from more than one plan, a problem that may be more prevalent when studying women. Although interrupted work careers lead to lower rates of vesting for women, job mobility and the lack of pension portability may increase the percentage of females eligible for multiple pensions. The effect of job mobility on lowering the probability of pension receipt has been investigated by a few; the effect on the incidence of multiple pension receipt of either men or women has not.

Differences between men and women in the type of plan in which they participate have not been investigated. Just as occupational choice affects pension coverage as such, it also affects the type of plan by which women who work are covered. Because women are more likely than men to interrupt paid work when raising children, and more likely to retire earlier and live longer after retirement, differences across plans in vesting and breaks in service rules, postretirement inflation adjustments, and the size of early retirement penalties may be more important to them in determining the value of pension coverage across different jobs. To illustrate, women are more likely to be in public sector jobs and thus more likely to be in plans that offer some form of inflation adjustment or limited portability (e.g., between statewide jobs). On the other hand, because women work in smaller firms and are less likely to be unionized, they may participate in pensions that are at risk of termination or are less able to offer any form of inflation adjustments or portability. ERISA regulations are implicated to some extent. What happens to women after pension plans fail is an important topic of research. So too is the effect of these terminations on lifetime compensation, on the income derived from pensions in retirement, and on occupational and job choices of younger women. An interesting area of research is whether particular pension plan provisions are considered by young women in making job choices and how these provisions affect their incomes in retirement.

Gains From Pension Coverage

The third and fourth pension issues listed above question the assumption that women will always gain from pension coverage. Although a one-time increase in pension income granted to women upon retirement would improve the economic status of older women, pension coverage while working does not necessarily improve the lifetime economic status of women. If other forms of compensation are altered in order to finance coverage, the net gain may be minimal. Because plans do not typically discriminate by sex (although they may subsidize benefits that are more likely to be elected by males — see below), women and men with similar earnings histories will receive comparable pensions.

However, for women in jobs with already lower wages than men, or who expect to interrupt work careers because of family responsibilities, pension coverage may exact an unacceptable sacrifice if they cannot expect to meet vesting requirements or are required to defer already low earnings from current to future consumption. The net advantage to low income earners of pension coverage needs to be investigated and the trade-off spelled out in careful detail.

Pension–Option Choice and Its Effects

Although the major role of pensions is to insure against income loss due to retirement, they may also be used to insure a member of a worker's family against the loss, upon the worker's death, of his earnings or pension payments. This may be done by choosing some form of a joint-and-survivor option.[5] Joint-and-survivor options may specify different percentages of the worker's benefits paid to the widow. Period-certain options specify payout periods of fixed time length. Which option is elected determines both the size of benefits received by retirees and the well-being of their survivors.

To date there has been little research on pension options that men and women elect when they retire and on subsequent well-being of retiree and survivor. For example, because women are less likely to choose a pension reduced to provide for a survivor, differences in pension amounts between men and women are understated to the extent that married men who choose a survivorship option have their pensions reduced. On the other hand, women are more likely to elect a lump-sum benefit and lump-sum distributions are more likely to be chosen by women with relatively low benefits. Because lump-sum distributions are often treated differently than income from an annuity when pension data are compiled, the number of female retirees with their own incomes from pensions is underestimated to an unknown degree [74].

Federal laws require the offer of a survivor option on all pensions and, since 1984, the approval by a spouse if that option is refused. The laws are based on the assumption that survivors of workers would be better off if this option were chosen. While it is admirable in its intent, there is little evidence for this assertion. Although prior to ERISA, widows of men who chose the survivor option were better off than widows of men who did not, it is also true that men who did not choose this option were more likely to have both relatively low pensions and low incomes. Even if they had chosen a joint-and-survivor pension, their widows would have been worse off than those whose husbands in fact did

---

[5] Under ERISA the joint-and-survivor option must be the default form of the pension, i.e., a payout schedule that is assumed unless the worker chooses otherwise. Thus, the worker doesn't formally choose a joint-and-survivor form. If he or she chooses a single-life annuity or some type of joint-and-survivor annuity that is different from the default, the worker must explicitly elect it. Under the Retirement Equity Act, the spouse must now approve this in writing.

choose the joint-and-survivor option [59]. We know little about how the situation has changed since ERISA and the REA, although there is some work in progress on this issue. A primary focus in this research must be the degree to which all assets are considered when workers select pension distribution plans. It may also be that workers who do not insure against their death through the purchase of survivor benefits are less likely to be in plans that subsidize this option. Also, they may be more likely to purchase other forms of life insurance, have other assets they can bequeath, be more likely to receive relatively low pensions and other income, or have higher need for current income (e.g., for health care needs for themselves or their spouse) than those who choose the survivor option.

Effects of Unexpected Events

Divorce reduces the probability that a married woman will share in her husband's pension. Although a married woman can expect to share in pension income after her husband's retirement, and if some form of a joint-and-survivor option is chosen, after his death, divorce may mean the loss of this sharing. Unless pension rights are specified in the division of property, financial hardships are likely to result. There is very little information on whether pensions are routinely considered in divorce settlements, either by awarding the wife some fraction of future benefits or by allocating to her a larger share of nonpension wealth than would otherwise be the case.

Pension Integration Rules and Women

The final issue concerns the effect of the integration of pensions with Social Security on the gains to women of pension coverage and benefit improvements. Internal Revenue Service rules allow integration of pension amounts or contribution schedules with Social Security, such that gains in Social Security benefits may be partially offset by pension reductions. Fewer years of covered service under any single pension and lower earnings may mean that offset rules disproportionately reduce the gains to women and minorities from pension coverage [77]. This occurs because the progressive benefit formula used to calculate Social Security benefits results in low-wage workers having a higher proportion of their lifetime earnings replaced by Social Security. Thus, for example, if the pension replaced a constant fraction of preretirement earnings across all wage levels, low income workers would have a higher proportion of their pension income reduced by integration rules. The effect of integration rules on the relative gains in retirement incomes of women and men has not been investigated.

A Summary of Research Issues
on Women and Pensions

There are two major issues that need to be addressed when investigating pensions among women. First, what are the explanations of lower pension incomes among women? Second, to what extent would improved pension coverage improve the lifetime economic status of women? In answering the first, improved descriptive statistics are necessary on the lifetime job patterns, current characteristics of women covered by pensions, and women who are receiving pension benefits. These studies are needed to enhance our understanding of how particular work decisions lead to different pension outcomes, and how pension plan provisions influenced those decisions. There are a growing number of studies of how pensions affect retirement timing among men but only a limited number looking at the same phenomena among women. Also lacking are studies on how pensions affect job choices of younger women. That pensions are associated with later retirement among some women has been discussed above. Whether women who are or who are not covered by pensions considered pensions in their employment decisions has not been investigated.

The second question, of whether women would be better off with pension coverage is an important one; it is typically assumed that requiring pension coverage would unambiguously benefit women. If low pension coverage and low vesting rates are, however, associated with their employment in low wage jobs, pension legislation compelling broader and costly pension coverage without complementary changes in total compensation may make women workers worse off. Because pensions reallocate income across a person's lifetime, higher pension coverage will come at the cost of lower take home pay during the working years. This cost may be a high one for working women with few alternative sources of current income. In plans in which pension benefits are integrated with and limited by Social Security benefits, women may realize lower pension returns from increased pension coverage than will men.

The study of the behavioral and income effects of pension plan provisions is made difficult because of the wide variety of pension plans in the U.S. There is not a unitary pension system but hundreds of retirement systems. In addition, the development of new retirement savings options, such as IRA accounts, makes it imperative that these "retirement systems" be included in a study of the effect of pensions on well-being. Because men's work patterns are less varied, the attention to detailed pension plan provisions may not be as important in the study of their economic decisions, though this too may be disputed. Precisely because career patterns determine the probability that women workers will receive a pension at retirement and affect the value of that pension, it is necessary to examine how specific provisions affect benefits among women.

Death of a spouse may sharply reduce income due to the loss of husband's pension benefits unless the deceased worker has elected a joint-and-survivor option. Only sparse information is available on the election of pension options. Because it may not be optimal for all workers to elect a survivorship, simple statistics on the number of workers electing joint-and-survivor options or the number of widows receiving benefits give an incomplete picture of whether husbands consider the well-being of the potential widow in making financial choices. A pension is only one of many ways to insure against financial hardships accompanying death of a spouse. Life insurance is an obvious alternative, as is the accumulation of other assets that can be passed on to the survivor. Whether those who do not elect a survivor option make their decision because of current income needs, because alternative forms of insurance are less costly, or because the potential survivor is already covered by her own job-related benefits is an issue that needs further study.

In short, we know little about why women receive lower pension income than do men beyond the obvious fact that past work histories are strongly correlated with particular pension outcomes. Whether those outcomes are due to long-time, middle income earners working at jobs that do not provide coverage or whose benefit schedules and vesting provisions are particularly disadvantageous to women, or whether generally lower compensation leads to those outcomes regardless of pension coverage and vesting provisions is an important issue that needs to be resolved before effective pension policies can be developed.

THE MEASUREMENT OF ECONOMIC STATUS: ALTERNATIVES

Studies of economic status typically define that status by absolute or relative income measures — not because income is identical to economic well-being, but because the value of money income is easily recalled by respondents, is easily aggregated over income sources, is comparable across consumption units, and is a high percentage of all resources available to households.

Ideally, economic status would be measured by either the actual consumption of goods and services or by their attainable level of consumption. Cash income is only one way by which families and individuals obtain the goods and services that determine their well-being. Cash income alone, however, is an inaccurate indicator of the absolute level of economic well-being if consumption possibilities are enhanced through in-kind transfers and tax and price subsidies. In addition, if noncash transfers and subsidies are not evenly distributed across families, cash income measures provide a misleading picture of the distribution of economic resources.

Non-income resources should be included in measures of economic status if they increase access by recipient families to a level of consumption that may not be attainable otherwise. Families and individuals who pay out of pocket for medical care, rents, and food are in a real sense worse off than are those with the same money income who have third party medical insurance, who own their own home or receive subsidized housing, or who receive subsidies through the Food Stamps program. In addition, households with assets that could provide income if other types of income fall (e.g., vested pensions that can replace lost earnings) are also better off than households with no such assets but with the same current income.

An economic status measure that included pension wealth, for example, would lower the relative well-being of elderly wage earners who are not eligible for pension income compared to workers with the same wage income but whose retirement income was insured by their pension eligibility. Thus more inclusive definitions of economic status will alter the position of some households in the distribution of measured economic resources and, therefore, are likely to suggest different program targets and lead to different judgments about the relative success of programmatic or economic change. Research that uses different definitions of economic status shows that definitions do matter, both in determining the relative economic status of older women and in identifying the economic risks they face.

In 1965 the Social Security Administration defined an income standard below which families would be unable "to enjoy even the minimal diet that could be expected to provide adequate nutrition and still have enough left over to pay for all other living essentials" [78, p. 4]. This "poverty threshold" was based on the actual purchasing patterns of low income families and was adjusted for family size, composition, and until recently, for rural-urban residence. This definition of poverty was a major improvement over the single income standard that had been applied across the board to all families and individuals. The charted prevalence of poverty by demographic group changed. The number of aged female headed households who were identified as poor declined since these household units were less likely to have children and were, therefore, on average smaller households. At the same time, the number of children in poverty rose as did the number of poor nonwhite families. This poverty threshold, adjusted for subsequent increases in prices, continues to be used to judge who is poor and who is not.

In keeping with the argument that what matters is not income alone but the resources that could be used to obtain goods and services, Moon calculated a measure of well-being that included the value of in-kind government transfers, tax benefits, intrafamily transfers, and the annuity value of net worth [10]. Even with these additions, almost 15 percent of elderly families remained below the poverty threshold in 1972, and the relative economic position of some elderly households changed. Because older, unmarried women are less likely than are couples to hold assets at retirement [24, 79] and less likely to hold pension wealth [55], their relative economic status on average was lowered by the inclusion of these wealth variables. By this measure they were worse off than some households that were poorer when income alone was used to measure well-being. Aged individuals who were less financially secure according to this more comprehensive measure of well-being were older, more likely to be females, and more likely to be in families headed by nonwhites.

Moon's adjusted measure of well-being identifies a group of elderly who may be particularly vulnerable to catastrophic events, given their lack of resources to supplement current income. To Moon's suggested components of economic status Smeeding has added the value of government in-kind programs to identify the elderly at risk of having to pay large medical bills or for unexpected increases in housing and energy costs [80]. Because these costs may be off-set in part through government or employee insurance programs, and by subsidized housing and rent free arrangements (10% of all elderly renters pay only for utilities), those persons who will be least able to pay for medical care or housing out of current income can be accurately identified only if the value to individuals of these programs are taken into account. The population who have to pay for all medical care and housing costs is not identical to the population that is currently poor. Smeeding defines this vulnerable group as "tweeners" — persons too poor to finance medical expenditures from their own assets, not covered by third party medical insurance, and whose incomes are too high to qualify for government subsidies. In this group are a disproportionate number of single females. Single females are concentrated both among the poor — that group that "lacked the where-with-all to live at anywhere near a tolerable level" [78, p. 4] — and in that group of persons whose near-poverty status places them at even greater risk of financial distress than is faced by those classified as poor.

Studies of economic status are increasingly concerned with ways to identify, measure, and define the value of these nonincome sources of current and future consumption. Although some elderly will be identified as better off (including some elderly women), a significant fraction will have their relative economic well-being lowered. Expanded measures of economic well-being are being used increasingly in statistical studies of economic status [1, 81]. The availability of better data on program eligibility will improve these measures. Longitudinal data will allow investigators to measure how status changes over time when individuals and families are classified by the broader definitions of well-being, and how groups such as the "tweeners" defined by Smeeding fare when catastrophic events occur.

To date, most studies of economic status, whether based on income or expanded definitions of resources, measure well-being at a given moment in time. Recent studies, however, indicate that economic status is not stable among the elderly. There is some evidence that incomes fluctuate to a greater extent than had been previously assumed and that characteristics of the population that is poor at one point are different from those of the population who are poor over a longer time period [82]. This may also be the case for the elderly population [57]. Thus, measures of economic status that reflect stability or change in income or all resources over time can provide additional information on lifetime well-being. Measures of economic status over a short accounting period do not reflect the security of that income and may be a misleading indicator of the relative economic status of particular individuals or population groups.

A resource measure of economic status is only useful, however, to the degree that it captures differences among individuals in attainable levels of well-being.

Consumption possibilities, given a level of income or in-kind services, depend, in addition, on ability and willingness to alter consumption patterns as resources change, on ability and willingness to participate in programs designed to alleviate economic distress, and on the existence of family and friends who can be called upon to share their own incomes or living space with an elderly person. Non-income assistance from other individuals will not alter the measured income position of any individual, but it will condition the effect of that position on her subjective well-being. More information on adaptive behavior of individuals and their family would identify both the salience of income status and those groups least able to draw on their own resources for the maintenance of well-being.

Health is a factor that, if good, can enhance the value of economic well-being of women in retirement and widowhood. If poor, it can reduce the ability of women to meet their needs even with otherwise adequate resources. The inter-action and joint determination of economic and health status is an area of relatively little research, due primarily to the lack of suitable data sources. Research on health is discussed in greater detail in an earlier chapter, as are some of the worklife factors that may affect health status. Here we briefly review these interactions from the perspective of research on the economic status of older women.

An important issue in any study of the relationship between health and economic status is the choice of the health measure that best captures the relationship with economic status. Anderson and Burkhauser argue that self-assessment measures may overstate the importance of health in economic studies since low wage earners are likely to overstate health problems as a rationale for their relatively disadvantaged economic position [83]. They assert that a more objective measure such as mortality is a better indicator of the health conditions affecting employment and earnings. On the other hand, subjective measures of health may be more important in explaining the different patterns of adaptation to age and economic status among the elderly.

There have been few theoretical discussions of the complex interaction over individuals' lifetimes between health and economic status. Clearly poor health limits economic activity, but low economic status will constrain the ability of families to seek medical care or participate in health enhancing activities. The relatively weak relationship found in some studies of health and economic status suggests that the relationship is complex. Anderson and Burkhauser hypothesized a joint determination of health and work activity of men where both are functions of wages, wealth, and related variables [83]. Because health requires investment of time and goods, market wages and wealth were hypothesized to affect both the marginal cost and benefits of time spent in health investments. Estimating a bivariate logistic model of work and health, they found their hypothesis supported. Wolfe and Haveman discovered that working mothers have poorer health because less time is allocated to health maintenance, supporting the contention of a joint determination [84]. This model of health has not been extended to the study of health among older women. These studies, however, do suggest that allocation of scarce resources to health maintenance is an issue that should be studied to understand fully the interaction between the health of older women and their economic status.

Living arrangements may also be a component of economic well-being. Changes in living arrangements may be one way in which women adjust to relatively low levels of economic well-being. Home ownership enables widows to remain in their own homes in spite of health problems [85]. The presence of children and other relatives to share living quarters enables the elderly to maintain community residence — an assumed preferred living arrangement [86, 87]. Children and other family members, even if not living under the same roof, are a potential source of intrafamily cash and in-kind transfers, expanding the number of options available to elderly with children as compared to those without [10, 88].

In summary, how economic status is measured will affect the position in the distribution of well-being of elderly women; some will appear better off, others worse off. More comprehensive measures of well-being are likely to identify additional groups of older women who are at risk of economic distress and the role of in-kind benefit programs in protecting them. Better data on consumption and on individuals' eligibility for in-kind transfers enable the more accurate measurement of economic well-being among the elderly. In the past, improved measures have indicated additional problems faced by some elderly groups. Specifically, more comprehensive measures have in general suggested that unmarried women may be even worse off compared to men and married women and more at risk of unexpected drains on their already meager economic resources than when income alone is used to measure economic well-being.

DATA

The discussion of available data will focus on two criteria: how amenable the data are to multiperiod analyses and the availability of variables allowing the development of broader measures of economic status and retirement behavior. The ideal data set with the ideal variables is hard to define, in part because there is little consensus within the research community on the best way to address particular research issues. Far more work is required on the meaning and accuracy of alternative measures of important economic variables — for example, the value of in-kind benefits, the health status of individuals, and the consumption needs of individuals and families. Concerns about the accuracy of survey data on asset income, on retrospective work histories, and on current pension coverage and income are not to be overlooked.

Many of the issues concerned with retirement and aging have been analyzed using data collected on males or male-headed households; it has been more difficult to find similar research on elderly women. In part this shortcoming is due to the lack of data collected on older women. For example, samples may be selected in such a way that married women are less likely to be sampled or are less likely to be asked for as complete information. The *Retirement History Study* is an example. Only males and women not living with a husband were chosen as primary respondents; wives were interviewed with their husband but were asked for far less information. Even though women who became widowed during the course of the ten years of the survey were followed as respondents, questions asked only of respondents (and not of wives) in previous years were never asked of widows. Thus studies over time of wives and widows suffer from the incomplete information gathered on these women.

Panel studies often fail to follow members of households after the initial respondent dies or is institutionalized. For example, the *National Longitudinal Survey* does not interview widows of the older men sampled. Thus, from these data one cannot determine how characteristics of a husband (including his health care needs prior to his death) affect economic outcomes for the widow. Virtually no longitudinal surveys follow respondents into institutions, limiting our ability to assess how this transition affects costs paid and the economic status of the rest of the family. The *Panel Study of Income Dynamics* and the *Survey of Income and Program Participation* do follow members of initial households as they form new families, but not if they become institutionalized.

Panel surveys can best address those research questions that look at lifetime patterns of change or the effect of initial characteristics on subsequent behavior and economic status. Hypotheses about the causes and consequences of economic events occurring late in life have moved beyond those derived from simple cross-sectional, static models. Testing dynamic models of behavior requires longitudinal data. The *Retirement History Study (RHS)*, the *National Longitudinal Survey (NLS)*, the *Panel Study of Income Dynamics (PSID)*, and the *Survey of Income and Program Participation (SIPP)* are four longitudinal files that gather detailed income, wealth, and work data on respondents and their immediate families. The *RHS* also has respondents' Social Security earnings records matched to the survey file. This allows estimation of the important Social Security wealth variable for retirement studies and provides data on the entire covered work history of male and female respondents. On the other hand, pension data rely on respondent-provided information.

The *NLS* sample of older women is still somewhat young to answer some of the questions raised in this chapter, although additional panels will begin to provide valuable data on women as they enter retirement and become widowed. The *PSID* follows family members as they leave households and form their own separate households or enter others, a feature particularly useful in the study of living arrangement transitions among aging women. The *PSID* has recently altered somewhat its procedure for interviewing husband--wife households; in both 1976 and 1985 detailed histories on wives were gathered.

Pension data to answer many of the issues raised are sadly inadequate. Understanding the reasons why some retirees receive pensions and others do not, then explaining differences among beneficiaries in the size of benefits received, requires information on life-time work patterns, the distribution across firms in pension coverage, and differences across plans in provisions with respect to coverage, vesting, contributions, and benefits at retirement. The complexity of the pension system makes statistics on pension characteristics difficult to collect and present in meaningful form. A serious barrier to the study of the determinants of pension income receipt and size of benefits is the lack of information on work histories that is adequate to estimate coverage and accrued pensions on all jobs. The variability in the work careers of women makes this information particularly important but more difficult to collect than in the case of males. For example, the *RHS* asks only about pension coverage on the current, last, and longest job. These jobs may include the entire work history of most men, but whether this is true for women is unknown.

Cross-sectional, time series data on pension coverage are available from publications of the Social Security Administration, American Council of Life Insurance, federal agencies that have jurisdiction over non-Social Security retirement systems, and the Employee Benefits Research Institute. The March 1972, 1979, and 1983 supplements to the *Current Population Survey* asked questions of current workers on pension coverage, vesting, and selected benefit provisions. Data were not gathered on persons who are currently out of the work force, a failure particularly unfortunate for researchers interested in how the varied work patterns of women affect pension eligibility. The 1979 Department of Labor *Survey of Pension Plan Beneficiaries* provides detailed pension plan data gathered from employers on individuals. Though currently not available for public use, these data provide the most accurate data on pension amounts and options selected by beneficiaries. The information is not available from other sources. Unfortunately, extremely limited information on nonpension characteristics of individuals is provided.[6]

Research on the relationship between health and economic status, on the costs of institutionalization to individuals and their families, and on the effects of health care choices by individuals (e.g., purchase of insurance, levels of health care, changes in living arrangements) on subsequent health and economic status are issues difficult to address with available data. In most cases detailed longitudinal data on both health characteristics and economic status are not provided. The panel studies mentioned above have only limited health data. The national health surveys contain limited information on financial variables. The *National Medical Care Expenditure Survey*, a longitudinal study in five waves, three months apart, is a source of information on the health care costs and insurance characteristics of elderly persons, but also has limited data on income and assets. Other data sets such as the *Consumer Expenditure Surveys* that include information on the consumption of households may be useful for the study of out-of-pocket health expenditures but fail to capture fully the effect of insurance on these expenditures.

[6] Note that this data set is not included in the Appendix.

SIPP may enable many of these issues to be addressed in ways that have not heretofore been possible. *SIPP* follows a panel of participants over a thirty-two-month period and provides detailed information on demographic characteristics, work and earnings, income, and the individual's participation in government transfer programs. Because the reference period is the four months prior to the survey, the accuracy of recall is expected to be higher than that in the *Current Population Survey*. Topical modules include those on health, disability, insurance coverage, and assets.

The *Survey of Consumer Finances*, 1983, offers information on vested pension and expected benefits, matched with data from identified plans and employers on pension characteristics and the accrued pensions of the survey respondents. The inclusion of formulae used by each pension plan to calculate pension benefits under various contingencies will allow researchers to project the pension wealth of individuals and how the wealth value would change given particular changes in earnings or retirement timing. A select sample of high income households may be useful in gaining a perspective on the status and decisions of these persons. Finally, because equally detailed information is gathered on husbands and wives, these data may not suffer from the unequal treatment of spouses in the interview process.

In 1982 the Social Security Administration interviewed a sample of persons who first began receiving Social Security retired worker, spouse, survivor, or disability benefits between mid-1980 and mid-1981. The *New Beneficiary Survey (NBS)* is restricted to this group and did not sample persons of similar age who were either already beneficiaries at that date or who were not yet receiving benefits. A sample of nonbeneficiary, Medicare eligibles sixty-five and older is available in the *NBS* file and in a limited way addresses the problem of having restricted the sample to new Social Security beneficiaries. Nevertheless, detailed information from survey and administrative data makes this a data set with information on elderly women that is not available elsewhere.

Finally, researchers should take note of new waves of data available out of the *NLS* and the *PSID*. Partially in response to developments in economic theory and changing policy concerns, additional waves are expected to gather more information on assets, including pensions. In addition, as these respondents age, household changes in social and economic variables can be studied.

Most of the discussion in this chapter has referred to studies using quantitative data. Yet one of the questions repeatedly raised was why people behave in ways that seemingly are not in their best economic interest. For example, why is the "best" insurance option not chosen when individuals have the choice of different health insurance and pension packages? Why do many eligible persons not enroll in means tested programs? Why aren't assets consumed during the retired lifetime of individuals? Why do elderly continue to save throughout their lives? Qualitative data are likely to give valuable insight into the decision-making process. In addition, qualitative data may indicate how individuals perceive their well-being, the congruence of standard economic measures with personal perceptions, the relative importance of savings versus consumption in subjective welfare, and the extent to which individuals use wealth measures versus annual income in evaluating their options and well-being.

FINAL NOTES AND SUMMARY

Among the aged, lifetime work patterns, command over economic resources, their health, and the willingness, if eligible, to participate in public income maintenance programs and to depend on friends and family members in times of economic need are conditioned by a lifetime of choices that are not easily measured by a single survey. Research on older women is handicapped by the lack of necessary lifetime data. Rapid changes in marital, childbearing, and work patterns make it difficult to infer life-cycle patterns from the more frequently available cross-sectional data. In their later years, women, like men, reap the rewards or losses from earlier choices about education, marriage, family, and work. Subsequent income status in old age cannot be understood without reference to the context within which these earlier choices were made. Yet the data, more often than not, are not sufficient to investigate the relationship between prior choices and current economic status. The variability in life-time earnings patterns among women makes the methodological issues even more complex than is apparently the case in studying economic behavior of men.

There is growing recognition that static models do not adequately represent life-cycle behavior. Current characteristics and work choices of elderly women are determined by their past experiences. For this reason, the lack of longitudinal data for both elderly women and men is a serious constraint on research that attempts to discover the causes of differences in economic and social conditions between elderly women and men and among elderly women now and in the future.

Research using longitudinal survey data is currently underway on the timing and life-cycle causes of major changes in the economic status of elderly women and on the insurance choices they and their families make against the likely occurrence of events that threaten economic well-being as individuals grow older. Models that adopt the more correct life-cycle approach in explaining economic well-being among elderly individuals must be tested with appropriate data. These models include variables that are difficult to estimate from cross-sectional data. For example, the estimation of the present value of accumulated pension wealth, a key variable in life-cycle models of retirement and economic status in old age, requires data on pension benefits that both current retirees and those individuals who continue to work would receive at alternative retirement ages.

Nevertheless, there remains much that can be done with current data sources and with continuing cross-sectional studies. As theory points to new relationships, or to better ways of defining variables, available data can be used to reestimate behavioral relationships or redefine often used measures of economic status and behavior.

This chapter has looked primarily at economic status issues related to the retirement, widowhood, and aging of women. The appropriate measurement of economic status accounted for a considerable amount of discussion. The isolation of research into separate disciplines is indicated by data sets that concentrate on either the social, the health-related, or the economic aspects of aging. What we need now are more interdisciplinary research efforts. As data gathering efforts have changed with theoretical developments, these efforts could be richly influenced by the professed need of persons working on retirement behavior, for example, for better data on health status or social relationships.

Not discussed in great detail above is the difficulty of projecting current behavioral relationships into the future. It is important to make projections in order to fashion appropriate public policies toward the future aged. Whether the longer work histories, higher rates of pension coverage, reduced occupational segregation, and greater likelihood of pension receipt predicted for women will be realized and will significantly improve the relative economic status of widows in the future is an issue upon which not everyone agrees. Because we do not know much about the financial planning decisions of women and their husbands, if married, it is not clear that private insurance programs can insure against the old age economic problems arising from unsteady work histories and early widowhood.

There are disturbing signs that women may not find their economic status significantly improved in the future despite predicted earnings gains. Higher divorce rates and the growing number of single parents who have their earnings limited by regulations of several income and in-kind transfer programs are expected to off-set the gains to women from higher earnings. In addition, divorce eliminates the ability of women to share in their spouses' income in old age. Smaller families and more childless women may reduce the availability of support from kin, even as it increases the earned resources of women by enabling them to work more. Cain argues that the lifetime income of women has not changed dramatically, since on average higher divorce rates and the longer length of time spent on welfare offset earnings gains [89]. More recently the very programs that were said to be one reason for the declining percentages of poor people have been increasingly criticized as the source of behavioral changes that retard preretirement earnings gains that would otherwise have taken place. The recent controversy over income transfers is critical of the very existence of these programs because of the presumed consequences of transfers on the earnings behavior of the nonelderly population [90]. Although a large body of literature has looked at the consequences of retirement income programs on the retirement timing and incomes of the current aged (see Aaron, as well as Danziger, Haveman, and Plotnick [4, 91]), few studies have looked at how retirement benefit programs affect preretirement earnings [92].

Increases in poverty in the preretirement years, whether due to major economic forces or induced by transfer programs themselves, will affect the probability of being poor in retirement. Thus, research on the economic status of older women can not be divorced from research on younger population groups. The effect of the greater dependence of young women on preretirement transfer programs (rather than on spouse or own earnings) on the economic position of these women in old age needs to be studied. If women in particular economic, ethnic, or marital status groups are less likely to benefit from labor market improvements prior to retirement, they are not likely to share in the expected higher retirement incomes that are predicted due to general economic gains. How large this group of "losers" are compared to the "gainers" is not known. Researchers in gerontology need to take a broad view of the determinants of economic status, expanding their models to include comprehensive measure of economic variables, to incorporate decisions made over the lifetime of individuals and to recognize the significance of characteristics and decisions of female members of households. Only then will we have a comprehensive and accurate view of the hardships faced by some groups of women in old age and be able to develop appropriate policy strategies for targeting these women.

REFERENCES

1. S. Danziger, J. van der Gaag, E. Smolensky, and M. Taussig, Implications of the Relative Economic Status of the Elderly for Transfer Policy, in *Retirement and Economic Behavior,* H. Aaron and G. Burtless (eds.), The Brookings Institution, Washington, D.C., 1984.
2. G. Myers, The Aging Population, in *International Perspectives on Aging: Population and Policy Changes,* R. H. Binstock, W. Chou and J. H. Schulz (eds.), United Nations, New York, 1982.
3. U.S. Bureau of the Census, Current Population Reports, *Characteristics of the Population Below the Poverty Level: 1982,* Series P-60, No. 144, U.S. Government Printing Office, Washington, D.C., 1984.
4. S. Danziger, R. Haveman, and R. Plotnick, How Income Transfer Programs Affect Work, Savings, and the Income Distribution: A Critical Review, *Journal of Economic Literature, 19,* pp. 975–1028, 1981.
5. P. Gottschalk and S. Danziger, A Framework for Evaluating the Effects of Economic Growth and Transfers on Poverty, *The American Economic Review, 75*:1, pp. 153–161, 1985.
6. S. Danziger and R. Plotnick, The Receipt and Antipoverty Effectiveness of Cash Income Maintenance Transfers: Differences Among White, Non-White and Hispanic Households, IRP Discussion Paper No. 683-81, Institute for Research on Poverty, Madison, Wisconsin, 1981.
7. R. M. Blank and A. S. Blinder, Macroeconomics, Income Distribution, and Poverty, in *Fighting Poverty: What Works and What Doesn't,* S. H. Danziger and D. H. Weinberg (eds.), Harvard University Press, Cambridge, 1986.

8. R. Borzilleri, The Need for a Separate Consumer Index for Older Persons, *The Gerontologist, 18,* pp. 230–236, 1978.
9. R. L. Clark and D. A. Sumner, Inflation and the Real Income of the Elderly: Recent Evidence and Expectations for the Future, *The Gerontologist, 25*:2, pp. 146–152, 1985.
10. M. Moon, *The Measurement of Economic Welfare–Its Application to the Aged Poor,* Academic Press, New York, 1977.
11. T. M. Smeeding, The Antipoverty Effects of In-Kind Transfers, *Policy Studies Journal, 10,* pp. 499–521, 1982.
12. U.S. Bureau of the Census, Current Population Reports, *Money Income of Households, Families and Persons in the U.S.: 1982,* Series P-60, No. 142, U.S. Government Printing Office, Washington, D.C., 1984.
13. S. E. Rix, *Older Women: The Economics of Aging,* Women's Research and Education Institute of the Congressional Caucus for Women's Issues, Washington, D.C., 1984.
14. M. Moon, Poverty Among Elderly Women and Minorities, Urban Institute Discussion Paper, Urban Institute, Washington, D.C., 1984.
15. S. Grad, *Income of the Population 55 and Over: 1982,* Office of Research, Statistics and International Policy, Social Security Administration, U.S. Government Printing Office, Washington, D.C., 1984.
16. C. Ross, S. Danziger, and E. Smolensky, The Level and Trend of Poverty in the United States: 1939–1979, *Demography,* in press.
17. B. Lingg, Social Security Benefits of Female Retired Workers and Two-Worker Couples, *Social Security Bulletin, 45*:2, pp. 3–24, 1982.
18. R. E. Marsh, The Income and Resources of the Elderly in 1978, *Social Security Bulletin, 44*:12, pp. 3–11, 1981.
19. T. J. Espenshade and R. E. Braun, Economic Aspects of an Aging Population and the Material Well-being of Older Persons, in *Aging in Society: Selected Reviews of Recent Research,* M. W. Riley, B. B. Hess, and K. Bond (eds.), Laurence Erlbaum Associates, Hillsdale, New Jersey, 1983.
20. R. L. Clark, J. Kreps, and J. Spengler, Economics of Aging: A Survey, *Journal of Economic Literature, 16*:3, pp. 927–930, 1978.
21. J. H. Schulz, *The Economics of Aging,* Wadsworth Publishing Company, Belmont, California, 1985.
22. A. O'Rand and J. C. Henretta, Midlife Work History and Retirement Income, in *Women's Retirement: Policy Implication of Recent Research,* M. Szinovacz (ed.), Sage, Beverly Hills, California, 1982.
23. A. O'Rand and R. Landerman, Women's and Men's Retirement Income Status: Early Family Role Effects, *Research on Aging, 6*:1, pp. 25–44, 1984.
24. L. D. Maxfield and V. P. Reno, Distribution of Income Sources of Recent Retirees: Findings from the New Beneficiary Survey, *Social Security Bulletin, 48*:1, pp. 7–13, 1985.
25. J. Warlick, Aged Women in Poverty: A Problem Without a Solution?, in *Aging and Public Policy: The Politics of Growing Old in America,* W. P. Brown and L. K. Olson (eds.), Greenwood Press, Westport, Connecticut, 1983.

26. K. C. Holden, Supplemental OASI Benefit to Homemakers Through Current Spouse Benefits, a Homemaker's Credit and Child-care Drop-out Years, in *A Challenge to Social Security: The Changing Roles of Women and Men in American Society*, R. V. Burkhauser and K. C. Holden (eds.), Academic Press, New York, 1982.

27. Center for the Study, Education and Advancement of Women, Black Working Women: Debunking a Myth: A Multidisciplinary Approach, University of California, Berkeley, California, n.d..

28. T. Tissue, Low Income Widows and Other Aged Singles, *Social Security Bulletin, 42*, pp. 3–10, 1979.

29. K. C. Holden, R. V. Burkhauser, and D. J. Feaster, The Timing of Falls into Poverty after Retirement: An Event-History Approach, Final Report to the AARP-Andrus Foundation, Part II, 1987.

30. R. V. Burkhauser and J. T. Wilkinson, The Effect of Retirement on Income Distribution: A Comprehensive Income Approach, *Review of Economics and Statistics, 65*:4, pp. 653–658, 1983.

31. K. C. Holden, R. V. Burkhauser, and D. Myers, The Dynamics of Poverty Among the Elderly: Income Transitions at Older Stages of Life, *The Gerontologist, 26*:3, pp. 292–297, 1986.

32. D. Hammermesh and A. Rees, *The Economics of Work and Pay*, Harper and Row, New York, 1984.

33. S. L. Hofferth, Long-term Economic Consequences for Women of Delayed Childbearing and Reduced Family Size, *Demography, 21*:2, pp. 141–156, 1984.

34. M. Corcoran, G. J. Duncan, and M. Ponza, Work Experience, Job Segregation, and Wages, in *Sex Segregation in the Workplace: Trends, Explanations, Remedies*, B. F. Reskin (ed.), National Academy Press, Washington, D.C., 1984.

35. S. J. Schieber and P. M. George, *Retirement Income Opportunities in an Aging America: Coverage and Benefit Entitlement*, Employee Benefit Research Institute, Washington, D.C., 1981.

36. J. H. Schulz, Private Pension and Women, in *Women in Mid-Life: Security and Fulfillment*, U.S. House Select Committee on Aging and the Subcommittee on Retirement Income and Employment, U.S. Government Printing Office, Washington, D.C., 1978.

37. A. H. Beller, Trends in Occupational Segregation by Sex and Race, 1960–1981, in *Sex Segregation in the Workplace: Trends, Explanations, Remedies*, B. F. Reskin (ed.), National Academy Press, Washington, D.C., 1984.

38. P. England, The Failure of Human Capital Theory to Explain Occupational Sex Segregation, *Journal of Human Resources, 17*:3, pp. 358–370, 1982.

39. K. C. Holden and W. L. Hansen, Part-Time Work, Full-Time Work, and Occupational Segregation, in *Gender in the Workplace*, C. Brown and J. A. Pechman (eds.), The Brookings Institution, Washington, D.C., 1987.

40. J. Sweet, *Women in the Labor Force*, Seminar Press, New York, 1973 (especially Chapter 7).

41. S. D. Lesnoy and D. R. Leimer, Social Security and Private Saving: Theory and Historical Evidence, *Social Security Bulletin, 48*:1, pp. 14–30, 1985.

42. H. Z. Lopata, Changing Commitments of American Women to Work and Family Roles, *Social Security Bulletin, 43*:6, pp. 3–14, 1980.

43. L. B. Bixby, W. W. Finegar, S. Grad, W. W. Kolodrubetz, P. Lauriat, and J. Murray, *Demographic and Economic Characteristics of the Aged: 1968 Social Security Survey*, Research Report No. 45, Office of Research and Statistics, Social Security Administration, U.S. Government Printing Office, Washington, D.C., 1975.

44. J. Treas, Women's Employment and Its Implications for the Status of the Elderly of the Future, in *Aging: Social Change*, S. B. Kisler, J. M. Morgan and V. K. Oppenheimer (eds.), Academic Press, New York, 1981.

45. A. H. Beller and K. K. Han, Occupational Sex Segregation, Prospects for the 1980s, in *Sex Segregation in the Workplace: Trends, Explanations, Remedies*, B. F. Reskin (ed.), National Academy Press, Washington, D.C., 1984.

46. V. Reno and A. D. Rader, Benefit for Individual Retired Workers and Couples Now Approaching Retirement Age, *Social Security Bulletin, 45*, pp. 25–31, 1982.

47. S. Polachek, Occupational Segregation Among Women: Theory, Evidence and a Prognosis, in *Women in the Labor Market*, C. Lloyd, E. Andrews, and C. Gilroy (eds.), Columbia University Press, New York, 1979.

48. E. B. Palmore, G. G. Fillenbaum, and L. K. George, Consequences of Retirement, *Journal of Gerontology, 39*:1, pp. 109–116, 1984.

49. E. B. Palmore, L. K. George, and G. G. Fillenbaum, Predictors of Retirement, *Journal of Gerontology, 37*:6, pp. 733–742, 1982.

50. S. R. Sherman, Reported Reasons Retired Workers Left Their Last Jobs: Findings from the New Beneficiary Survey, *Social Security Bulletin, 48*:3, pp. 22–30, 1985.

51. M. E. Szinovacz, Beyond the Hearth: Older Women and Retirement, in *Older Women*, E. W. Markson (ed.), Lexington Books, Lexington, Massachusetts, 1983.

52. S. Masters and I. Garfinkel, *Estimating the Labor Supply Effects of Income Maintenance Alternatives*, Academic Press, New York, 1977.

53. J. Henretta and A. O'Rand, Joint Retirement in the Dual Worker Family, *Social Forces, 62*, pp. 504–520, 1983.

54. R. L. Clark, T. Johnson, and A. A. McDermed, Allocation of Time and Resources by Married Couples Approaching Retirement, *Social Security Bulletin, 43*:4, pp. 3–16, 1980.

55. H. M. Iams, Characteristics of the Longest Job for New Retired Workers, *Social Security Bulletin, 48*:3, pp. 5–21, 1985.

56. R. L. Clark and A. McDermed, Inflation, Pension Benefits, and Retirement, *Journal of Risk and Insurance*, pp. 19–38, March, 1982.

57. R. V. Burkhauser, K. C. Holden, and D. Myers, Marital Disruption and Poverty: the Role of Survey Procedures in Artificially Creating, *Demography, 23*:4, pp. 621–631, 1986.

58. A. J. Auerbach and L. J. Kotlikoff, Life Insurance of the Elderly: Its Adequacy and Determinant, in *Work, Health, and Income Among the Elderly*, G. Burtless (ed.), The Brookings Institution, Washington, D.C., 1987.

59. K. C. Holden and R. V. Burkhauser, Pensioners' Annuity Choice: Is the Well-Being of Widows Considered? IRP Discussion Paper No. 802-86, Institute for Research on Poverty, University of Wisconsin, Madison, 1986.
60. D. Hammermesh, Consumption During Retirement: The Missing Link in the Life Cycle, *Review of Economics and Statistics, 66*, pp. 1-7, 1984.
61. J. Wolfe, Perceived Longevity and Early Retirement, *Review of Economics and Statistics, 65*:4, pp. 544-551, 1983.
62. P. J. Taubman and S. Rosen, Healthiness, Education and Marital Status, in *Economic Aspects of Health,* V. R. Fuchs (ed.), University of Chicago Press, Chicago, 1982.
63. L. W. Thompson, J. N. Breckenridge, D. Gallagher, and J. Peterson, Effects of Bereavement on Self-Perceptions of Physical Health in Elderly Widows and Widowers, *Journal of Gerontology, 39*:3, pp. 309--314, 1984.
64. R. V. Burkhauser, K. C. Holden, and D. J. Feaster, Incidence, Timing and Events Associated with Poverty: A Dynamic View of Poverty in Retirement, *Journal of Gerontology* (in press).
65. M. David and P. Menchik, Distribution of Estate Wealth and its Relationship to Intergenerational Transfers, *ASA Proceedings, 1982,* pp. 103-108, 1982.
66. T. Mirer, The Wealth-Age Relation Among the Aged, *American Economic Review, 69*:3, pp. 435-443, 1979.
67. C. E. McConnel and F. Deljavan, Consumption Patterns of the Retired Household, *Journal of Gerontology, 38*:4, pp. 480-490, 1983.
68. J. Davies, Uncertain Lifetime, Consumption and Dissaving in Retirement, *Journal of Political Economy, 89,* pp. 561-577, June 1981.
69. M. Darby, *The Effects of Social Security on Income and the Capital Stock,* The American Enterprise Institute, Washington, D.C., 1979.
70. Y. P. Chen, Economic Status of the Aging, in *Handbook of Aging and the Social Sciences* (2nd Edition), R. H. Binstock and E. Shanas (eds.), Van Nostrand Reinhold, New York, 1985.
71. O. S. Mitchell and G. S. Fields, The Effects of Pensions and Earnings on Retirement: A Review Essay, in *Research in Labor Economics,* R. Ehrenberg (ed.), *5,* JAI Press, Greenwich, Connecticut, 1982.
72. U.S. Department of Justice, *The Pension Game: American Pension System from the Viewpoint of the Average Woman,* Task Force on Sex Discrimination, Civil Rights Division, U.S. Government Printing Office, Washington, D.C., n.d..
73. M. Upp, Relative Importance of Various Income Sources of the Aged, 1980, *Social Security Bulletin, 46*:1, pp. 3-10, 1983.
74. J. J. Kotlikoff and D. E. Smith, *Pensions in the American Economy,* The University of Chicago Press, Chicago, 1983.
75. President's Commission on Private Pensions, *Coming of Age: Toward a National Retirement Income Policy,* President's Commission on Private Pensions, U.S. Government Printing Office, Washington, D.C., 1981.
76. C. Ross, Income Transfer and the Relative Economic Status of the Elderly, 1967, 1974, and 1981, Discussion Paper No. 760-84, Institute for Research on Poverty, Madison, Wisconsin, 1984.

77. J. H. Schulz, T. H. Leavitt, S. Litkouhi, and J. M. Strate, The Impact of Pension Integration on the Income of Minority Persons in Later Years, National Aging Policy Center on Income Maintenance, Working Paper No. 11, Brandeis University, Waltham, Massachusetts, 1983.

78. M. Orshansky, Counting the Poor: Another Look at the Poverty Profile, *Social Security Bulletin, 28,* pp. 3-29, 1965.

79. L. Mallan, Women's Worklives and Future Social Security Benefits, *Social Security Bulletin, 39*:5, pp. 3-13, 1976.

80. T. M. Smeeding, Nonmoney Income and the Elderly: The Case of the "Tweeners," *Journal of Policy Analysis and Management, 5*:4, pp. 707-724, 1986.

81. U.S. Bureau of the Census, Alternative Methods for Valuing Selected In-Kind Transfer Benefits and Measuring Their Effects on Poverty, Technical Paper No. 50, U.S. Government Printing Office, Washington, D.C., 1982.

82. G. J. Duncan, R. D. Coe, M. E. Corcoran, M. S. Hill, S. D. Hoffmann, and J. N. Morgan, *Years of Poverty, Years of Plenty: The Changing Economic Fortunes of American Workers and Families,* Institute for Social Research, The University of Michigan, Ann Arbor, 1984.

83. K. H. Anderson and R. V. Burkhauser, The Retirement-Health Nexus: A New Measure of an Old Puzzle, *Journal of Human Resources, 20*:3, pp. 315-330, 1985.

84. B. Wolfe and R. Haveman, Time Allocations, Market Work, and Changes in Female Health, *American Economic Review; Papers and Proceedings of the Ninety-Fifth Annual Meetings of the American Economic Association, 73*:2, pp. 134-139, 1983.

85. S. Schwartz, S. Danziger, and E. Smolensky, The Choice of Living Arrangements by the Elderly, in *Retirement and Economic Behavior,* H. Aaron and G. Burtless (eds.), The Brookings Institution, Washington, D.C., 1984.

86. L. E. Troll, The Family of Later Life: A Decade Review, *Journal of Marriage and the Family, 33,* pp. 263-290, 1971.

87. B. Soldo, M. Sharma, and R. T. Campbell, Determinants of the Community Living Arrangements of Older Unmarried Women, *Journal of Gerontology, 39*:4, pp. 492-498, 1984.

88. R. J. Lampman and T. M. Smeeding, Interfamily Transfers as Alternatives to Government Transfers to Persons, *Review of Income and Wealth,* Series 29, 1, pp. 45-66, 1983.

89. G. Cain, Welfare Economics of Policies Toward Women, *Journal of Labor Economics, 3*:1, Part 1, pp. S375-S396, 1985.

90. C. Murray, *Losing Ground,* Basic Books, New York, 1984.

91. H. J. Aaron, *Economic Effects of Social Security,* The Brookings Institution, Washington, D.C., 1982.

92. R. V. Burkhauser and J. A. Turner, A Time Series Analysis on Social Security and its Effects on the Market Work of Men at Younger Ages, *Journal of Political Economy, 86*:4, pp. 701-716, 1978.

PART THREE
Methodological Issues

CHAPTER
6

Methodological Issues in Research on Older Women[1]

A. Regula Herzog

Discussions at the conference "Older Women: Research Issues and Data Sources," although focusing on health and economic issues, returned frequently to the many ways in which features of a study's methodology can contaminate the substantive conclusions. Methodological features thought to be important include the nature of the assumptions underlying the research, the design of the study, the design of the sample, the measurement instruments, and the data analysis. These features will be briefly described in this chapter and their potential impact on conclusions will be suggested.

An issue of terminology merits a brief note. "Sex" and "sex differences" are used throughout this chapter to denote men and women and the differences between them. The use of this terminology is not meant to imply anything about the nature of the differences, i.e., whether they are biologically or culturally determined.

ASSUMPTIONS

Implicit assumptions about the nature of women and men and about aging often guide the hypotheses to be tested, the data collected and, thus, ultimately affect the research results. For example, in past investigations women were often

[1] The author would like to thank all the participants of the conference for their invaluable intellectual contribution and Andrew Achenbaum, Nancy Fultz, Linda George, Jersey Liang, Elizabeth Mutran, Willard Rodgers, and Marcia Ory for critical reading of earlier drafts of this paper. All remaining errors are the author's responsibility. The writing of this chapter was supported by Grant R13 AG03458 from the National Institute on Aging.

either omitted altogether or included only if they held their own jobs or were not married – presumably because a married woman's situation was believed to be primarily determined by her husband's situation, particularly if she was not employed outside of the home. More recently emerging research on older women continues to focus on issues assumed to be of particular importance to women's lives, such as menopause or the empty nest, while aspects such as employment-related and economic issues are still assumed to be of lesser importance and have garnered less attention by researchers. It must be emphasized that in order to design relevant research on older women we need to think creatively about the diverse situations of women in our society and avoid errors resulting from accepting outmoded or inaccurate social stereotypes.

STUDY DESIGN

Although few studies are explicitly designed to test sex differences, most of the more recent studies do include both women and men on the assumption that findings may differ by sex. As a result, many studies now available lend themselves to investigating sex differences. Nevertheless, the design of any such study must be carefully examined to determine whether it is appropriate for the research question that is to be addressed.

Cross-Sectional Design

Cross-sectional designs, which survey a particular population or subgroup of the population at a particular point in time, are best suited to investigating the current health and economic status of women and men, and how they differ. Although less well suited to investigating the processes by which such differences were established, cross-sectional data are often used for this purpose because appropriate longitudinal data bases are unavailable.

Data – There are many available cross-sectional sample surveys on physical health, mental health, and economic status that include large numbers of older adults and are suitable for investigating differences between older men and women. They include, for example, the *Myth and Reality of Aging in America* and *America in Transition,* conducted by Harris in 1974 and 1981, respectively; the 1975 *National Survey of the Aged,* by Shanas; the *Survey of the Low-Income Aged and Disabled,* conducted by the Bureau of the Census in 1974; the *Aging Supplement* of the *Health Interview Survey,* conducted by the Bureau of the Census for the National Center for Health Statistics in 1984; the *Aging in Manitoba* study conducted in 1971, 1976, and 1983; and the *Establishment of Populations for Epidemiologic Studies of the Elderly (EPESE)* studies sponsored by the National Institute on Aging. These and other surveys are described in Appendix A. Many other cross-sectional surveys cover the entire adult age range and can be used to establish sex differences across age levels, although often the number of respondents at the upper age levels are not large enough to sustain detailed analyses.

Longitudinal Design

Investigators are often interested in examining changes over time in health or economic status, the processes by which such changes come about, and how the processes vary for women and men. A longitudinal design is more appropriate than a cross-sectional one for studying change and for unraveling the processes leading to change.

In a longitudinal design the same persons are surveyed repeatedly at various intervals and over periods ranging from a few weeks to many years. A longitudinal survey can provide data that describe the actual age-related changes individuals undergo over time, while data from cross-sectional studies require that age-related changes be inferred from differences between cohorts of different ages. Because of the time ordering inherent in the data, longitudinal designs also permit a better specification of certain causal effects and the ruling out of others. However, even a longitudinal design does not necessarily resolve all the questions concerning causal direction. While a detailed discussion of longitudinal designs is clearly beyond the scope of this chapter, interested readers are referred to Baltes, Reese, and Nesselroade, and Schaie and Hertzog [1,2].

Data — Few longitudinal surveys are available. Moreover, of those that do exist, few cover more than ten to fifteen years, too short a time span to observe such long-term effects as the impact of life style on morbidity or mortality. It is important, therefore, to conceptualize the appropriate time lag for the influence of a causal factor, in addition to the nature of its influence. Some of the most promising longitudinal data sources in the area of work and economic issues include the Social Security Administration's *Retirement History Survey* and the *Longitudinal Survey of the Labor Force Experience of Mature Women.* In health and mental health, important sources are the *Alameda County Study,* the *Baltimore Longitudinal Study of Aging,* the *Duke Second Longitudinal Study,* the *EPESE* studies sponsored by the National Institute on Aging, the *Epidemiological Catchment Area Program (ECA)* studies sponsored by the National Institute of Mental Health, the *Tecumseh Community Health Study,* and the *Framingham Heart Study.*

For longitudinal investigations of the causes of mortality a new tool has recently become available in the form of the *National Death Index.* This index can be used to trace deaths (and their proximal causes) of survey respondents from existing U.S. studies, as long as their names, birth dates, and preferably Social Security numbers are known.[2] In this way a longitudinal data base for

---

[2] Names and other identifying information are of course only available to the agency that collected the original data.

investigating death as an outcome can be built from an existing cross-sectional study without recontacting the respondents. The design and use of the *National Death Index* are discussed by Rogot et al. and Wentworth et al. [3, 4].

Age–Period–Cohort Design

While intraindividual change, the causes of such change, and sex differences in the change and related processes may be observed in a given longitudinal study, the findings may not be generalizeable across different time periods, because observed patterns may depend on historical and social contexts specific to the particular period studied. Only patterns that do not differ across time periods can be said to be truly universal. For example, results obtained from a study of the effects of work history on women's economic status in old age that included a period when women spent much of their married life without paid employment might differ from results obtained later when many married women hold paid employment and sex differences in status and type of occupations are slowly diminishing.

Data — In order to establish generality or cohort-specificity of age-related changes and cause–effect relationships, multiple longitudinal surveys from different time periods, or at least repeated cross-sections, are needed [1, 2]. Among the few publicly available data sources that fulfill these data requirements are the *Health Interview Survey (NHIS)*, the *Health and Nutrition Examination Survey (NHANES)*, the *Quality of Life Surveys*, the *Americans View Their Mental Health* surveys, the *Survey of Income and Program Participation*, and the three *National Surveys of the Aged*.

It is now generally acknowledged, however, that even these designs do not permit unique estimation of the effects of aging, cohort membership, and time period because the three effects are not uniquely identified. The nature of the necessary assumptions and choice of appropriate analytical techniques to deal with this problem have spurred a great deal of controversy. For an introduction to the issues and the various stands on it see, for example, Fienberg and Mason, Kosloski, and Rodgers [5-7].

Experimental and Quasi-Experimental Design

The ultimate test of the causal impact of a certain factor is provided by a controlled intervention or an experimental design. In these designs the causal factor is experimentally manipulated and research "subjects" are assigned randomly to an experimental or a control group. Inferences about causation are clearer in experimental than in longitudinal designs. In the longitudinal design the natural occurrence of the causal factor is exploited; however, it most certainly does not occur randomly to participants in longitudinal surveys but instead is often a function of preexisting differences. In the experiment, on the other hand, random assignment results in control of preexisting differences. Of course, sex cannot be randomly assigned to persons, but other factors that are confounded with sex in nonexperimental studies can be experimentally controlled. Many of the explanatory concepts discussed in other chapters of this volume — such as nutrition, exercise, cash payments, in-kind benefits, health care benefits, and even social support and coping styles — might lend themselves to intervention or experimental manipulation. An experimental design is rarely used in the kinds of research discussed in this publication but deserves more frequent use. One example of a large-scale experiment is the Health Insurance Experiment; two examples of smaller-scale experiments are a study by Schulz in which the degree of control available to residents over some aspects of the institutional environment was manipulated and a study by Rodin in which coping style was manipulated in order to test effects on residents' health [8, 9]. It should be noted that most experiments use small numbers of experimental subjects and test specific hypotheses. Thus, experimental data generally are not made available for use by other investigators.

Data — Although typically lacking a control group, a few studies offer quasi-experimental designs in the form of measures collected before and after major policy and program changes. One of these is the *Survey of the Low-Income Aged and Disabled* that was conducted before and after the institution of the Supplemental Security Income program in 1974. More generally, ongoing cross-sectional series (e.g., *Health Interview Survey*) or longitudinal studies (e.g., *Panel Study of Income Dynamics*) that use the same measures over time could be used as "before" and "after" measures for certain naturally occurring events such as policy changes or changes in medical technology. Another quasi-experimental design may be provided by using cross-state studies to approximate variations in experimental manipulation when state-controlled programs are being studied. For a general discussion of various quasi-experimental designs and their potentials and pitfalls, see Cook and Campbell [10].

SAMPLING AND NONRESPONSE

Much gerontological research is based upon volunteers from the community or from retirement organizations. If young comparison groups are used, they are typically college students who participate as part of a course requirement, or community volunteers. Camp, West, and Poon, and Lachman, Lachman, and Taylor have provided systematic assessments of the selection of subjects in memory research and have carefully documented the biased selection [11, 12]. A cursory survey of journals on aging suggests that the respondent selection procedures are not very different for other areas of gerontological research; and most likely a similar criticism holds for many other research disciplines. This state of the art implies that experimental subjects are often not representative of the population of old or young persons, and that, as a consequence, sex and age differences may be biased in any number of ways.

Other data on women and men stem from records of physicians, hospitals, and other health care and social service agencies. These types of data provide uniquely detailed information on the institutionalized population or on those receiving medical assistance, Supplemental Security Income, or food stamps, to name just a few examples. These data yield biased sex differences for the general population because they include only persons who sought these services and the two sexes, in particular, appear to differ in their use of services. For example, women may be more likely than men to use health care services earlier in life, although little or no sex difference might exist in late life [13, 14].

No matter what the design, properly designed and implemented probability samples are critical in arriving at estimates of characteristics and relationships that represent the population values within well-specified error limits. For an introduction to sampling see the chapters by Frankel and by Sudman in the *Handbook of Survey Research* [15]; for a classic text on survey sampling see Kish [16]. There are several possible sampling errors that may jeopardize representativeness and these must be evaluated when a data set is chosen for further analysis. A sample can fail because the frame from which it was drawn did not represent the entire population of older persons, because persons were improperly selected, or because selected persons did not participate in the study. Let us first examine issues of incomplete frames and how they might bias the representation of women and men and thus might confound sex comparisons.

Most samples are designed to represent the noninstitutionalized population living in private households of a certain region or of the entire nation. The exclusion of people living in institutions, however, creates likely biases in samples of the very oldest age groups. Although it is typically stated that only about 5 percent of all persons over sixty-five live in institutions, among those seventy-five and older the percentage is about 7 percent, and among those eighty-five and older it is 22 percent [17]. Samples of noninstitutionalized populations over eighty-five will therefore routinely exclude 22 percent of the target population. Furthermore, since the nursing home population is predominantly female,[3] this exclusion may confound analyses of sex differences. While nursing home residents are generally less healthy and closer to death than are the community-dwelling older adults, older women living in institutions are likely to have less severe forms and levels of health problems than do older men in institutions because community-dwelling men are more likely to be living with wives and able to delay institutionalization even in the face of serious physical and mental health problems. At any rate, only sampling frames that

---

[3] It is not clear from the literature with which the author is familiar whether the proportion of women is higher in the nursing home than in the noninstitutionalized of equal age, or whether it is just equally high.

include all older adults — those living in the community as well as those living in institutions — can represent the entire older population and lead to unbiased estimates of sex differences in health-related characteristics among the old. Coverage of institutionalized and noninstitutionalized populations in the same survey is rare, and the required samples are difficult to draw. One survey that includes an institutional as well as a noninstitutional sample is the *Epidemiologic Catchment Area Program (ECA)*.

There is one group that neither household nor institutional sampling frames can include because they do not live in either setting; these are the people who dwell in alleyways or temporary shelters. Although these people admittedly represent a small proportion of the population, they are most likely to have some very special mental health and economic problems, and the failure to include them into population samples may result in biased health and economic estimates. It is also likely that most transients are men, although little good data seem to be available on this. A recent study by Rossi and his colleagues represents the first scientifically based attempt to learn about homeless people in Chicago [18]. This study shows that the homeless average a very small proportion, i.e., about one-tenth of a percent of Chicago's population at any one time, that they are predominantly male, very poor, and burdened with many physical and mental health problems.

As noted above, the selection of respondents represents another step in drawing a sample where bias can be introduced. For example, in a household sample respondent(s) should be selected in random fashion from all eligible persons living in the household; otherwise, those more readily found at home — more likely women and older persons — may be overrepresented in the sample and those rarely found at home — more likely men and younger persons — may be underrepresented.

Once sample persons are selected, however, some of those selected are unwilling or unable to participate in the research. Even the best sample will result in biased findings if some of the sampled persons do not participate *and* if those who do not participate are systematically different from those who do. Yet, except with Federal Government sponsorship, it is extremely difficult to obtain participation by nearly all selected respondents. Research ethics require that participation in all scientific investigations be voluntary and that this condition be made clear to all prospective participants. Participation in well-conducted surveys, as expressed by the measure of response rate, is usually not much higher than 70 percent. Furthermore, such response rates have been declining over the last few decades and they are lower than average among certain subgroups of the population such as the elderly and men [19-21]. The lower response rates among these subgroups suggests potential biases in representing the elderly and men in social surveys.

Nonresponse among the older population tends to generate other systematic and predictable biases. Seriously ill, disturbed, or demented people often cannot be subjected to a formal interview. They must therefore be deleted from the study even though they were properly sampled, resulting in a sample biased towards healthy older adults. Furthermore, to the extent that the health problems responsible for the deletion are related to the sex of the respondent, sex differences estimated from the responses of the interviewed respondents may be biased. As discussed in more detail in the chapter on health, debilitating health problems may be more frequent among older women than older men. There are also some suggestions, albeit inconsistent, that older women experience more cognitive and emotional impairment.[4] As a consequence, sex differences in health may be attenuated when assessed in surveys.

After completion of the survey, larger weights are often assigned to the underrepresented respondents than to the overrepresented ones, in order to adjust for differential nonresponse across sampling areas and for deviations from the population on standard sociodemographic characteristics, including sex and age. Such adjustments are effective only to the extent that nonrespondents are similar to respondents, an assumption which is questionable and notoriously difficult to prove.

Another source of possible bias that is often overlooked is item nonresponse. When respondents fail to answer certain questions in a survey by saying "I don't know," by providing an uncodable answer, or by refusing to answer, their responses are reported as missing in the data set and are often excluded from specific analyses. The resulting bias in a specific analysis depends on the number of respondents who fail to respond to a question and the degree to which their responses would be different from the responses of those who do give an answer. Again, older respondents are more likely to fail to answer a question than are other age groups [22, 23], and women are more likely to do so than are men [24]. It is also suspected that respondents who fail to respond differ systematically in their attitudes and behaviors from those who give answers. If the latter is true — which is usually difficult to substantiate — the imputation procedures utilized routinely in some of the large surveys conducted by the U.S. Government or major survey organizations to remedy item nonresponse may not solve the problem, because imputation procedures are usually based on respondents who have provided answers but who are otherwise similar to those who have not provided answers. For a distinguished panel's comprehensive assessment of the problem of item nonresponse in surveys and a discussion of methods for dealing with item nonresponse, see Madow, Olkin, and Rubin [25].

To summarize, samples of older adults may not represent older men and older women equally well. Some of the problems seem to affect samples of older women disproportionately; these include the exclusion of institutionalized populations from the sampling frame and women's higher likelihood for item nonresponse. Other problems disproportionately affect the sampling of older

---

[4] Of course, these sex differences are themselves based on data from surveys.

men; these include the lower response rate among men and the numbers of transient people. In either case, sex comparisons may be affected by bias in the sample of one or the other sex. Such biases should be kept in mind as possible alternative explanations when sex differences are interpreted. Their potential significance may be evaluated by carefully reviewing sampling design and study procedures and by examining nonresponse patterns and potential adjustment and imputation procedures for nonresponse, where such information is available.

MEASUREMENT

Two measurement issues — the conceptualization of measures by the investigator and the meaning of measures to the respondent — have already been touched upon in the chapters on health and economic status and shall be discussed here only briefly. Two other measurement issues — accuracy of reporting and reporting by proxy — have not been discussed.

First, the conceptualization of measures is important because of the many different ways in which health and economic status can be operationalized. As a result, different surveys may yield different patterns of sex differences. An example from research on health is used to illustrate this point. Whereas in some studies self-assessed health shows only minor differences between older women and men [26, 27; but see 28 for males reporting worse health], mortality and more objective measures of morbidity show a quite different picture. Sex differences in mortality indicate that older women live longer than older men [29, 30]. Sex differences in morbidity suggest that older women have more illness conditions and impairments than do older men, and that women's illness conditions are more painful and debilitating [27, but see 13 for a contrasting view]. Thus, one might reach a different conclusion about existing sex differences depending on which measure of health one decided to use. From mortality measures one would conclude that older women are healthier than older men; from morbidity one might conclude that they are less healthy; and at least from some self-report data, that they are no different. Obviously, comprehensive and well-reasoned measures of health and economic status and consensus about operationalizing these concepts are needed for a meaningful assessment of sex differences.

Second, differences in the meaning of health phenomena and of relevant survey measures to respondents may also confound observed sex differences. Women and men may differ in the ways in which they perceive their health and react to health problems. For example, women may be more aware of health problems because childbearing made them earlier and more frequent users of health care services and thus more knowledgeable about their own health; because they are often responsible for the health of all family members; or because weakness is more compatible with the traditional female than male role. Or, women and men may understand the survey questions in different ways, because they view health and illness differently. As was argued elsewhere in this book, researchers know little about how older persons perceive, think about, and talk about their health and whether the sexes differ in this regard. Such differences, if they do exist, are likely to jeopardize the equivalence of standardized questions across the sexes.

A number of procedures are available to examine the equivalence of meaning or structure of concepts between the sexes. These analytical methods include ethnographic, anthropological, and content-analytic methods for the analysis of open-ended materials and relevant statistical analyses of the frequencies of the codes. They also include factor-analytical models of multiple measures of the same concepts and their analysis by structural modeling techniques utilized in computer programs such as LISREL for subgroup analysis. For a discussion of the LISREL approach to subgroup comparisons, see Jöreskog and Jöreskog and Sörbom [31, 32]; for an example of an analysis testing the equivalence of the structure of morale for the sexes see Liang and Bollen [33].

Third, another factor that possibly confounds sex differences in health and economic assessment is the accuracy of reporting. Survey researchers are quite concerned about possible inaccuracies that may derive from survey respondents' inability to recall accurately the information requested and/or from their unwillingness to disclose fully the requested information [34, 35]. For example, it is well known that specific health conditions are systematically underreported, most likely because respondents do not recall them accurately. It is also known that information on "embarrassing" health conditions and on financial characteristics of the respondent's situation is often reported inaccurately or not at all, presumably because of the respondent's unwillingness to disclose the information [36].

It is possible that men and women are not equally accurate in their answers to survey questions. Women have been found by some to report health conditions more accurately than men [37]. A recent review of sex differences in the accuracy of health reporting and a systematic evaluation of measurement error in survey responses have found no systematic sex differences, however [30, 38]. More generally, a recent review of response errors in surveys concluded that inaccuracy is largely a function of the format of surveys (i.e., the mode of administration, the order and format of the questions, the memory processes required to produce the answers) rather than a function of respondent characteristics [39]. Based on this conclusion, women would be expected to be less accurate only in reporting information that is inherently more complex and thus more difficult to remember. For example, one might speculate that women would report their work histories less accurately than men would because, on average, women's work histories are much less continuous and more fragmented and thus more difficult to recall in detail.

Fourth, it has been suggested that proxy responding may confound sex differences in health and economic assessments. In surveys that permit reporting by proxy respondents, women are more likely to become proxy respondents and proxy respondents are less accurate than self-respondents. The argument is summarized in Wingard [30]. It is, however, not clear whether this argument that women report about men more often than men report about women applies in old age when adults of either sex often become proxy respondents for their older parents of either sex.

To summarize, the sexes could potentially differ in the validity of the information they report in the interview. Such differences are most likely specific to the particular topics being measured and the questions being used to measure them. No consistent sex differences in response quality have emerged so far from the available evidence. Yet, at this point, it is probably a good idea for researchers comparing women and men to examine carefully the measurement quality of variables at the core of the research question, with particular attention to possible sex differences.

DATA ANALYSIS AND PRESENTATION

Not only must data be collected on appropriate samples of women and men, using equivalent questions and scales, but these data must be organized and analyzed such that they yield relevant results for sex comparisons. Quite obviously, data need to be reported separately for men and women and, if age variations in sex differences are to be investigated, separately for each age level.

Sex comparisons should be evaluated by a statistical test. Various statistical tests are available, depending on the level of measurement of the variables on which the sexes are to be compared. Because sex is related to many other characteristics and cannot be experimentally manipulated, multivariate techniques controlling for these other characteristics are often the appropriate analytical strategy. For example, in samples of older men and women, women are, on the average, somewhat older than men. Failure to control for this age difference could affect the size of the sex difference for many health conditions. Older women are also more likely to live alone, and failure to adjust for such sex-specific variations could confound comparisons on such characteristics as independent functioning or economic status, the latter of which is based on the household unit.

Many investigators are interested in whether sex differences vary across age levels, whether they diminish or become accentuated in older age. Instead of estimating sex differences for different age levels and then comparing them by inspection, a systematic assessment of the differences across age levels might be made. A test of the change in sex differences across age levels might be accomplished by including interaction terms between sex and age in a regression analysis. For a discussion on testing interaction effects in multiple regression analysis see Pedhazur [40]. Other independent variables might be included in the form of additional predictors in the regression analysis. For an example of a multivariate analysis of life satisfaction that used age-by-sex interaction terms, see George, Okun, and Landerman, but note that these authors did not find any significant age-by-sex interactions [41].

A still different research question addresses the explanation of observed sex differences in health or economic status. Such explanations may be sought in previously established predictors of the particular characteristic on which the sex difference was observed and tested in a multivariate framework. Two different forms of explanations, however, need to be distinguished. Either 1) the probability or frequency of exposure to the explanatory factor is different for men and women, or 2) the strength of the relationship between the explanatory variable and the characteristic in question is different for the two sexes. Statistically speaking, in the former case the factor explains the relationship, in the latter case the interaction between the factor and sex explains it. For an illustration of one means of handling the decomposition of a sex difference in distress in terms of these two explanations see Kessler and McLeod [42].

Although age comparisons are often carried out with cross-sectional data, as noted earlier, panel or longitudinal data are more appropriate for investigating change across the life-span. Because panel data involve repeated measures of the same persons, a repeated-measures analysis of variance design might be the analytical method of choice [1, 2, 43]. This approach readily permits the inclusion of sex-by-age interactions and thus a systematic assessment of sex differences in age-related changes is possible. For an explication of this approach, and an example of an analysis of race differences in age-related changes in retirement status, that may be used as a model for the assessment of sex differences see Campbell, Mutran, and Parker [43].

While much remains to be learned about sex differences in age-related changes, some investigators are particularly interested in the predictors of change, and how these might differ for the two sexes. Structural equation-type models are more appropriate techniques for this type of research question because the use of predictors is more flexible and the interpretation of their effects is clearer than in the analysis of variance. For an introduction to structural equation models for research on aging, see Alwin [44]. The LISREL methodology mentioned before may be used to analyze covariance structures involving measures from two or more points in time. Since the methodology also allows one to analyze effects between unmeasured concepts that are indexed by imperfect measures, it embraces at the same time a measurement model and a causal model, controlling in this way for measurement errors in the causal analysis. Advantages of the LISREL methodology for longitudinal data analysis include the ability to examine structural invariance over time; to analyze separately changes in means, variances, and causal effects over time; and to handle autocorrelations between residuals over time. More detailed presentations of the LISREL methodology for the analysis of longitudinal data are provided by Campbell and Mutran and by Schaie and Hertzog [2, 45]. An example of testing measurement equality within a panel analysis is given in Mutran [46].

An advantage of the LISREL methodology for sex comparisons is that it provides specific options for subgroup comparisons. More specifically, any component of the model, including measurement estimates and causal effect estimates, can be constrained to be equal across men and women and the fit of such a model can be evaluated. In a set of hierarchical models the location of the lack of equality between men and women can then be pinpointed.

Unlike standard panel data, where the occurrence of an event is inferred from a change in status measured in two consecutive data collections, event history analysis models the exact date of the event. An example that is provided by Campbell, Mutran, and Parker is retirement status [43]. In a traditional panel study each respondent's employment status is assessed during each interview, and change in status is assumed when the reports differ. For an event history analysis, the event of retirement and its exact timing is assessed during the interview and thus the time line of retirement can be analyzed in more detail. The drawback is that the potential for measurement error is more serious for the exact dating of an event than for the assessment of whether the event occurred or not. For a readable brief introduction into event history analysis and a comparison of this analytical method to structural equation and analysis of variance models, see Campbell, Mutran, and Parker [43]; for a general introduction, see Allison [47]; and for a more comprehensive but technically more demanding exposition, see Tuma and Hannan [48].

CONCLUSION

The foregoing is a set of methodological considerations for research on older women and their comparison with older men. It is not claimed that the discussion is exhaustive, but it is hoped that the reader has become sensitized to potential artifactual sex differences arising from unarticulated assumptions about the nature of women and men and their roles in this society, from the procedures used in design and data collection, and from the form of the data analyses. A careful researcher must consider these alternative explanations and, wherever possible, control them in the analyses.

REFERENCES

1. P. B. Baltes, H. W. Reese, and J. R. Nesselroade, *Life-Span Developmental Psychology: Introduction to Research Methods,* Brooks/Cole, Monterey, California, 1977.
2. K. W. Schaie and C. Hertzog, Longitudinal Methods, in *Handbook of Developmental Psychology,* B. B. Wolman (ed.), Prentice-Hall, Englewood Cliffs, New Jersey, 1982.
3. E. Rogot, M. Feinleib, K. A. Ockay, S. H. Schwartz, R. Bilgrad, and J. E. Patterson, On the Feasibility of Linking Census Samples to the National Death Index for Epidemiologic Studies: A Progress Report, *American Journal of Public Health, 73,* pp. 1265-1269, 1983.

4. D. N. Wentworth, J. D. Neaton, and W. L. Rasmussen, An Evaluation of the Social Security Administration Master Beneficiary Record File and the National Death Index in the Ascertainment of Vital Status, *American Journal of Public Health, 73*, pp. 1270–1274, 1983.
5. S. E. Fienberg and W. M. Mason, Identification and Estimation of Age-Period-Cohort Models in the Analysis of Discrete Archival Data, in *Sociological Methodology*, K. F. Schuessler (ed.), Jossey-Bass, San Francisco, California, 1979.
6. K. Kosloski, Isolating Age, Period, and Cohort Effects in Developmental Research: A Critical Review, *Research on Aging, 8*, pp. 460–479, 1986.
7. W. L. Rodgers, Estimable Functions of Age, Period, and Cohort Effects, *American Sociological Review, 47*, pp. 774–787, 1982.
8. R. Schulz, The Effects of Control and Predictability on the Physical and Psychological Well-Being of the Institutionalized Aged, *Journal of Personality and Social Psychology, 33*, pp. 563–573, 1976.
9. J. Rodin, Behavioral Medicine: Beneficial Effects of Self Control Training in Aging, *International Review of Applied Psychology, 32*, pp. 153–181, 1983.
10. T. D. Cook and D. T. Campbell, *Quasi-Experimentation*, Houghton Mifflin, Boston, 1979.
11. C. J. Camp, R. L. West, and L. W. Poon, Recruitment Practices for Gerontological Research, *Special Methodologies in Gerontological Research*, M. P. Lawton and A. R Herzog (eds.), (forthcoming).
12. R. Lachman, J. L. Lachman, and D. W. Taylor, Reallocation of Mental Resources over the Productive Lifespan: Assumptions and Task Analyses, in *Aging and Cognitive Processes*, F. I. M. Craik and S. Trehub (eds.), Plenum, New York, 1982.
13. C. A. Nathanson and G. Lorenz, Women and Health: The Social Dimensions of Biomedical Data, in *Women in the Middle Years*, J. Z. Giele (ed.), John Wiley and Sons, New York, 1982.
14. F. D. Wolinsky, R. M. Coe, D. K. Miller, J. M. Prendergast, M. J. Creel, and N. M. Chavez, Health Services Utilization Among the Non-Institutionalized Elderly, *Journal of Health and Social Behavior, 24*, pp. 325–337, 1983.
15. P. H. Rossi, J. D. Wright, and A. A. Anderson, *Handbook of Survey Research*, Academic Press, New York, 1983.
16. L. Kish, *Survey Sampling*, John Wiley and Sons, New York, 1965.
17. K. G. Manton and B. J. Soldo, Dynamics of Health Changes in the Oldest Old: New Perspective and Evidence, *Milbank Memorial Fund Quarterly, 63*, pp. 206–285, 1985.
18. P. H. Rossi, J. D. Wright, G. A. Fisher, and G. Willis, The Urban Homeless: Estimating Composition and Size, *Science, 235*, pp. 1336–1341, 1987.
19. C. G. Steeh, Trends in Nonresponse Rates, 1952–1979, *Public Opinion Quarterly, 45*, pp. 40–57, 1981.
20. T. J. DeMaio, Refusals: Who, Where and Why, *Public Opinion Quarterly, 44*, pp. 223–233, 1980.
21. T. W. Smith, Sex and the GSS, Technical Report No. 17, National Opinion Research Center, Chicago, 1979.

22. K. J. Gergen and K. W. Back, Communication in the Interview and the Disengaged Respondent, *Public Opinion Quarterly, 30,* pp. 385–398, 1966.

23. N. D. Glenn, Aging, Disengagement, and Opinionation, *Public Opinion Quarterly, 33,* pp. 18–33, 1969.

24. J. D. Francis and L. Busch, What We Now Know About "I Don't Knows," *Public Opinion Quarterly, 39,* pp. 207–218, 1975.

25. W. G. Madow, I. Olkin, and D. B. Rubin, *Incomplete Data in Sample Surveys, Volume 2: Theory and Bibliographies,* Academic Press, New York, 1983.

26. Chartbook on Aging in America, Prepared for the 1981 White House Conference on Aging, 1981.

27. L. M. Verbrugge, A Health Profile of Older Women with Comparisons to Older Men, *Research on Aging, 6,* pp. 291–322, 1984.

28. K. F. Ferraro, Self-Ratings of Health Among the Old and the Old-Old, *Journal of Health and Social Behavior, 21,* pp. 377–383, 1980.

29. L. M. Verbrugge, Men and Women: Mortality and Health of Older People, in *Aging and Society: Selected Reviews of Recent Research,* M. W. Riley, B. B. Hess, and K. Bond (eds.), Lawrence Erlbaum, Hillsdale, New Jersey, 1983.

30. D. L. Wingard, The Sex Differential in Morbidity, Mortality, and Lifestyle, *Annual Review of Public Health,* Annual Reviews, Palo Alto, California, 1984.

31. K. G. Jöreskog, Simultaneous Factor Analysis in Several Populations, in *Advances in Factor Analysis and Structural Equation Models,* J. Magidson (ed.), Abt Books, Cambridge, Massachusetts, 1979.

32. K. G. Jöreskog and D. Sörbom, *LISREL IV: Analysis of Linear Structural Relationships by the Method of Maximum Likelihood,* National Educational Resources, 1978.

33. J. Liang and K. A. Bollen, Sex Differences in the Structure of the Philadelphia Geriatric Center Morale Scale, *Journal of Gerontology, 40,* pp. 468–477, 1985.

34. R. Andersen, J. Kasper, M. R. Frankel, and associates, *Total Survey Error,* Jossey-Bass, San Francisco, 1979.

35. C. F. Cannell and R. L. Kahn, Interviewing, in *The Handbook of Social Psychology* (2nd Edition), G. L. Lindzey and E. Aronson (eds.), Addison-Wesley, Reading, Massachusetts, 1968.

36. C. F. Cannell, G. Fisher, and T. Bakker, Reporting of Hospitalization in the Health Interview Survey, *Health Statistics,* Series D, No. 4, U.S. Department of Health, Education, and Welfare, Washington, D.C., 1961.

37. W. G. Madow, Interview Data on Chronic Conditions Compared with Information Derived from Medical Records, National Center for Health Statistics, Series 2, No. 3, U.S. Government Printing Office, Washington, D.C., 1967.

38. F. M. Andrews, Construct Validity and Error Components of Survey Measures: A Structural Modeling Approach, *Public Opinion Quarterly, 48,* pp. 409–442, 1984.

39. N. M. Bradburn, Response Effects, in *Handbook of Survey Research*, P. H. Rossi, J. D. Wright, and A. B. Anderson (eds.), Academic Press, New York, 1983.

40. E. J. Pedhazur, *Multiple Regression in Behavioral Research* (2nd Edition), Holt, Rinehart and Winston, New York, 1982.

41. L. K. George, M. A. Okun, and R. R. Landerman, Age as a Moderator of the Determinants of Life Satisfaction, *Research on Aging, 7,* pp. 209–233, 1985.

42. R. C. Kessler and J. D. McLeod, Sex Differences in Vulnerability to Undesirable Life Events, *American Sociological Review, 49,* pp. 620–631, 1984.

43. R. T. Campbell, E. Mutran, and R. N. Parker, Longitudinal Design and Longitudinal Analysis: A Comparison of Three Approaches, *Research on Aging, 8,* pp. 480–504, 1986.

44. D. F. Alwin, Structural Equation Models in Research on Human Development and Aging, in *Methodological Issues in Aging Research*, K. W. Schaie, R. T. Campbell, W. M. Meredith, and S. C. Rawlings (eds.), Springer, New York, 1987.

45. R. T. Campbell and E. Mutran, Analyzing Panel Data in Studies of Aging: Applications of the LISREL Model, *Research on Aging, 4,* pp. 3–41, 1982.

46. E. Mutran, The LISREL Approach to Multiple Occasion Research, *Special Methodologies in Gerontological Research,* M. P. Lawton and A. R. Herzog (eds.), forthcoming.

47. P. D. Allison, *Event History Analysis,* Sage University Paper Series on Quantitative Applications in the Social Sciences, Series No. 07-046, Sage, Beverly Hills, California, 1984.

48. N. B. Tuma and M. T. Hannan, *Social Dynamics: Models and Methods,* Academic Press, New York, 1984.

CHAPTER
7

Sources and Uses
of Qualitative Data[1]

Jeanne E. Miller

In articulating the nature of aging, Sally Gadow tells us that "It is at heart subjective" [1, p. 131]. This statement reminds us of the importance of looking at the non-objective, non-quantifiable side of aging, of learning from the object of our study — the individual.

The search for understanding of human behavior is at best difficult; at worst one wonders if it is possible. The use of multiple methods to gather information — of more than one research strategy or design — enables us to gain a more complete picture of the complexities of human nature. We need not only numbers and other descriptive data at particular points in time, but information about how those numbers think about themselves and their experiences. How do they describe and explain themselves? What do they see as cause and effect? This chapter focuses on the use of qualitative research methods and strategies as an invaluable approach to examining and learning more about health and economic aspects of old women's lives. Only in tapping this dimension can social scientists identify the logic-in-use by their respondents. Quantitative and qualitative methods can supplement one another, permitting us to see a broader and more complex reflection of old women's realities. As Filstead points out [2, p. 5] :

> To acknowledge the unique prerogative of the behavioral scientists is to understand that which he (sic) studies — to combine both the inner and outer perspectives of knowing — in no way detracts from the scientific nature of the behavioral sciences. This dual perspective is of great utility in trying to assess the possible forms of behavior . . . .

[1] I would like to thank Carol Hollenshead for helpful discussions and suggestions concerning this chapter.

In recent years there has been an increase in qualitative research in the field of aging. Certainly Myerhoff's book, *Number Our Days* and a more recent anthropological account by Kaufman, *The Ageless Self* let us hear, in their own words, how old women (and men) view their own aging and their lives [3, 4] .

Qualitative research is no less scientific nor less rigorous than is quantitative. The reality it identifies may be more factual for older persons than that isolated by survey research. Using different techniques including observation, interviews, content analysis, or the examination of other human products (e.g., literature, art, the media), its sources and methods offer a perspective unlike that of traditional quantitative research. The value of such research and its different perspective may be found in any of its components: the focus on the whole, the focus on the meaning of the data to the individual who provides it — whether through an interview or a written record, or the aim of reflecting the world as seen through the eyes of the "subject." Qualitative research is involved with the informants or the research participants; interpretation of these research data thus demands a recognition that such data reflect the cultural, social, and interior lives of those people providing information.

This chapter also identifies resources and methods for acquiring this information. Sources of qualitative data on older women range from archival resources such as women's diaries to ethnographies which document the roles of older women in particular societies. These data sources are scattered and are often not readily identified, since they may not be exclusively about older women. Primary sources include manuscript or other archival collections, which are frequently historical, often addressing women in general. Within such archives, the researcher will need to find the specific collections that highlight the older woman or issues pertaining to aging. Some of the best approaches to archival resources are through the many guides now available.

The definitive guide to collections in the United States is the *National Union Catalog of Manuscript Collections,* which inventories each registered collection in American archives [5] . More specifically, sources such as *Women's History Sources: A Guide to Archives and Manuscript Collections in the United States, Women's Collections: Libraries, Archives, and Consciousness,* and the regional sources, for example, *Women's History: Resources at the State Historical Society of Wisconsin, Bibliography of Sources Relating to Women* (Michigan), and Georgia's *Women's Records: A Preliminary Guide,* lead the researcher to individual collections of manuscripts produced by or relating to women [6-11] . Many archives have inventories of their collections, and many have inventories relating to specific subjects such as women or work.

Manuscript sources can be used in a variety of ways. Individual lives and experiences are documented in personal or family collections, or autobiographies prepared for familial use. Terri Premo's work on older women in early America uses such collections [12, 13] . The archives of organizations (corporations, hospitals, universities) provide quantitative information or may, through content analysis, offer a means of identifying trends or cultural effects in the experiences of women.

In terms of older women and work, the holdings of archives specific to labor may be the most useful source. (See, for example, *Women and Work: A Preliminary Guide to Primary Sources,* from the M. P. Catherwood Library, Cornell [14].) Collections relating to specific industries, such as textile manufacture, in which large numbers of women are employed, may have information not only on women's work patterns but also on health issues of woman workers. (See the Amoskeag Manufacturing Company collection, Manchester Historic Association, New Hampshire.) Finally, collections of individuals may document their own work or refer to issues of women's work (including part-time and home work). The Isabel Bacon LaFollette papers, held in the Schlesinger Library at Radcliffe, include information on an employment agency for mature women. Periodicals such as the nineteenth-century *New England Offering,* a forum for working women, also allow the researcher to approach the experiences of those women being studied.

Health concerns of older women may be approached in a number of ways, including the collections of medical colleges and associations (Medical College of Pennsylvania Archives and Special Collections on Women in Medicine) as well as the records of hospitals (Women's General Hospital, Cleveland). State archives may provide rich collections for the study of older women's health. The Kentucky State Archives, for example, hold over 1,000 cubic feet of records from the only hospital in the state that served the indigent. Similar collections from other institutions (e.g., prisons, mental hospitals) offer considerable data across time. Many nineteenth-century hospitals, mental asylums and almshouses still hold patient records that may be used to trace the effects of variables such as age and gender on therapy, data used, for example, by Pernick [15]. Among the few examples that use such records coded in machine-readable form is an article by Rosenkrantz and Vinovskis on "Invisible Lunatics" [16]. Additional information on the health of older women may be found in personal reminiscences as well as in letters, journals, and the like.

For a historical perspective on printed sources, the *Index-Catalogue of the Library of the Surgeon General's Office, U.S. Army,* Series 1–3, is recommended [17]. Journal articles and books making up what later became the National Library of Medicine are cumulated in an author/subject index.

In addition to archival records and print materials, other types of qualitative sources exist and can be used in research on older women. Qualitative data are frequently obtained through in-depth, open-ended interviews. These may exist in transcript form only, or may form the text of a completed work, such as Rubin's *Women of a Certain Age* [18]. Such interviews may yield a "richness and depth of observation and interpretation which is the hallmark of good [qualitative] research" [19, p. 5]. Interviews on audio or videotape as well as in transcripts provide a source for secondary analysis of qualitative data. The data archive of the Henry A. Murray Research Center at Radcliffe College includes sources of this kind. The 1984 Center conference on "The Use of Archival Data to Study Women's Lives" offers an example of increased interest in an exploration of such sources [20]. Oral histories may provide a rich source of information and may be held not simply in archives, but also in special collections and public libraries. For example, the *Black Women Oral History Project* transcripts are held by the Schlesinger Library at Radcliffe College. Other non-print collections, such as photographic archives, may be used by researchers in a number of ways. In addition to the collections at the Library of Congress and the National Archives, there are the George Eastman House Collections, Smithsonian collections, and additional collections held in many repositories around the country. The "Images of Old Age in America" project, for example, used photographic and other images such as engravings to document a thesis of attitudinal change across time toward the roles of older Americans [21].

Ethnographic data and studies may not focus specifically on older women in a society but may be a rich source of information concerning their roles, work, or other aspects of their lives if the researcher is willing to seek the information throughout the document. Linguistic data also provide information and may be used to document societal attitudes about women through terminology and processes of communication. Useful to anthropologists may be the *Human Relations Area Files* indexing vast amounts of literature in the social sciences. These files are available in numerous libraries across the country and are now computerized, offering easier access to the ethnographic studies and literature in anthropology and focusing on cross-cultural information. Also useful is the *Standard Cross-Cultural Sample* which allows the researcher to compare selected societies in cross-cultural study. The Murray Research Center conference papers include several on the use of ethnographies and other anthropological data and on qualitative approaches to research on women [20].

Frequently, qualitative data sources are those which were not intentionally created as data sources. Their use enables the researcher to examine a natural process or to place a person or experience within a particular milieu. Public sources, such as legislative testimony, depositions, and court records, document the process of changing political and social values. They can illuminate specific changes affecting older women (for example Social Security or age and sex discrimination laws) or provide a measure of the cultural perceptions that affect conditions of life, work, and health of older women as well as the perceptions and assumptions underlying earlier research on older women. Popular culture itself provides a vast number of sources — songs, literature, and technologies in addition to art forms — that reflect the notions and beliefs impacting the lives of those within that culture.

Diaries or letters between women could be used to investigate such topics as the health practices and attitudes of older women of a particular time, whereas the use of archival materials of a labor organization may offer information on the practices of labor organizers, the interest of the union in older women and their issues — or, conversely, attempts to exclude women from the workforce — and indeed specifics of women's work life and workforce behaviors as documented by such records. One of the greatest values of qualitative sources is their ability to reflect the experience of the individual, offering considerable depth or detailed information. Beyond the use of manuscript collections for data about older women, there is their use as a source of information deposited directly *by* older women. The individual woman may, in such a collection, speak through diaries or letters directly to the subjects of work or health as experiences in her life, and changes with age/period may thereby be documented through a single life. As Eva S. Moseley says of women's letters and diaries, "Now those words can be read from a new perspective to answer questions about health, . . . to study in microcosm the changing patterns of marriage, childrearing, and work — household, volunteer, and paid work" [22, p. 184] .

Thus, the combination of the data produced by quantitative methodology with the data and viewpoints of qualitative methodologies may result in further amplification and resolution of many of those gaps and discrepancies found in research on older women.

REFERENCES

1. T. S. Cole and S. A. Gadow (eds.), *What Does It Mean to Grow Old? Reflections from the Humanities,* Duke University Press, Durham, NC, 1986.

2. William Filstead (ed.), *Qualitative Methodology: Firsthand Involvement With the Social World,* Markham Publishing Company, Chicago, 1970.

3. B. Myerhoff, *Number Our Days,* E. P. Dutton, New York, 1970.

4. S. R. Kaufman, *The Ageless Self: Sources of Meaning in Late Life,* University of Wisconsin Press, Madison, 1986.

5. *National Union Catalog of Manuscript Collections,* Library of Congress, Washington, D.C., 1959.

6. A. Hinding (ed.), *Women's History Sources: A Guide to Archives and Manuscript Collections in the United States,* Bowker, New York, 1979.

7. S. Hildenbrand and L. Ash, *Women's Collections: Libraries, Archives, and Consciousness,* Haworth Press, New York, 1985. (Also published as *Special Collections, 3,* 3/4, 1986.)

8. J. P. Danky, et al. (eds.), *Women's History: Resources at the State Historical Society of Wisconsin* (rev. Edition), State Historical Society of Wisconsin, Madison, 1982.

9. *Bibliography of Sources Relating to Women,* 2nd Edition, Michigan History Division, Michigan Department of State, Lansing, 1978.

10. D. R. Roth and V. Shadion (comp.), *Women's Records: A Preliminary Guide,* Georgia Department of Archives and History, n.p., [1979].
11. E. Thomas, C.S.J. (ed.), *Women Religious History Sources: A Guide to the Repositories in the United States,* Bowker, New York, 1983.
12. T. Premo, *Women Growing Old in the New Republic: Personal Responses to Old Age 1785-1835,* Doctoral dissertation, University of Cincinnati, Cincinnati, Ohio, 1982.
13. T. Premo, "A Blessing to Our Declining Years": Feminine Responses to Filial Duty in the New Republic, *International Journal of Aging and Human Development, 20,* pp. 69–74, 1984–85.
14. M. C. Buckley (comp.), *Women and Work: A Preliminary Guide to Primary Sources,* Cornell University, M. P. Catherwood Library, Ithaca, New York, 1975.
15. M. S. Pernick, *A Calculus of Suffering,* Columbia University Press, New York, 1984.
16. B. G. Rosenkrantz and M. Vinovskis, The Invisible Lunatics: Old Age and Insanity in Mid-19th Century Massachusetts, in *Aging and the Elderly,* Spicker et al. (eds.), Humanities Press, New York, pp. 95–126, 1978.
17. *Index-Catalogue of the Library of the Surgeon-General's Office, United States Army,* Series 1–3, USGPO, Washington, D.C., 1880–1932.
18. L. B. Rubin, *Women of a Certain Age: The Midlife Search for Self,* Harper & Row, New York, 1979.
19. C. Hollenshead, The Human Science Research Paradigm: Underlying Assumptions, paper, Annual Meeting of The Gerontological Society of America, Boston, November, 1982. (mimeo)
20. The Use of Archival Data to Study Women's Lives, Conference, The Henry Research Center, Radcliffe College, October 7–8, 1984.
21. W. A. Achenbaum and P. A. Kusnerz, *Images of Old Age in America: 1970 to the Present* (rev. Edition), Institute of Gerontology, The University of Michigan, Ann Arbor, 1982.
22. E. S. Mosley, Sources for the "New Woman's History," *The American Archivist, 43,* pp. 180–190, 1980.

PART FOUR
Conclusion

CHAPTER 8

Conclusion

Mildred M. Seltzer

This concluding section highlights some issues that permeate earlier discussions but could not be addressed fully within the confines of the previous chapters. Specifically, it addresses: 1) the intersections between health and economic issues, and 2) selected major themes that are touched upon at various points in the other chapters. There will be no attempt, however, to summarize materials presented in those other chapters. This section also contains a series of unanswered questions as well as recommendations for future research. It continues to build on conference discussions and the ideas stimulated by participants and by information in the body of this volume.

LOOKING BACK

One of the major contentions of those whose work is presented here is that there are significant differences between older men and older women in the economic and health components of life. It is also clear that many of the issues discussed so far are not solely problems for older women but for older men as well. On the other hand, and equally important, many of the reported findings are based on aggregate data and may not be true for all older women. Older women include Black, Hispanic, Oriental, and White women; they include "young-old" and "old-old" women; they include widowed, married, divorced, and never-married women. While legitimate comparisons can be made on the basis of statistical means, it is well to remember the large variations that produce considerable overlaps between the sexes. For example, while older women in general have lower incomes than older men, there are some older women whose incomes are quite high and some older men whose incomes are very low. Of equal relevance is the need to understand not only sex differences, but also cohort, race, ethnic, and other social differences. With these caveats in mind, we can move to a discussion of some of the major themes and important questions raised.

Although materials in this volume are organized around the two distinct and discrete areas of health and economics, it is readily apparent that people's lives are not so neatly organized. Moreover, the discussion of economic issues focuses consciously on only two aspects of the economics of old age: retirement income and poverty. Herzog and Holden point out the interrelationships of health and economics. We alluded earlier to the importance of health and income to the quality of life. It is easy to see how one's illness affects one's economic status because of medical bills, time off from work, and the possible need for temporary home care. In addition, being sick affects the quality of one's life. Sickness makes it difficult to perform well on the job, in the tasks of everyday living, and in interpersonal relationships. The interrelationships of health and economics can also be seen in those instances where one's occupation is physically hazardous and/or emotionally stressful. Underemployment can be tension producing as can an overly demanding employer. Illness often accompanies poverty because of inadequate housing. Being poor and sick affects the quantity of life as well as its quality, and the quantity and kinds of medical care received. Insufficient income affects nutrition, which in turn affects health. The ordering of interrelationships between these various aspects of life are complex. The complexity of these phenomena helps to account for difficulties in undertaking and implementing research. Indeed, our research techniques and methods for measuring health and economic status are interrelated. To illustrate, many measures of ability, disability, and impairment tend to be oriented toward labor force participation. This suggests the need to develop new measures of health and economic well-being that are both reflective of everyday life and less oriented toward the market place.

DEFINITIONS AND DYADS

Problems of measurement are further complicated by difficulties of definitions. We measure disability and impairment, we do not measure health — in fact, as noted earlier, we have no definition of health. Health can be viewed as the absence of disease or illness or it can be defined subjectively by the individual. If the latter option is taken, we may not know how the individual formed this subjective definition. To what extent are such definitions influenced by the age of the individual? By his or her ethnic background? Sex? Social class? Some combination of these variables? We know that there are differences between the perception of illness, its subjective experience, and its objective evaluation by health care providers. How these different perceptions might influence the type of treatment offered and the care plan followed is not clear. We know little about how an individual's perceptions of his/her health influence perceptions of symptoms and the decision to seek treatment. We do not yet know much about the dyadic relationships between patient and health care providers and how they influence each other with respect to treatment, compliance, respective role definitions, and the achievement of goals.

The lack of adequate information about the dyad of patient and health care provider is similar to the lack of information about other dyadic relationships in the lives of older women. Many of these relationships are particularly important in the areas of health and economics. Others are significant within the family and as these relate to one's social support system. The "social convoys" about which Antonucci writes often consist of a series of dyads within which much of our social lives take place [1]. In the economic realm specifically, we would benefit greatly from increased information about the interactions between employer and employee and how these affect the decisions to continue working full- or part-time, or to retire. An older woman's perceptions of options are strongly influenced by those with whom she interacts on a daily basis.

Just as there are problems with definitions relating to health conditions, so too, are there problems in dealing with definitions relating to economic issues. What, for example, is poverty and how is it measured for individuals and groups? How do subjective and objective definitions of poverty match one another? How, when, and under what circumstances do people define themselves as impoverished? Currently, we measure annual income, but it is questionable whether this single-shot picture accurately reflects the processes of those "moving into and out of poverty" annually, or whether it necessarily provides us with accurate data about those "at risk" of becoming poor. Do people "slide into" or "drop precipitously into" poverty? Much of our research about the economics of old age is cross-sectional, and as a consequence, we rarely see other than a single snippet of the economic realities of old age.

STILL MORE QUESTIONS

Similar process-related questions can be raised about retirement. At what point and how do people begin planning concretely for retirement, and how do they do it? Data suggest that previous conceptions regarding sex differences in the timing of retirement may be inaccurate. For example, women are planning retirement in terms of their own pension eligibility rather than merely their husbands' eligibility. Moreover, the timing of wives' retirement is not dependent solely on their husbands' retiring.

It is apparent that additional research is needed on the nature, timing and the impact of life-stage and role transitions. We have before and after pictures; we measure the consequences of these. To date, our research focus has been on "stages," "conditions," and "events" — relatively static aspects of life — rather than upon measurement of more difficult phenomena such as processes. While we know some of the typical events people experience throughout the life-cycle, such as retirement, death of spouse, or launching of children, we know less about how people anticipate these events and how they insure against undesirable events and outcomes.

There is also a need to learn more about the specific choices women make early in their lives and how such choices affect and even determine late-life outcomes. Are poor old women poor because they made, either consciously or unconsciously, economically disadvantaged occupational choices in young adulthood? Were such decisions made because of social structural constraints, lack of information, or few alternative opportunities? Or, was it because these earlier choices had unanticipated consequences, or did not turn out as expected? For many, particularly members of minority groups, being poor in old age is the continuation of a life-long pattern of economic deprivation. Despite the fact that some social science models implicitly assume that people make rational decisions and choices, data suggest that this may not necessarily be so. One's position in the social structure and the results of earlier decisions often limit and/or determine the available choices. The answers to many of these questions about economic behaviors can have important implications for the development and implementation of policy. If growing old results in a woman's becoming poor, then policies need to rectify the economic problems of old age. If, on the other hand, being poor in old age is the continuation of a life-long pattern, then changes in the conditions of old people can best be remedied by changing their early life circumstances.

There is a broad range of factors that influence people's behaviors. Some were alluded to above. Others include significant persons in one's life — fellow employees, union members, social workers — while other kinds of influential factors include social policies, legislation, and particular programs and services available to older people. We have noted previously the importance of dyadic relationships in influencing behaviors. Our emphasis was upon the nature of the interactions in these dyads. We know relatively little about the people who influence individuals' choices. How do health care providers, employers, and others provide formal and informal advice that aids individuals in making decisions about health and economic matters? The pervasive sex differences in health and economic status discussed throughout the book suggest that women make better decisions regarding health outcomes than do men, while men make better decisions regarding economic issues. Why?

SOCIOCULTURAL AND STRUCTURAL FACTORS

The dearth of data is unrelenting as we move from the perspective of individual persons in the social environment to that of those impersonal structural forces such as the impact of existing policies and programs on people's personal health and economic status. What, for example, is the differential impact of health policies and programs on men and on women? What is the differential impact on specific subcategories of women, rural and urban? Black and white? Married, widowed, never-married? Childless or with children? Policies, legislation, and programs rarely, if ever, have the same impact on everyone in society. They are implemented by individuals for and on other individuals. As a result, sexism, racism, and ageism may influence how policies and legislation are developed and implemented and how programs are conducted. Development and implementation also reflect conflicting sociocultural values. On the one hand, our society stresses the importance of marriage and the family but, on the other, stresses individuals. We value independence but cultivate, through various of our welfare programs, dependence; we stress honesty, but maintain eligibility requirements for some programs that make dishonesty a necessity. Such conflicting values result in inconsistencies in policies and legislation which are reflected, for example, in the differential impact of legislation on different subcategories of women. Social Security benefits, for example, for a widow who had never been employed in the labor force are based on her husband's eligibility. A never-married woman employed in the labor force throughout her adult life will receive benefits based on her eligibility. The former could conceivably receive a higher pension benefit than the latter under these circumstances, or alternatively, the formerly employed woman could receive higher benefits than the woman who worked within the home as a housewife. We have still to learn the extent to which sex is a significant variable affecting the impact of programs and policies. It may be that lack of information rather than discriminatory barriers influence women's behaviors and decision-making activities. An important research question then is: Does awareness of services change throughout the life cycle? If so, what factors are related to changing levels of awareness and how do these affect decisions women make?

In summary, then, there are two important areas about which additional research is needed. First, we need information about how policies and programs influence economic and health outcomes without necessarily affecting conscious decision-making. Second, information is needed about how awareness of programs and policies affect decision-making processes. Neither is an area in which research can be easily undertaken, yet more information is needed about both topics.

THE ROLE OF THE OTHER

We have been emphasizing the importance of relationships in influencing perceptions and behaviors in the areas of economics and health. We now draw attention to the importance of other sometimes impersonal third parties, as these influence the choices and behaviors of people. For example, we have little information about the roles, regulations, and functions of private insurance programs, Tax-deferred Annuities (TDAs), employer's personnel practices, and the effects of eligibility criteria of other industries and organizations on the choices made by individual older women. We know little about how such third parties may impose perceived and actual constraints upon women's decisions, choices and other behaviors in health and economic areas. We also have not taken full advantage of existing opportunities to undertake research in such areas. For example, there is little information available on the role of TDA salespeople in providing information that assists in making decisions about retirement. We do not know the extent to which private insurance company salespeople and claims adjustors influence decisions about obtaining health care. To some extent, we have a natural laboratory in the everyday world in which to measure some of the impact of these third parties on behaviors. We could, for example, collect data from those selling TDAs and their clients in an effort to learn more about the influence of available information about specific TDAs on a client's decision to retire.

The data about mental health problems in late life raise a series of additional questions about sex differences in this area. First, there are differences in how physicians diagnose and treat the same or similar symptoms when these are presented by men and by women, thus suggesting that mental health care providers interpret the same behaviors differently depending upon the sex of the individual expressing the symptoms. A related issue is that the same behaviors may be interpreted differently at different times in the life-cycle. What is viewed as withdrawn behavior in the early years of one's life can be interpreted as adaptive behavior in later life. The fact that similar behaviors are interpreted, diagnosed, and treated differently at different points raises questions about the validity of our data on mental illness in late life.

RESEARCH ISSUES REVISITED

As noted in Herzog's chapter, difficulties in interpreting such data are further complicated by the Neugarten and Gutmann hypothesis regarding personality "cross over" changes in men and women as they age [2-4]. These authors suggest that women become more assertive and independent as they age, while men become more nurturant and expressive. They also suggest that sex role behaviors become less distinct in later years. If, indeed, this is an accurate statement, we need to know whether declines in sex differences are a general phenomenon, representative of an aging or a cohort effect, or whether there are societal expectations regarding such role changes. It would also be interesting to learn whether the increased assertiveness of women combined with their increased involvement in the labor force will bring about any significant changes in the market place itself.

Attention was drawn not only to areas where research is lacking or where contradictory findings abound, but also to methodological issues. Using both quantitative and qualitative methods is necessary to provide a more complete picture of the everyday lives of everyday old women. Cross-sectional accounts are not always appropriate; longitudinal research is needed but is more difficult to conduct. Archival materials are available to supplement numerical descriptions. The choices are plentiful.

There is also a need to draw upon the research skills and knowledge of those in a variety of disciplines and with a variety of approaches. In order to be effective in such undertakings, it is important to understand the vocabularies and models colleagues use in disciplines other than our own. Different research strategies may ask different questions or hold different assumptions. Rather than viewing one approach as "better than" another, seeing quantitative data as more accurate than qualitative findings for example, we can use varying approaches to supplement one another and thus enrich our perspectives and increase our knowledge about aging in general and older women in particular. With the advent of new quantitative methodologies, structural equations being but a single example, the impact of previously unexamined variables can be highlighted. A further discussion of sources and potential uses of quantitative and qualitative data is found in Herzog's and Miller's chapters. Our overall measures and methods can stand some improvements. Some of our conceptualizations need refinement; our samples are not always representative. We need more research documenting the existence or lack of sex differences in old age.

We have called attention to the importance of data in the development of policies and programs for older women. We have also emphasized the importance of accurate information in meeting the everyday needs of older women. The material presented earlier calls attention not only to research findings, but also to sources of data which can be used for further analysis. We have referred to a number of data sources. Information concerning these sources is found in Appendix A. We periodically called attention to opportunities to use these data for secondary analysis. This call for action becomes particularly important as the costs of research activities increase, and as federal actions have decreased both the opportunities to engage in new research and the availability of federal data specifically about aged people. Maximum use of such information is, therefore, a must. At the same time, there are problems and cautions in using such material for secondary analysis. Among other considerations are those having to do with where and how to store archival material as it accumulates. To what extent can secondary analysis data collected for one purpose be useful for another purpose? For some purposes, such data will be outdated while for others they provide an historical perspective.

THEMES AND VARIATIONS

There have been a number of persistent themes permeating the material in this book. Among the more important ones are: 1) the emphasis on transitions, transformations and interactions, on processes rather than on structure of events; 2) the importance of early life precursors and decisions on late-life circumstances; 3) the need to disaggregate our aggregated data; 4) the relationships between behavioral and biological aspects of behavior; 5) the lack of adequate information about some of the decision-making aspects of behavior; and 6) the need for more precise and comparable definitions in our research.

Another theme is the recognition that relationships, illnesses, health, and other aspects of one's life are interrelated and that these relationships wax and wane throughout the life-cycle. We see this in interpersonal relationships, in sex differences themselves, in health concerns, and in economic issues. The waxing and waning is also apparent in problems that are faced and help that is sought. There are times when health issues are more salient to the quality of life, while economic issues are dominant at other times. There is also a waxing and waning in the degree to which government, various programs and services, and other third parties are involved at specific times in individuals' life-cycles.

Despite a fair amount of knowledge, there are still broad areas concerning health and economic issues of older women about which we know relatively little. Some of what we do know contributes to our basic understanding of the processes of aging as well as to our knowledge about the ramifications of health and economic circumstances. Other of our findings have particular significance to policy development and planning issues. Still other findings are proving to be incomplete as we broaden our definition of needed research pertaining to older women. While we have come a long way since research about older women first became recognized as an important academic endeavor, we still have a way to go.

REFERENCES

1. T. C. Antonucci, Personal Characteristics, Social Support, and Social Behavior, in *Handbook of Aging and the Social Sciences*, R. H. Binstock and E. Shanas (eds.), Van Nostrand Reinhold Co., New York, 1985.
2. B. L. Neugarten and D. Gutmann, Age-sex Roles and Personality in Middle Age: A Thematic Apperception Study, *Psychological Monographs: General and Applied, 72,* No. 470, 1958.
3. D. Gutmann, A Key to the Comparative Study of the Life Cycle, in *Life-Span Developmental Psychology,* N. Datan and L. Ginsburg (eds.), Academic Press, New York, 1975.
4. D. Gutmann, The Cross-cultural Perspective: Notes Toward a Comparative Psychology on Aging, in *Handbook of the Psychology of Aging,* K. W. Schaie and J. E. Birren (eds.), Van Nostrand Reinhold Co., New York, 1977.

Appendices

APPENDIX
A

Descriptions of Survey Data Sets

Nancy H. Fultz

This appendix briefly describes data sets appropriate for investigations of health and economic issues concerning older women. The datasets are listed in alphabetical rather than topical order because a number of the studies include both health and economic measures. Included in the description of each study, where possible, are the name(s) and affiliation(s) of the Principal Investigator(s) or other contact person, the person(s) or archive distributing the data, a summary of the design and substantive focus of the study, and a selection of related publications.

Several of these data sets are not archived for general release and must be accessed through direct arrangements with the Principal Investigators. In some cases restrictions are placed on the distribution of the data. For example, studies may require a collaborative arrangement between a staff researcher and an outside user before the data are made available. Often this is because primary analyses of the data are still underway. Studies that are not generally distributed are noted with a "PI" for the archive, and the potential user should contact the persons listed. The full names and addresses of archives represented by other abbreviations are listed below.

The abstracts presented here are meant to provide an *overview* of available resources that address the topics of older women's health and economic status; they are not intended as an exhaustive compilation of useful data sets. Therefore, the omission of a survey cannot be construed as a reflection of data quality or utility. Nor does the inclusion of a data set necessarily represent an endorsement of the study. In planning any secondary analysis of survey data the investigator is advised to evaluate the study population, the sample design and size, the response rate, the wording of the questions, the field period, and data collection procedures to determine if they are appropriate for the planned research.

166 / HEALTH AND ECONOMIC STATUS OF OLDER WOMEN

Every effort was made to ensure that the information presented here is accurate at the time of its preparation (Spring 1985). However, by the time of publication, some of this information may already be dated. This is especially true of the names and affiliations of contact persons.

In preparing these descriptions, documentations from the Data Archive for Aging and Adult Development, the Inter-university Consortium for Political and Social Research, the Henry A. Murray Research Center, and the Louis Harris Data Center were utilized [1–4]. Other sources consulted were articles citing relevant studies, other published summaries of datasets [5, 6], and researchers experienced in analyzing these data. Principal Investigators of studies that are not archived were contacted for permission to include their data sets and for approval of the abstracts. Materials and assistance from these sources are gratefully acknowledged.

Names and Addresses of Archives:

Data Archive for Aging and Adult Development (DAAAD)
Box 3003
Duke University Medical Center
Durham, NC 27710
(919) 684-3204

Henry A. Murray Research Center
Radcliffe College
10 Garden Street
Cambridge, MA 02138
(617) 495-8140

Inter-university Consortium for Political and Social Research (ICPSR)
Institute for Social Research
P.O. Box 1248
Ann Arbor, MI 48106
(313) 763-5010

Louis Harris Data Center
Institute for Research in Social Science
Manning Hall 026A
University of North Carolina
Chapel Hill, NC 27514
(919) 966-3346

NAME:	*Aging in Manitoba*
INVESTIGATORS:	Manitoba Department of Health Contact: Betty Havens Office of the Provincial Gerontologist 7th floor — 175 Hargrave Street Winnipeg, Manitoba, Canada R3C 3R8
ARCHIVE:	PI
DESCRIPTION:	In 1971, 1976, and 1983, cross-sections of Manitoba's older population (aged sixty-five and over in 1971, sixty and over in 1976 and 1983) were administered face-to-face interviews to assess their status and needs. The 1971 sample included both community-based and institutionalized respondents (2,542 women, 2,263 men). The 1976 sample (637 women, 665 men) and the 1983 sample (1,492 women, 1,362 men) consisted only of noninstitutionalized persons. Interview questions covered housing, community activities, employment, health and personal care, interests, attitudes, morale, social supports, and economic well-being. The 1976 and 1983 interview schedules were shorter than the first and a majority of these questions were repeated from the first schedule. Reinterviews with surviving respondents (N = 2,303) from 1971 and 1976 took place in 1983–1984; selected information on the deceased (N = 3,381) was obtained. Agencies acting as resources for the senior community were also surveyed in all three years.
PUBLICATIONS:	N. L. Chappell and B. Havens, Old and Female: Testing the Double Jeopardy Hypothesis, *The Sociological Quarterly, 21,* pp. 157–171, 1980. N. L. Chappell, Measuring Functional Ability and Chronic Health Conditions Among the Elderly: A Research Note on the Adequacy of Three Instruments, *Journal of Health and Social Behavior, 22,* pp. 90–102, 1981. B. Havens, Differentiation of Unmet Needs Using Analysis by Age/Sex Cohorts, in *Aging in Canada: Social Perspectives,* V. W. Marshall (ed.), Fitzhenry and Whiteside Ltd., Don Mills, Ontario, 1980. B. Havens, Possibilities and Problems in Using Service Generated Data for Longitudinal Research on Aging, in *Canada's Changing Age Structure: Implications for the Future,* G. M. Gutman (ed.), SFU Publications, Burnaby, British Columbia, 1982.

B. Havens and N. L. Chappell, Triple Jeopardy: Age, Sex and Ethnicity, *Canadian Ethnic Studies, 15,* pp. 119–132, 1983.

Manitoba Department of Health and Social Development, *Aging in Manitoba: Vols. I–IX,* Winnipeg, Manitoba, 1973.

J. M. Mossey and E. Shapiro, Self-Rated Health: A Predictor of Mortality Among the Elderly, *American Journal of Public Health, 72,* pp. 800–808, 1982.

NAME: *Alameda County Study*

INVESTIGATORS: Human Population Laboratory (HPL)
                    California State Department of Health Services
                    2151 Berkeley Way
                    Berkeley, CA 94704
                    Contact: Terry Camacho Dickey

ARCHIVE: PI

DESCRIPTION: An area probability sample of the Alameda County, California noninstitutionalized adult population was surveyed in 1965 with follow-ups in 1974 and 1982 (50% sample). Households were contacted in person and questionnaires were left to be completed and mailed back. The information obtained for the 6,928 respondents (including approximately 500 women aged sixty-five years and older) includes chronic health conditions, health behaviors, social involvements, and psychological characteristics. Mortality data were collected from 1965 to 1982. Major analyses of this data set are currently underway at the HPL; however, collaborative projects may be possible if they do not duplicate current or planned portions of the HPL research program. Informal inquiry is recommended as a first step for interested parties. Subsequently, written proposals describing the planned work in some detail must be submitted to the HPL.

PUBLICATIONS: L. F. Berkman and L. Breslow, *Health and Ways of Living,* Oxford University Press, New York, 1983.

                    J. R. Hochstim, Health and Ways of Living: The Alameda County, California, Population Laboratory, in *The Community as an Epidemiologic Laboratory: A Casebook of Community Studies,* I. I. Kessler and M. L. Levin (eds.), The Johns Hopkins Press, Baltimore, 1970.

L. Vincente, J. A. Wiley, and R. A. Carrington, The Risk of Institutionalization Before Death, *The Gerontologist, 19,* pp. 361–367, 1979.

D. Wingard, The Sex Differential in Mortality Rates: Demographic and Behavioral Factors, *American Journal of Epidemiology, 115,* pp. 205–216, 1982.

NAME:	*American Women's Opinion Poll*
INVESTIGATORS:	Conducted for the Virginia Slims division of Liggett and Meyers, Inc. by Louis Harris and Associates, Inc. (1970 and 1972) and by the Roper Organization (1974 and 1980).
ARCHIVE:	Louis Harris Data Center (1970), ICPSR (1972), Roper Center for Public Opinion Research, University of Connecticut, Storrs, CT 06268 (1974 and 1980)
DESCRIPTION:	This series of cross-sectional surveys measured the attitudes of American women and men on issues of women's roles and rights. About 4,000 respondents, ages eighteen and over, were interviewed for each study. The topics have included women's status, women and work, motherhood, discrimination, women's groups, women in politics, and evaluations of prominent women. Some questions were repeated in some years.
PUBLICATIONS:	*The 1970 Virginia Slims American Women's Opinion Poll: A Survey of the Attitudes of Women on Their Roles in American Society,* Louis Harris and Associates, New York, New York, 1971.
	The 1972 Virginia Slims American Women's Opinion Poll: A Survey of the Attitudes of Women on Their Roles in Politics and the Economy, Louis Harris and Associates, New York, New York, 1972.
	The 1980 Virginia Slims American Women's Opinion Poll, The Roper Organization, Storrs, Connecticut, 1980.
NAME:	*Americans View Their Mental Health, 1976*
INVESTIGATORS:	Joseph Veroff, Elizabeth Douvan, and Richard Kulka, The University of Michigan
ARCHIVE:	ICPSR
DESCRIPTION:	This 1976 survey is a partial replication of a study conducted in 1957 by Gurin, Veroff, and Feld. The face-to-face interviews focused on psychosomatic

symptoms, happiness, worries, role performance, satisfactions, stresses, personal competence, self-esteem, formal and informal help-seeking, coping responses, and social interactions. The probability sample of the U.S. noninstitutionalized adult population included approximately 2,250 persons.

PUBLICATIONS: J. Veroff, E. Douvan, and R. A. Kulka, *The Inner American,* Basic Books, New York, 1981.

J. Veroff, R. A. Kulka, and E. Douvan, *Mental Health in America,* Basic Books, New York, 1981.

NAME: *Baltimore Longitudinal Study of Aging (BLSA)*

INVESTIGATORS: Richard C. Greulich
Gerontology Research Center, NIA
Francis Scott Key Medical Center
Baltimore, MD 21224

ARCHIVE: PI

DESCRIPTION: The *BLSA* was initiated in 1958 to permit repeated observations of the same subjects over a long period of time in order to quantify true age changes and elucidate underlying mechanisms. The subjects are community-dwelling volunteers, ranging in age from their twenties to nineties, who now return every two years for an intensive two-and-one-half-day evaluation and are enrolled for their lifetimes. Recruitment of the male cohort began in 1958. Since 1978, women (many of whom are wives or daughters of the male *BLSA* members) have been systematically added to the *BLSA.* New subjects continue to be introduced to maintain the population. About 1,200 men have been tested at least once and 380 women; currently, there are 583 participating males and 323 females. As of February, 1985, 131 active women subjects were sixty-five or over; only a very few of these women were eighty-five years or older. Observations include medical, genetic, biochemical, physiological, and behavioral variables. *BLSA* data are active working files rather than archival data bases, and access is conditioned upon establishment of a collaborative arrangement with an NIA intramural scientist.

PUBLICATIONS: The recently published, *Normal Human Aging: The Baltimore Longitudinal Study of Aging,* provides a comprehensive description of the history, structure, methodology, and research accomplishments of the

BLSA. This book addresses the first twenty-five years of the study, and therefore, is directed to the male cohort. There are numerous publications on specific *BLSA* studies. Contact the Gerontology Research Center Information Office for additional information.

NAME:	*Census of Population and Housing*
INVESTIGATORS:	U.S. Department of Commerce, Bureau of the Census
ARCHIVE:	ICPSR
DESCRIPTION:	Every ten years the Bureau of the Census conducts an enumeration of the U.S. population, collecting detailed information on the housing and demographic characteristics of the country's residents. Summaries of this information by varying geographic regions are widely available as published tabulations and in machine-readable form. Also available are public-use microdata files from the 1900 and 1960–1980 censuses. These tapes contain sampled response records at the household and individual levels, allowing researchers to perform analyses of their own design.

NAME:	*Consumer Expenditure Survey* (*CES*)
INVESTIGATORS:	U.S. Department of Labor, Bureau of Labor Statistics
ARCHIVE:	ICPSR
DESCRIPTION:	This series of studies about the spending patterns of U.S. consumers provides data used in calculating weights for the Consumer Price Index. Begun in 1888, the *CES* more recently had been conducted about every ten years. Since 1980, it has been run on a continuous basis. Nationwide probability samples of the noninstitutionalized population provide information on expenses such as food, clothing, and consumer durables. Demographic characteristics, including detailed income measures, are also recorded. Data from the 1960–1961 and 1972–1973 surveys are currently available. In the earlier study, 13,728 families were administered face-to-face interviews. In the 1972–1973 survey, approximately 10,000 households were interviewed every three months over a fifteen month period in 1972–1973, and another 10,000 were interviewed quarterly for fifteen months in 1973–1974. A separate 20,000 households completed diaries

of purchases and expenses during two week periods in 1972–1973 and 1973–1974.

NAME:	*Continuous Longitudinal Manpower Survey* (*CLMS*)
INVESTIGATORS:	U.S. Department of Labor
ARCHIVE:	*CLMS* data can be obtained by contacting the CLMS Information Office, Westat, Inc. at 1650 Research Blvd., Rockville, MD 20850 or (301) 251-8259.
DESCRIPTION:	This continuous longitudinal survey of national samples of Comprehensive Employment and Training Act (CETA) enrollees was developed to evaluate the effectiveness of CETA funded programs. New enrollees were sampled quarterly from January 1975 through September 1983, but only those selected before or during Fiscal Year 1981 were interviewed. Up to four face-to-face interviews were conducted with each sampled enrollee. At the first interview (conducted during the quarter following entry) questions were asked about employment and earnings histories, the primary reason for enrolling in CETA, and the receipt of public benefits prior to enrollment. The follow up interviews (usually six months after the first, then eighteen and thirty-six months after entry) focused on earnings and employment status. Additional information on demographic and background characteristics, services received, and termination was collected from sponsors' records. When possible, an earnings history (as reported to the Social Security Administration) was also appended to the data record. The public use data currently available are for persons newly enrolled in CETA between January 1975 and September 1978 (January–June 1975 entry cohort $N = 6,650$; July 1975–June 1976 entry cohort $N = 13,283$; July 1976–September 1977 entry cohort $N = 18,640$; July 1977–September 1978 entry cohort $N = 25,027$). About .5 percent of the enrollees were women aged sixty-five or over. Data for persons who enrolled between October 1978 and September 1981 will be made available at a later date.
PUBLICATIONS:	Westat, *Handbook for CLMS Public Use Tapes: January 1975–September 1978 Enrollees*, Rockville, Maryland, 1983.

NAME: *Coping and Adaptation in Older Black Women, 1980*

INVESTIGATORS: The Henry A. Murray Research Center and the Arthur and Elizabeth Schlesinger Library on the History of Women in America, Radcliffe College

ARCHIVE: Murray Center

DESCRIPTION: Oral histories from outstanding older black women and comparable white women were coded and analyzed to reveal coping styles and evidence of successful psychological adaptation to aging. Sixty highly achieving black women, aged sixty and older, were interviewed about their educational, family, and employment histories; current life situations; personality characteristics; and coping strategies. The thirty-one white women's oral histories were taken from those in possession of the Schlesinger Library.

NAME: *Coping with Stress and Challenge in Later Life*

INVESTIGATORS: Linda K. George and Ilene C. Siegler, Duke University

ARCHIVE: DAAAD

DESCRIPTION: Participants in this 1980 study completed a battery of paper-and-pencil inventories designed to assess locus of control, anomie, self-rated health, self-esteem, behavioral orientations to coping, and subjective well-being. In addition, semi-structured interviews probed for stress and coping styles in three time frames: whole life, previous ten years, and present. The nonprobability sample of 100 white, noninstitutionalized, central North Carolina residents (ages fifty-five to eighty) was equally divided between upper middle class and working class, and between males and females. All the respondents had previously participated in the *Duke Second Longitudinal Study.*

PUBLICATIONS: L. K. George and I. C. Siegler, Stress and Coping in Later Life, *Educational Horizons, 60,* pp. 147–154, 1982.
                    L. K. George and I. C. Siegler, *Coping with Stress and Challenge in Later Life,* Duke University Center for the Study of Aging and Human Development, Durham, North Carolina, 1981.

NAME:	*Current Population Survey (CPS)*
INVESTIGATORS:	U.S. Department of Commerce, Bureau of the Census
ARCHIVE:	ICPSR
DESCRIPTION:	The *CPS* is the principal source of data on employment and unemployment in the U.S. Probability samples of approximately 58,000 households from the noninstitutionalized civilian population are interviewed monthly. All persons fourteen years of age or older at the selected households are enumerated. The continual sample rotation system specifies that a household is interviewed once a month for four consecutive months and is then reinterviewed once a month during the corresponding period one year later. Variables measured each month include employment status, occupation, hours worked during the previous week, reasons for leaving the previous employment, duration of unemployment, methods used in locating work, reasons for not seeking work, and demographic characteristics. Supplemental data are collected regularly on topics like food stamp participation, smoking, fertility, and pension plan coverage. There are also files in which *CPS* data are matched with Social Security earnings records for sampled respondents.
PUBLICATIONS:	U.S. Bureau of the Census, *The Current Population Survey: Design and Methodology*, by R. H. Hanson, Technical Paper No. 40, U.S. Government Printing Office, Washington, D.C., 1978.
NAME:	*Duke Second Longitudinal Study (DSLS)*
INVESTIGATORS:	Center for the Study of Aging and Human Development, Duke University
ARCHIVE:	DAAAD
DESCRIPTION:	This multidisciplinary longitudinal study measured demographic, biomedical, psychological, and social variables through a variety of data collection methods: face-to-face interviews, physical examinations, medical histories, self-administered inventories, performance tests, and laboratory analyses. Standardized instruments and scales such as WAIS, Affect Balance Scale, and scales of anomie, self-concept, and internal–external locus of control were included in the four waves of data collection (1969, 1971, 1973, and 1975)

as were measures of social interaction, work and retirement, and life events. The sample of 502 white men and women, ages forty-six to seventy-one, was selected predominantly from the enrollment list of a major North Carolina medical insurance company. Volunteers from local churches and organizations supplemented the enrollees. Men and older persons were oversampled.

PUBLICATIONS: E. Palmore (ed.), *Normal Aging II,* Duke University Press, Durham, North Carolina, 1974.

E. Palmore, *Social Patterns in Normal Aging: Findings from the Duke Longitudinal Study,* Duke University Press, Durham, North Carolina, 1981.

E. Palmore, W. P. Cleveland, J. B. Nowlin, D. Ramm, and I. C. Siegler, Stress and Adaptation in Later Life, *Journal of Gerontology, 34,* pp. 841–851, 1979.

NAME: *Epidemiologic Catchment Area Program (ECA)*

INVESTIGATORS: National Institute of Mental Health
5600 Fishers Lane
Rockville, MD 20857
Contact: Darrel Regier

ARCHIVE: PI

DESCRIPTION: The objectives of the *ECA* Program are to estimate the prevalence and incidence of specific mental disorders, to identify causes of these disorders, and to provide data for planners of health care services. Two waves of face-to-face interviews and one of telephone interviews are being taken with probability samples of community dwelling and institutionalized adults at five sites: Los Angeles, California; St. Louis, Missouri; New Haven, Connecticut; Baltimore, Maryland; and Durham and surrounding North Carolina counties. The Baltimore, New Haven, and North Carolina samples include oversamples of the aged population. Approximately 3,000 community and 500 institutionalized respondents, per site, are expected. All specific diagnoses are as defined by the DSM-III and measured by the NIMH's Diagnostic Interview Schedule. Both psychotic and nonpsychotic disorders are included. Data from this program are not yet available; release is likely around 1988.

PUBLICATIONS:

W. W. Eaton, D. A. Regier, B. Z. Locke, and C. A. Taube, The Epidemiologic Catchment Area Program of the National Institute of Mental Health, *Public Health Reports, 96,* pp. 319–325, 1981.

W. W. Eaton, C. E. Holzer, III, M. Von Korff, J. C. Anthony, J. E. Helzer, L. K. George, M. A. Burnam, J. H. Boyd, L. G. Kessler, and B. Z. Locke, The Design of the Epidemiologic Catchment Area Surveys: The Control and Measurement of Error, *Archives of General Psychiatry, 41,* pp. 942–948, 1984.

B. Z. Locke, The Epidemiologic Catchment Area Program of NIMH, in *Nature and Extent of Alcohol Problems Among the Elderly,* Research Monograph No. 14, G. Maddox, L. N. Robins, and N. Rosenberg (eds.), U.S. Department of Health and Human Services, Rockville, Maryland, 1984.

J. K. Myers, M. M. Weissman, G. L. Tischler, C. E. Holzer, III, P. J. Leaf, H. Orvaschel, J. C. Anthony, J. H. Boyd, J. D. Burke, Jr., M. Kramer, and R. Stoltzman, Six-Month Prevalence of Psychiatric Disorders in Three Communities: 1980 to 1982, *Archives of General Psychiatry, 41,* pp. 959–967, 1984.

D. A. Regier, J. K. Myers, M. Kramer, L. N. Robins, D. G. Blazer, R. L. Hough, W. W. Eaton, and B. Z. Locke, The NIMH Epidemiologic Catchment Area Program: Historical Context, Major Objectives, and Study Population Characteristics, *Archives of General Psychiatry, 41,* pp. 934–941, 1984.

L. N. Robins, Introduction to the ECA Project as a Source of Epidemiological Data on Alcohol Problems, in *Nature and Extent of Alcohol Problems Among the Elderly,* Research Monograph No. 14, G. Maddox, L. N. Robins, and N. Rosenberg (eds.), U.S. Department of Health and Human Services, Rockville, Maryland, 1984.

L. N. Robins, J. E. Helzer, M. M. Weissman, H. Orvaschel, E. Gruenberg, J. D. Burke, and D. A. Regier, Lifetime Prevalence of Specific Psychiatric Disorders in Three Sites, *Archives of General Psychiatry, 41,* pp. 949–958, 1984.

S. Shapiro, E. A. Skinner, L. G. Kessler, M. Von Korff, P. S. German, G. L. Tischler, P. J. Leaf, L. Benham, L. Cottler, and D. A. Regier, Utilization of Health and Mental Health Services: Three Epidemiologic Catchment Area Sites, *Archives of General Psychiatry, 41,* pp. 971–978, 1984.

NAME: *Establishment of Populations for Epidemiologic Studies of the Elderly (EPESE)*

INVESTIGATORS: National Institute on Aging
National Institutes of Health
Bethesda, MD 20205
Contact: Joan Cornoni-Huntley

ARCHIVE: PI

DESCRIPTION: This research project comprises four prospective epidemiologic surveys of probability samples of persons sixty-five years old and over (approximately 2,800–3,800 respondents per site, about 62% female). The four study sites are East Boston, Massachusetts; New Haven, Connecticut; Iowa and Washington Counties, Iowa; and Durham, North Carolina. The baseline survey (conducted in 1982) and five annual follow-ups will provide information on the prevalence and incidence of chronic conditions among the elderly as well as on general trends in their physical well-being. Questions about functional health; impairments and disabilities; hospitalization; longterm care; and histories of cancer, stroke, high blood pressure, diabetes, and cardiovascular disease are common to all four sites. Mortality information is also collected. The investigators at each site included questions pertaining to their particular research interests: cognitive functioning and medical care utilization at East Boston, socioeconomic status and dental health at Iowa, and psychosocial characteristics at New Haven. Data are actively being collected and the earliest possible release is in 1990.

PUBLICATIONS: J. Cornoni-Huntley, Research Design and Demographic Characteristics of the EPESE, Paper presented at the American Public Health Association Meeting, Dallas, November 1983.

NAME: *Framingham Heart Study*

INVESTIGATORS: William B. Kannel
Boston University Medical Center
School of Medicine
80 East Concord St.
Boston, MA 02118

William P. Castelli
Epidemiology and Biometry Program
National Heart, Lung, and Blood Institute
118 Lincoln St.
Framingham, MA 01701

ARCHIVE: PI

DESCRIPTION: This ongoing prospective community study has followed a probability sample of Framingham, Massachusetts residents for over thirty years. The first of the biannual data collections was in 1951 when the 5,200 respondents were thirty to fifty-nine years of age. The original sample contained 1,256 spouse pairs, and 5,135 of the respondents' adult children were later included. The study involves physical examinations, laboratory tests, and face-to-face interviews. Information on medical history, health behaviors, life events, psychological stress, and social environments is collected as a possible predictor of coronary disease risk.

PUBLICATIONS: A set of monographs presents the study's methodology and the output from numerous analyses of the data. This series is recommended as a starting point for researchers interested in utilizing the data base. See: *The Framingham Study: An Epidemiological Investigation of Cardiovascular Disease*, U.S. Department of Health, Education, and Welfare, National Institutes of Health, Bethesda, Maryland.

T. R. Dawber, *The Framingham Study: The Epidemiology of Atherosclerotic Disease*, Harvard University Press, Cambridge, Massachusetts, 1980.

T. Gordon and W. B. Kannel, The Framingham, Massachusetts, Study Twenty Years Later, in *The Community as an Epidemiologic Laboratory: A Casebook of Community Studies*, I. I. Kessler and M. L. Levin (eds.), The Johns Hopkins Press, Baltimore, 1970.

S. G. Haynes and M. Feinleib, Women, Work and Coronary Heart Disease: Prospective Findings From the Framingham Heart Study, *American Journal of Public Health, 70*, pp. 133–141, 1980.

M. W. Higgins, The Framingham Heart Study: Review of Epidemiological Design and Data, Limitations and Prospects, in *Genetic Epidemiology of Coronary Heart Disease: Past, Present and Future*, Alan R. Liss, Inc., New York, 1984.

W. B. Kannel and T. Gordon, Cardiovascular Risk Factors in the Aged: The Framingham Study, in

S. G. Haynes and M. Feinleib (eds.), *Second Conference on the Epidemiology of Aging,* NIH Publication No. 80-969, U.S. Government Printing Office, Washington, D.C., 1980.

NAME: *General Social Survey*

INVESTIGATORS: National Opinion Research Center, University of Chicago

ARCHIVE: ICPSR

DESCRIPTION: This national survey has been more or less annual since 1972. A cross-section of the U.S. adult (ages eighteen and over) noninstitutionalized population is selected for each survey. Since 1977, the approximately 1,500 respondents per study year have been sampled using a full probability design. Samples selected through 1974 were chosen using a modified probability scheme and those during the transitional years of 1975 and 1976 were half modified and half full probability. *General Social Survey* interviews cover a broad range of sociological topics including life events, organizational participation, satisfactions, social contacts, and attitudes. Most of the items are replicated in some or all of the years.

PUBLICATIONS: E. F. Borgatta and R. G. Foss, Correlates of Age: The NORC General Social Survey, *Research on Aging, 1,* pp. 253–272, 1979.

E. F. Borgatta, R. J. V. Montgomery, and M. L. Borgatta, Alcohol Use and Abuse, Life Crisis Events, and the Elderly, *Research on Aging, 4,* pp. 378–408, 1982.

T. W. Smith, The Hidden 25 Percent: An Analysis of Nonresponse on the 1980 General Social Survey, *Public Opinion Quarterly, 47,* pp. 386–404, 1983.

NAME: *Harris 1978 Retirement and Pensions Survey*

INVESTIGATORS: Louis Harris and Associates, Inc.

ARCHIVE: Louis Harris Data Center

DESCRIPTION: The 1,699 respondents sampled nationwide for this survey were twenty-one years of age or over and received pension benefits, worked full-time, or were retired. Topics of the face-to-face interview included inflation, the quality of retired life, alternatives to retirement, planning for retirement, and pension plan reporting and funding. Two hundred twelve business leaders were also interviewed about similar issues.

PUBLICATIONS: Louis Harris and Associates, *1979 Study of American Attitudes Toward Pensions and Retirement: A Nationwide Survey of Employees, Retirees, and Business Leaders,* Johnson and Higgins, New York, 1979.

NAME: *Harris 1981 Aging in the Eighties Survey: America in Transition*

INVESTIGATORS: Louis Harris and Associates, Inc. for the National Council on Aging

ARCHIVE: Louis Harris Data Center

DESCRIPTION: In 1981, Louis Harris and Associates, Inc. interviewed 3,427 adults (aged eighteen and over) about their beliefs about aging, the experience of aging, attitudes toward and preparation for retirement, social activities, finances, employment after age sixty-five, and health care. The sample, a national cross-section, included oversamples of two age groups (fifty-five to sixty-four and sixty-five or over), Blacks, and Hispanics.

PUBLICATIONS: National Council on Aging, *Aging in the Eighties: America in Transition,* Washington, D.C., 1981.

NAME: *Life Patterns Survey, 1980*

INVESTIGATORS: Grace Huffaker with Marjorie Platt and Julie Breskin, Radcliffe College

ARCHIVE: Murray Center

DESCRIPTION: In October 1979, members of the Radcliffe College Class of 1947 were mailed questionnaires asking about their family backgrounds, educational histories, work and volunteer experiences, children, future plans, attitudes, and husbands' attitudes. Of the 228 women who could be located by the Alumnae Office, eighty-one responded. The average age of the respondents was approximately fifty-five years.

NAME:

Longitudinal Study of Transitions in Four Stages of Life

INVESTIGATORS:

Marjorie Fiske (Lowenthal), Majda Thurnher, and David Chiriboga, University of California at San Francisco

ARCHIVE:

Murray Center

DESCRIPTION:

This study followed respondents as they prepared for and coped with four common transitions in the adult life-cycle. The 216 participants represented four groups: high school seniors, newlyweds, middle-aged parents expecting an "empty nest" transition, and preretirees. Respondents were residents of a West Coast community and were predominantly white and of middle and lower-middle class background. Some were selected from school and other records, others were the friends and relatives of those individuals. Data collection in 1969–1970, 1971, 1975, 1977, and 1979 involved focused interviews, health histories, and projective tests. Information was collected on values, goals, social contacts, and psychological well-being.

PUBLICATIONS:

D. A. Chiriboga, Evaluated Time: A Life Course Perspective, *Journal of Gerontology, 33,* pp. 388–393, 1978.

M. F. Lowenthal, Psychosocial Variations Across the Adult Life Course: Frontiers for Research and Policy, *The Gerontologist, 15,* pp. 6–12, 1975.

M. F. Lowenthal, M. Thurnher, D. Chiriboga, and Associates, *Four Stages of Life: A Comparative Study of Women and Men Facing Transitions,* Jossey-Bass, San Francisco, 1975.

NAME:

Massachusetts Health Care Panel Study

INVESTIGATORS:

Laurence G. Branch
Harvard Medical School
643 Huntington Ave.
Boston, MA 02115

ARCHIVE:

PI

DESCRIPTION:

A probability sample of 1,625 Massachusetts community residents aged sixty-five or over was interviewed in 1974–1975 and reinterviewed in 1976 ($N = 1,317$), 1980 ($N = 825$), and 1985. Interview questions covered the areas of food shopping and preparation, transportation, housekeeping, activities of daily living, social activities, emergency assistance, health care utilization, and functional status. Particular attention was paid to measuring needs and resources in these areas. The 1976 interview also included some questions on morale, dietary habits, smoking, and alcohol consumption.

PUBLICATIONS:

L. G. Branch, *Understanding the Health and Social Service Needs of People Over 65*, Report to the Administration on Aging, HEW, Center for Survey Research, University of Massachusetts and the Joint Center for Urban Studies of MIT and Harvard University, Boston, Massachusetts, 1977.

L. G. Branch, S. Katz, K. Kniepmann, and J. A. Papsidero, A Prospective Study of Functional Status Among Community Elders, *American Journal of Public Health, 74,* pp. 266–268, 1984.

NAME: *McBeath Institute Aging Women Project, 1978-1979*

INVESTIGATORS: Jane Traupmann, Wellesley College

ARCHIVE: Murray Center

DESCRIPTION: A sample of 480 female Madison, Wisconsin residents aged fifty and over was interviewed in the summer of 1978. One year later, 400 were reinterviewed. Variables assessed include demographic characteristics, health, depression, political attitudes, work history, friendships, and family relationships. Both household interviews and self-administered questionnaires were used for data collection.

NAME: *Myth and Reality of Aging*

INVESTIGATORS: Louis Harris and Associates, Inc. for the National Council on Aging

ARCHIVE: ICPSR, DAAAD

DESCRIPTION: Louis Harris and Associates interviewed approximately 4,250 respondents for this study during June and July 1974. Eighteen- to sixty-four year olds were asked for their perceptions of aging, respondents sixty-five and over were questioned about the experience of aging.

Also addressed were attitudes toward work and retirement, morale, self-concept, religiosity, and financial resources. To ensure adequate numbers of older persons and older black respondents, oversamples of these groups augmented the nationwide sample of noninstitutionalized adults.

PUBLICATIONS: L. Harris and Associates, *The Myth and Reality of Aging in America,* National Council on Aging, Washington, D.C., 1975.

J. C. Henretta, R. T. Campbell, and G. Gardocki, Survey Research in Aging: An Evaluation of the Harris Survey, *The Gerontologist, 17,* pp. 160–167, 1977.

J. Liang, A Structural Integration of the Affect Balance Scale and the Life Satisfaction Index A, *Journal of Gerontology, 40,* pp. 552–561, 1985.

J. Liang, Dimensions of the Life Satisfaction Index A: A Structural Formulation, *Journal of Gerontology, 39,* pp. 613–622, 1984.

NAME: *National Ambulatory Medical Care Survey* (*NAMCS*)

INVESTIGATORS: National Center for Health Statistics

ARCHIVE: DAAAD, ICPSR

DESCRIPTION: Begun in 1973, this study of patient visits to a national probability sample of office-based physicians has been annual since 1975. Prior to a sample physician's designated random week for data collection, trained interviewers teach the doctor/office staff to prepare a standardized listing of all patient visits for that week. Records are systematically sampled from the resulting frame. Each year, approximately 48,000 records are selected from about 1,900 sampled doctors. The study provides information on the volume of office visits by demographic characteristics of the patients and by properties of the doctors (such as specialty and geographic location). Records include the patient's problem or symptoms, diagnostic procedures used, the diagnosis, treatments prescribed, duration of the visit, and whether the patient had been seen before.

PUBLICATIONS: J. B. Tenney, K. L. White, and J. W. Williamson, National Ambulatory Medical Care Survey: Background and Methodology, *Vital and Health Statistics,* Series 2, No. 61, U.S. Department of Health, Education, and Welfare, Public Health Service, Rockville, Maryland, 1974.

NAME: *National Health and Nutrition Examination Survey (NHANES)*

INVESTIGATORS: National Center for Health Statistics

ARCHIVE: ICPSR

DESCRIPTION: With the addition of a nutritional surveillance component, the *National Health Examination Survey* became the *NHANES* series. Interviews, medical examinations, and laboratory tests were used to obtain detailed information on dietary habits and nutritional adequacy, health care needs, health behaviors, general well-being, specific medical conditions, and the use of food stamps and home meal delivery. For *NHANES I* (1971–1975) a national multistage stratified probability sample of 32,331 noninstitutionalized individuals aged one to seventy-four years was selected. Of those, 31,973 were interviewed and 23,808 examined. *NHANES II* (1976–1980) examined 20,325 of the 27,803 selected individuals and interviewed 25,286. Respondents to *NHANES II* were ages six months to seventy-four years. Young people, older persons, women of childbearing ages, and low-income persons were oversampled for both waves of data collection. In 1982–1984, the *Hispanic HANES (HHANES)* surveyed respondents from families of Mexican-American, Cuban, or Puerto Rican origin or descent. It is anticipated that data collection for *NHANES III* will begin in 1988.

PUBLICATIONS: H. W. Miller, Plan and Operation of the Health and Nutrition Examination Survey: U.S. 1971–1973, *Vital and Health Statistics,* Series 1, No. 10a and b, U.S. Department of Health, Education, and Welfare, Public Health Service, Rockville, Maryland, 1973.

    A. Engel, R. S. Murphy, K. Maurer, and E. Collins, Plan and Operation of the HANES I Augmentation Survey of Adults 25–74 Years: United States, 1974–1975, *Vital and Health Statistics,* Series 1, No. 14, U.S. Department of Health, Education, and Welfare, Public Health Service, Hyattsville, Maryland, 1978.

NAME: *National Health Examination Survey (NHES)*

INVESTIGATORS: National Center for Health Statistics

ARCHIVE: DAAAD

DESCRIPTION: Cycle 1 of the *National Health Examination Survey* collected health status information on a nationwide probability sample of 6,672 noninstitutionalized civilian adults (eighteen to seventy-nine years old) through face-to-face interviews, medical and dental examinations, and laboratory tests. A set of eight tapes, indexed for merging, was prepared for release from this 1959–1962 cycle. The Data Archive for Aging and Adult Development, Duke University, holds tapes on cardiovascular conditions and on psychological distress. Two subsequent cycles were devoted solely to children under eighteen years of age and, in 1971, the *NHES* was expanded to become the *National Health and Nutrition Examination Survey* (*NHANES*).

PUBLICATIONS: National Center for Health Statistics, Plan and Initial Program of the Health Examination Survey, *Vital and Health Statistics,* Series 1, No. 4, U.S. Department of Health, Education, and Welfare, Public Health Service, Washington, D.C., 1965.

NAME: *National Health Interview Survey* (*NHIS*)

INVESTIGATORS: National Center for Health Statistics

ARCHIVE: ICPSR, DAAAD

DESCRIPTION: Since 1957 the *NHIS* has involved continuous probability sampling and interviewing, with annual data publication. Respondents are sampled from the U.S. noninstitutionalized civilian population; information is collected on about 110,000 members of the approximately 40,000 households selected each year. Census Bureau staff administer questionnaires concerning chronic and acute conditions, disabilities and impairments, and utilization of health services. Several measures of social status are also included. Additional topics are added in single years. These include smoking behavior, drinking behavior, health habits, exercise, and health insurance coverage. Especially pertinent to research on older women is the recently conducted *Aging Supplement* to the *NHIS*.

PUBLICATIONS: National Center for Health Statistics, Health Interview Survey Procedure, *Vital and Health Statistics,* Series 1, No. 11, U.S. Department of Health, Education, and Welfare, Public Health Service, Rockville, Maryland, 1975.

L. M. Verbrugge, NCHS Data and Studies of Differential Morbidity and Mortality, *Research on Aging, 3,* pp. 429–458, 1981.

NAME: *National Longitudinal Survey of the Labor Market Experience of Mature Women*

INVESTIGATORS: Kenneth Wolpin, Ohio State University (H. S. Parnes was principal investigator until his retirement)

ARCHIVE: ICPSR

DESCRIPTION: This survey began in 1967 with a national probability sample of 5,083 women thirty through forty-four years of age (including an oversample of black women). Since then, reinterviews have been conducted at one or two year intervals. The interviews focus on labor force experience, socioeconomic and human capital variables, and environmental characteristics of the labor market. The *National Longitudinal Survey of Labor Market Experience* involves three additional cohorts — young women, young men, and mature men. These groups can be used for comparison purposes.

PUBLICATIONS: Center for Human Resource Research, *The National Longitudinal Surveys: Handbook,* The Ohio State University, Columbus, Ohio, 1983 (revised).
B. Gratton and M. R. Haug, Decision and Adaptation: Research on Female Retirement, *Research on Aging, 5,* pp. 59–76, 1983.
H. S. Parnes and R. S. Spitz, A Conceptual Framework for Studying Labor Mobility, *Monthly Labor Review, 91,* pp. 55–58, November 1969.
H. S. Parnes, The National Longitudinal Surveys: New Vistas for Labor Market Research, *American Economic Review,* pp. 244–249, May 1975.
L. B. Shaw, *Unplanned Careers: The Working Lives of Middle-Aged Women,* Lexington Books, Lexington, Massachusetts, 1983.

NAME: *National Medical Care Utilization and Expenditure Survey*

INVESTIGATORS: National Center for Health Statistics and Health Care Financing Administration

ARCHIVE: ICPSR

DESCRIPTION: The sample of households for this 1980–1981 survey was drawn in two parts. One part was a national probability sample of the civilian noninstitutionalized population (about 6,600 households). The other part was selected from the Medicaid enrollment lists for New York, California, Texas, and Michigan (about

1,000 households per state). A core of questions about health services utilization and expenditures was repeated at each of the five interviews conducted per household (at approximately twelve week intervals). Variables measured by the survey include hospital admissions, doctor and dental visits, number of bed-days, health problems, medicines purchased, charges for medical services, and insurance coverage. A 1987 *National Medical Care Utilization and Expenditure Survey* is planned.

NAME:	*National Nursing Home Survey*
INVESTIGATORS:	National Center for Health Statistics
ARCHIVE:	DAAAD, ICPSR
DESCRIPTION:	This series of cross-sectional studies, conducted in 1969, 1973–1974, and 1977, provides data on selected nursing home facilities, residents, and staff. A stratified two-stage probability design was used to select 1) the nationwide samples of nursing homes, and 2) residents, staff, and discharges (in 1977) from the sampled facilities. Facility information such as the number of beds and types of services and therapies provided was gathered through personal interviews with administrators. Expense and income information was obtained from facility accountants (in 1973–1974 and 1977). Staff completed self-administered questionnaires. Data on the health and behavior characteristics of the residents were provided by nurses based on their personal experience and medical records.
PUBLICATIONS:	National Center for Health Statistics, Design and Methodology for a National Survey of Nursing Homes, *Vital and Health Statistics*, Series 1, No. 7, U.S. Department of Health, Education, and Welfare, Public Health Service, Washington, D.C., 1968.

NAME:	*National Senior Citizen Survey*
INVESTIGATORS:	Kermit Schooler, Syracuse University
ARCHIVE:	ICPSR
DESCRIPTION:	Kermit Schooler used face-to-face interviews with about 4,000 persons aged sixty-five and older to gather data on morale, life satisfaction, age-identification, general health status, functional health, assistance

needs and provision, social contacts, and residential environment. The probability sample from the U.S. older population was interviewed in 1968. A subset of approximately 500 respondents was reinterviewed in 1971 using mostly identical questions.

PUBLICATIONS: J. Liang, Sex Differences in Life Satisfaction Among the Elderly, *Journal of Gerontology, 37,* pp. 100–108, 1982.

J. Liang and B. L. Warfel, Urbanism and Life Satisfaction Among the Aged, *Journal of Gerontology, 38,* pp. 97–106, 1983.

K. K. Schooler, Effect of Environment on Morale, *The Gerontologist, 10,* pp. 194–197, 1970.

K. K. Schooler, Environmental Change and the Elderly, in *Human Behavior and Environment: Advances in Theory and Research,* Vol. 1, Plenum Press, New York, 1976.

NAME: *National Survey of Access to Medical Care*

INVESTIGATORS: Ronald Andersen and Lu Ann Aday, Center for Health Administration Studies, University of Chicago

ARCHIVE: ICPSR

DESCRIPTION: These cross-sectional surveys were conducted in 1975–1976 and in 1982 to study respondents' experiences and problems with accessing medical services. The 7,787 persons interviewed in 1975–1976 were sampled from the entire U.S. noninstitutionalized population. The 1982 sample of 6,610 was selected from U.S. households with telephones (using a random digit dialing design) and included a low income oversample. Survey questions measured patient's symptoms, reasons for seeking or not seeking medical care, doctor's office visits, hospital stays, satisfaction with medical services, financial problems, dental examinations, and attitudes regarding medical care.

NAME: *National Survey of Black Americans*

INVESTIGATORS: James S. Jackson
Institute for Social Research
P.O. Box 1248
Ann Arbor, MI 48106

ARCHIVE: PI

DESCRIPTION: Aspects of social, psychological, and physical well-being in the U.S. adult black population were examined in this 1979–1980 survey. Topics covered include self-esteem, personal efficacy, anxiety, satisfaction, happiness, coping strategies, recent problems, health conditions, disabilities, group and personal identity, social activities, religion, social support, and neighborhood concerns. The probability sample of 2,107 Black Americans responded to face-to-face interviews conducted by Black interviewers. Three hundred sixty-six of the respondents were women aged fifty-five and above, from a total of 581 persons in that age range.

PUBLICATIONS: L. M. Chatters, R. J. Taylor, and J. S. Jackson, Size and Composition of the Informal Helper Networks of Elderly Blacks, *Journal of Gerontology, 40,* pp. 605–614, 1985.

J. S. Jackson, L. M. Chatters, and H. W. Neighbors, The Mental Health Status of Older Black Americans: A National Study, *The Black Scholar: The Black Elderly, 13,* pp. 21–35, 1982.

J. S. Jackson and R. C. Gibson, Work and Retirement Among the Black Elderly, in *Work, Leisure, Retirement, and Social Policy,* Z. Blau (ed.), JAI Press, Greenwich, Connecticut, 1985.

NAME: *National Survey of Institutionalized Persons, 1976*

INVESTIGATORS: U.S. Department of Commerce, Bureau of the Census

ARCHIVE: ICPSR, DAAAD

DESCRIPTION: The purpose of this study was to collect information on a probability sample of U.S. longterm care facilities, a sample of residents within those facilities, and a sample of the residents' families. Data for the 851 institutions include the types of care provided, the number of beds, occupancy rates, ownership, and programs offered. Information on 9,090 residents includes demographic characteristics, the reasons for institutionalization, functional health, and treatments received. Approximately 3,300 of the residents' relatives were interviewed; these data describe visitation patterns, demographics, and attitudes toward the residents and their institutionalization. The sampling frame was the *1973 Master Facility Inventory* maintained by the National Center for Health Statistics. Penal and juvenile detention facilities were not included in the sample.

PUBLICATIONS: B. J. Soldo, The 1976 SIP: Research Opportunity for Gerontologists, *Research on Aging, 3,* pp. 459–474, 1981.

NAME: *National Survey of the Aged*

INVESTIGATORS: Ethel Shanas, University of Illinois at Chicago Circle

ARCHIVE: ICPSR

DESCRIPTION: The functional health, finances, services utilization, health conditions, social and family contacts, and morale of a cross-section of Americans aged sixty-five and over were measured in 1975. The probability sample of about 2,150 noninstitutionalized older persons included an oversample of Blacks. In addition to the personal interviews, there are data from a few proxy respondents and some information on non-respondents. Two earlier national surveys of the aged, conducted by Dr. Shanas in 1957 and 1962, used many of the same questions and are also available.

PUBLICATIONS: E. Shanas, Self-Assessment of Physical Function: White and Black Elderly in the United States, in *Second Conference on the Epidemiology of Aging,* S. G. Haynes and M. Feinleib (eds.), NIH Publication No. 80-969, U.S. Government Printing Office, Washington, D.C., 1980.

E. Shanas, *Older Women: Retired Workers and Housewives,* Final Report to the Social Security Administration, Project No. HEW SSA 10-P-98020-5-01, The University of Illinois at Chicago Circle, Chicago, June 1981.

NAME: *National Women's Study, 1975*

INVESTIGATORS: Market Opinion Research Co., Inc.

ARCHIVE: ICPSR

DESCRIPTION: Attitudes about labor market discrimination, day care centers, the ERA, and divorce were covered in this survey of American women. In addition, respondents were asked about their work patterns, labor union memberships, mass media use, and leisure pursuits. The geographically stratified probability sample of 1,522 adult females included 221 aged sixty-five or older.

NAME: *New Beneficiary Survey*

INVESTIGATORS: Social Security Administration

ARCHIVE: Social Security Administration, ICPSR

DESCRIPTION: From October through December 1982, the *New Beneficiary Survey* collected information from new recipients of social security benefits (first payment in mid-1980 through mid-1981) and their spouses. This information includes employment history, recent income, and health data. In addition, respondents' and spouses' Master Beneficiary Records and Summary Earnings Records are appended to the questionnaire records. The study includes a comparison sample of persons who had established entitlement to Medicare and were eligible for, but had not yet received, social security benefits. There are 18,599 records in the data set.

NAME: *Ohio Longitudinal Survey*

INVESTIGATORS: Robert C. Atchley, Scripps Foundation Gerontology Center, Miami University

ARCHIVE: DAAAD

DESCRIPTION: Self-administered questionnaires were mailed in 1975 to all Oxford Township, Ohio residents born on or before July 1, 1925. The approximately 1,600 eligible persons (identified by Board of Elections records and a postcard census) returned 1,003 usable questionnaires. Three additional waves of data collection were completed in 1977, 1979, and 1981. The questionnaires focused on the perceived and actual impact of retirement, health, leisure activities, morale, self-concept, and demographic characteristics.

PUBLICATIONS: R. C. Atchley, *The Sociology of Retirement,* Schinkman, Cambridge, Massachusetts, 1976.
                         R. C. Atchley, The Process of Retirement: Comparing Men and Women, in *Women's Retirement,* M. Szinovacz (ed.), Sage Publications, Beverly Hills, California, 1982.

NAME: *Panel Study of Income Dynamics*

INVESTIGATORS: James N. Morgan, The University of Michigan

ARCHIVE: ICPSR

DESCRIPTION: The heads of approximately 5,000 families have been interviewed annually since 1968 in an attempt to understand the determinants of family income and of changes in economic status. Survey items address employment, income, housing, food expenditures, home maintenance, car ownership, time use, attitudes, and personality characteristics; there are plans for the addition of a few health measures. In addition to the survey data, information on employment conditions is obtained for each of the counties where respondents reside. The probability sample of U.S. families is supplemented by an oversample of low-income families. Split-off households are retained in the study.

PUBLICATIONS: G. J. Duncan, *Years of Poverty, Years of Plenty*, Institute for Social Research, Ann Arbor, Michigan, 1984.

NAME: *Quality of American Life, 1978*

INVESTIGATORS: Angus Campbell and Philip E. Converse, The University of Michigan

ARCHIVE: ICPSR

DESCRIPTION: Respondents to this study reported their satisfactions or disappointments with various aspects of American life including housing, employment, social interactions, family, leisure activities, economic status, and health. Also asked were questions about happiness, personal competence, and life events over the previous five years. The national probability sample of 3,692 respondents included persons eighteen to ninety-seven years of age, many of whom had participated in the *Quality of American Life, 1971* survey. Interviewer observation data on neighborhoods and living conditions enhance the self-reported information.

PUBLICATIONS: A. Campbell, P. E. Converse, and W. L. Rodgers, *The Quality of American Life: Perceptions, Evaluations, and Satisfactions*, Russell Sage, New York, 1976.
A. Campbell, *The Sense of Well-Being in America: Recent Patterns and Trends*, McGraw-Hill, New York, 1981.

NAME: *Quality of Canadian Life: Social Change in Canada*

INVESTIGATORS: Tom Atkinson, Bernard R. Blishen, Michael D. Ornstein, and H. Michael Stevenson, York University

ARCHIVE: ICPSR

DESCRIPTION: This five-year project began in 1976 with the objective of developing time-series measures of the perceived quality of Canadian life and of other subjective social indicators. Cross-sectional samples of about 3,000 noninstitutionalized Canadians aged eighteen and over were interviewed in 1977, 1979, and 1981. A panel of approximately 2,200 respondents was surveyed in all three years. Decision makers from government, business, labor, the media, and academics were interviewed in 1977 (N = 650) and 1981 (N = 1,150) to allow a comparison of their opinions with those of the general population. In addition to the quality of life measures, respondents were asked questions regarding personal and social values and political ideology.

NAME: *Quality of Employment Survey, 1977*

INVESTIGATORS: Robert Quinn and Graham Staines, The University of Michigan

ARCHIVE: ICPSR

DESCRIPTION: This survey was designed to provide an overview of working conditions in the United States. A probability sample of 1,515 employed Americans responded to questions about job satisfaction, tension, employment conditions, physical health, and financial status. Many of these questions were replicated from the *Survey of Working Conditions, 1969-1970* and the *Quality of Employment Survey, 1972-1973*.

PUBLICATIONS: R. P. Quinn and G. L. Staines, *The 1977 Quality of Employment Survey: Descriptive Statistics with Comparison Data from the 1969-1970 and the 1972-1973 Surveys*, Institute for Social Research, The University of Michigan, Ann Arbor, 1979.

                        G. L. Staines and R. P. Quinn, American Workers Evaluate the Quality of Their Jobs, *Monthly Labor Review, 102*, pp. 3-12, January 1979.

NAME: *Quality of Life of Older Age Groups*

INVESTIGATORS: John C. Flanagan
                        American Institutes for Research
                        P.O. Box 1113
                        Palo Alto, CA 94302

ARCHIVE: PI

DESCRIPTION:

This 1975 survey used face-to-face interviews and case studies to obtain indicators of respondents' general well-being. One thousand men and women fifty years of age and another 1,000 seventy-year olds were selected via a stratified-random probability sampling of the United States. Relations with others, current activities, personal development, and self-fulfillment were some of the concepts measured. Retrospective questioning was used to reconstruct the respondents' quality of life at ages thirty and fifty.

PUBLICATIONS:

J. C. Flanagan, *Identifying Opportunities for Improving the Quality of Life of Older Age Groups,* (AIR-53500-6/79-FR), American Institutes for Research, Palo Alto, California, 1979.

J. C. Flanagan, *New Insights to Improve the Quality of Life at Age 70,* (AIR-88800-5/82-FR), American Institutes for Research, Palo Alto, California, 1982.

NAME:

Rancho Bernardo Study

INVESTIGATORS:

Elizabeth Barrett-Connor and Deborah L. Wingard
Dept. of Community and Family Medicine M-007
University of California at San Diego
La Jolla, CA 92093

ARCHIVE:

PI

DESCRIPTION:

The entire community of Rancho Bernardo, California was invited to participate in this ongoing prospective research program. Eighty-two percent ($N = 6,110$) of the upper middle class community participated in 1972, including 1,100 women sixty-five years of age or older. Subsamples were followed up in 1974–1975 and are currently being recontacted (1984–1986). The study involves physical examinations on up to three occasions, an extensive questionnaire administered on three occasions, and one page self-administered questionnaires completed annually. Blood pressure, cholesterol levels, fasting blood glucose, height, and weight were measured in the examination; and an EKG was done. The questionnaire covers medical history, health behaviors, medical services utilization, and demographic characteristics.

PUBLICATIONS:

E. Barrett-Connor, D. L. Wingard, Sex Differential in Ischemic Heart Disease Mortality in Diabetics: A Prospective Population-Based Study, *American Journal of Epidemiology, 118,* pp. 489–496, 1983.

D. L. Wingard. L. Suarez, and E. Barrett-Connor, The Sex Differential in Mortality From All Causes and Ischemic Heart Disease, *American Journal of Epidemiology, 117,* pp. 165–172, 1983.

NAME: *Retirement History Longitudinal Survey*

INVESTIGATORS: Social Security Administration

ARCHIVE: ICPSR, DAAAD

DESCRIPTION: The Social Security Administration designed this longitudinal study to investigate trends in the social and economic characteristics of older persons as they approached and entered the retirement years. A panel of 11,153 respondents aged fifty-eight to sixty-three years was first interviewed in 1969. Reinterviews followed in 1971, 1973, 1975, 1977, 1979, and 1981. The multistage area probability sample of the U.S. represented all men and unmarried women. Widows of original panel members were retained in the study. Substantive survey areas included work history, income and sources of income, health, expenditures, retirement preparation and expectations, family contacts, leisure activities, and morale.

PUBLICATIONS: L. E. Bixby and L. M. Irelan, The Social Security Administration Program of Retirement Research, *The Gerontologist, 9,* pp. 143–147, 1969.

B. Gratton and M. R. Haug, Decision and Adaptation: Research on Female Retirement, *Research on Aging, 5,* pp. 59–76, 1983.

L. M. Irelan, D. K. Motley, K. Schwab, S. R. Sherman, J. H. Murray, and K. Bond, *Almost 65: Baseline Data From the Retirement History Study,* U.S. Government Printing Office, Washington, D.C., 1976.

L. M. Irelan and K. Schwab, The Social Security Administration's Retirement History Study, *Research on Aging, 3,* pp. 381–386, 1981.

NAME: *Status of the Elderly, 1972*

INVESTIGATORS: Social Security Administration

ARCHIVE: ICPSR

DESCRIPTION: Data from the March 1972 *Current Population Survey* were matched with data from the Social Security Administration's benefit record system to construct a file containing information on work rates, sizes and sources of income, and beneficiary characteristics of the U.S. population aged sixty and older. The 14,724 records are for all individuals aged sixty and older included in the nationwide multistage probability sample of households selected for the March 1972 *CPS*.

NAME:	*Study of the Well-Being of Older People in Cleveland, Ohio*
INVESTIGATORS:	U.S. General Accounting Office
ARCHIVE:	ICPSR, DAAAD
DESCRIPTION:	The original goals of this project were to assess the general well-being of an older population using multiple indicators; to document any changes in well-being over a one year interval; and to identify the need for and impact of services. The sample of noninstitutionalized Cleveland residents aged sixty-five and over was composed of two parts. The first was a random scientific sample of the older population. The second was a sample of Supplemental Security Income (SSI) recipients. Face-to-face interviews, employing the *OARS* instrument, were taken with 1,834 respondents in 1975. Reinterviews with 1,519 persons were done in 1976. Matching information on services provided by eighty-eight agencies is included in the file. Additional data collection expanded the study to cover a nine-year span.
PUBLICATIONS:	Conditions of Older People: National Information System Needed — HRD-79-95, September 20, 1979.
	Home Health: The Need for a National Policy to Better Provide for the Elderly — HRD-78-19, December 30, 1977.
	The Well-Being of Older People in Cleveland, Ohio — HRD-77-70, April 19, 1977.
	U.S. General Accounting Office Distribution Section, Room 1518, 441 G Street, NW, Washington, D.C. 20548.
NAME:	*Support Systems Involving Widows, 1974*
INVESTIGATORS:	Helena Lopata, Loyola University of Chicago
ARCHIVE:	Murray Center

DESCRIPTION: Face-to-face interviews were conducted with 1,169 Chicago-area widows who were selected from Social Security lists to include five types of current or former beneficiaries. The data set contains measures of the respondents' psychological, social, and financial well-being. A series of interview questions also asked the women to compare conditions before and after their husbands' deaths. Some of the respondents had re-married and questions addressing the advantages and disadvantages of second marriages were included.

NAME: *Survey of Consumer Finances, 1983*

INVESTIGATORS: Richard T. Curtin
Institute for Social Research
P.O. Box 1248
Ann Arbor, MI 48106

ARCHIVE: PI

DESCRIPTION: Detailed information on the financial activities of American consumers is contained in this recent data set. Included are measures of savings behaviors, credit behaviors, pension coverage, assets, and debts. The national probability sample of households was augmented with a sample of high income families selected from federal agency records. Face-to-face interviews were held with 4,280 adults, ages eighteen and over. Respondents were free to consult their spouses and/or check household records to ensure accurate data. A telephone follow-up of respondents is now underway (1985).

NAME: *Survey of Health Services Utilization and Expenditures*

INVESTIGATORS: National Center for Health Services Research and Center for Health Administration Studies/National Opinion Research Center, University of Chicago

ARCHIVE: ICPSR

DESCRIPTION: These studies were conducted in 1963 and 1970 so that conditions could be compared with the findings of similar studies done in 1953 and 1958. In 1963, interviews were conducted with 7,803 members of 2,367 randomly selected U.S. families. In 1970, oversamples of the aged, urban poor, and rural residents were included with respondents from 3,763 families to produce 11,619 cases. Records from hospitals, insurance companies, and employers supplemented the interview reports of medical care visits, hospitalizations, expenses for services and drugs, health status, and health attitudes and beliefs.

PUBLICATIONS: R. Andersen, et al., *Expenditures for Personal Health Services: National Trends and Variations, 1953–1970,* Health Resources Administration, HEW: DHEW Publication No. (HRA)74-3105, October, 1983.

R. Anderson, J. Kravits, and O. W. Anderson (eds.), *Equity in Health Services: Empirical Analysis in Social Policy,* Ballinger Press, Cambridge, Massachusetts, 1975.

R. Anderson, J. Lion, and O. W. Anderson (eds.), *Two Decades of Health Services: Social Survey Trends in Use and Expenditures,* Ballinger Press, Cambridge, Massachusetts, 1976.

R. Anderson, J. Kasper, M. R. Frankel and Associates, *Total Survey Error,* Jossey-Bass, San Francisco, 1979.

NAME: *Survey of Income and Program Participation* (*SIPP*)

INVESTIGATORS: U.S. Department of Commerce, Bureau of the Census

ARCHIVE: ICPSR

DESCRIPTION: The ongoing *Survey of Income and Program Participation* is a panel study of the amounts and sources of income and program benefits received by U.S. households and individuals. A new panel of approximately 20,000 households from the U.S. civilian noninstitutionalized population is introduced each year; households are interviewed eight times at four-month intervals. Every person fifteen years old or older at a selected address provides personal income and program information. Panel members who move to new addresses are followed and persons who move in with panel members are interviewed (although the latter are not followed). At each face-to-face interview, basic household information is updated; a core of questions is asked about labor force activity, earnings, receipt of noncash benefits, assets, and receipt of government and private transfer payments; and (depending upon the wave) "modules" of questions about related topics are introduced. Modules on health and disability, work history, pension and retirement issues, and housing conditions and costs (among others) have been scheduled for inclusion.

PUBLICATIONS: D. Nelson, D. B. McMillen, and D. Kasprzyk, An Overview of the Survey of Income and Program Participation (SIPP Working Paper Series No. 8401), U.S. Bureau of the Census, Washington, D.C., 1984.

NAME: *Survey of Low-Income Aged and Disabled (SLIAD)*

INVESTIGATORS: Social Security Administration

ARCHIVE: ICPSR, DAAAD

DESCRIPTION: Seventeen thousand five hundred fifty-one noninstitutionalized low income aged and disabled adults were interviewed both before and after the implementation of the Supplemental Security Income (SSI) program. The major objectives of this study were to describe the economic and social characteristics of persons most likely to be affected by SSI and to evaluate the program's impact. The initial face-to-face interviews were conducted in 1973 with respondents sampled from four populations — recipients of Old Age Assistance, recipients of disability payments, and general population low income aged and disabled. Reinterviews were done in 1974. The survey focused on housing and neighborhood, household composition, expenditures, employment, income and assets, health, diet, and social activities.

PUBLICATIONS: K. F. Ferraro, Self-Ratings of Health Among the Old and the Old-Old, *Journal of Health and Social Behavior, 21,* pp. 377–383, 1980.
K. F. Ferraro, The Health Consequences of Relocation Among the Aged in the Community, *Journal of Gerontology, 38,* pp. 90–96, 1983.
T. Tissue, The Survey of the Low-Income Aged and Disabled: An Introduction, *Social Security Bulletin, 40,* pp. 3–11, February 1977.

NAME: *Survey of Needs of Boston's Elders*

INVESTIGATORS: Laurence G. Branch
Harvard Medical School
643 Huntington Ave.
Boston, MA 02115

ARCHIVE: PI

DESCRIPTION: An area probability sample of Boston, Massachusetts housing units was screened to identify all noninstitutionalized members aged sixty years or over in preparation for this 1978 survey. Seven hundred six respondents participated in the assessment of needs related to transportation, food shopping and preparation, social activities, housekeeping, activities of daily living, and emergency assistance. The interview also included questions about the use and cost of health services, morale, employment and retirement, satisfactions with housing and neighborhood, and self-assessed health status.

PUBLICATIONS: L. G. Branch, *Boston Elders: A Survey of Needs, 1978,* Report to the Massachusetts Department of Elder Affairs, Center for Survey Research, University of Massachusetts and the Joint Center for Urban Studies of MIT and Harvard University, Boston, 1978.

NAME: *Survey of Newly-Entitled Social Security Beneficiaries*

INVESTIGATORS: Social Security Administration

ARCHIVE: ICPSR

DESCRIPTION: In 1970, a sample of 19,108 persons who were newly entitled Social Security beneficiaries or recent Medicare enrollees responded to mailed questionnaires concerning the extent to which the Social Security program was meeting their needs and expectations. The survey covered respondents' employment histories, health, attitudes toward Social Security benefits, pension plans, and income.

NAME: *Survey of Older People in Virginia*

INVESTIGATORS: Virginia Office on Aging

ARCHIVE: DAAAD

DESCRIPTION: The *OARS* methodology was the foundation of this 1979 survey. The sample of 2,146 noninstitutionalized adults ages sixty years and older was selected from a multistage probability sample of Virginia households headed by persons sixty years of age or older. The questionnaire focused on social and economic resources, physical and mental health, the respondent's capacity for self-care, and services utilization and needs.

NAME:	*Tecumseh Community Health Study*

INVESTIGATORS: Department of Epidemiology
School of Public Health
The University of Michigan
Ann Arbor, MI 48109
Contact: The Chairman, Tecumseh Management
Committee

ARCHIVE: PI

DESCRIPTION: The *Tecumseh Community Health Study* is a prospective epidemiologic research program that has focused on cardiovascular diseases (especially atherosclerosis), diabetes, rheumatic disorders, and respiratory disease. Special investigations concerned exercise physiology, nutrition, genetics, serology and biochemistry, environmental factors, and social/demographic characteristics. The target population was the approximately 10,000 residents (about 6,000 adults) of Tecumseh, Michigan — a predominantly white, middle class community. In the first wave of data collection (1959–1960) 8,641 persons were examined; 9,226 individuals (including 2,499 new residents) participated in the second wave that ended in 1965. A third study wave reached completion in 1969. Data collection methods included face-to-face interviews, physical examinations and laboratory tests, medical histories, and self-administered health questionnaires. Hospital admissions, death certificates, and school absence records were monitored to identify cases of the conditions of interest. There was also an attempt to obtain medical information about respondents who moved from the area.

PUBLICATIONS: F. H. Epstein, et. al., The Tecumseh Study: Design, Progress and Perspectives, *Archives of Environmental Health, 21,* pp. 402–407, 1970.
J. A. Napier, B. C. Johnson, and F. H. Epstein, The Tecumseh, Michigan Community Health Study, in *The Community as an Epidemiologic Laboratory: A Casebook of Community Studies,* I. I. Kessler and M. L. Levin (eds.), The Johns Hopkins Press, Baltimore, 1970.

NAME:	*Two Generation Study of Postparental Women*

INVESTIGATORS: Ida Davidoff and Marjorie Platt, Radcliffe College

ARCHIVE: Murray Center

DESCRIPTION: Family, work, leisure, future plans, physical and emotional well-being, sources of stress, sources of satisfaction, coping strategies, and self-concept are some of the topics covered in this study comparing two generations of older women. The twenty-five respondents interviewed in 1957 were recruited from suburban Connecticut alumnae, political, and civic organizations and met four criteria: 1) had at least a bachelor's degree, 2) lived with husband, 3) had never worked permanently, full-time during the childrearing years, and 4) youngest child had left home at least one year prior to the interview. In 1978–1979 the nineteen survivors of this group were reinterviewed. A second group of thirty women recruited from similar sources and meeting the original eligibility criteria was also interviewed at that time.

NAME: *Widowhood in an American City, 1968*

INVESTIGATORS: Helena Lopata, Loyola University of Chicago

ARCHIVE: Murray Center

DESCRIPTION: The social and psychological implications of widowhood were explored in this survey of 301 Chicago-area women. The respondents, who fell almost equally into the fifty to sixty-four and sixty-five or over age ranges, had not remarried and were living in private dwellings. The face-to-face interview covered such topics as the major problems of widowhood, the type and extent of help offered by family and friends, the changes in lifestyle and social/familial relationships associated with widowhood, and personal plans for the future.

PUBLICATIONS: H. Lopata, The Social Involvement of American Widows, *American Behavioral Scientist, 14,* pp. 41–57, 1970.
                    H. Lopata, On Widowhood: Grief Work and Identity Reconstruction, *Journal of Geriatric Psychiatry, 8,* pp. 41–55, 1975.

Other potential sources of data regarding the health and economic well-being of older women are state government agencies. The Older Americans Act, as amended in 1969, gave the states a mandate to evaluate the needs of their older citizens. Several states — for example, Michigan, Minnesota, Ohio, Washington, and Wisconsin — have conducted assessment surveys, the data from which may be available for further analysis by interested researchers.

REFERENCES

1. B. M. Burchett and L. K. George, *Duke University Data Archive for Aging and Adult Development: Reference Guide,* Survey Data Laboratory, Center for the Study of Aging and Human Development, Duke University, Durham, North Carolina, 1983.

2. Henry A. Murray Research Center, *A Guide to the Data Resources of the Henry A. Murray Research Center,* Henry A. Murray Research Center, Radcliffe College, Cambridge, Massachusetts, 1984.

3. Inter-university Consortium for Political and Social Research, *Guide to Resources and Services,* Inter-university Consortium for Political and Social Research, Ann Arbor, Michigan, 1984.

4. Louis Harris Data Center, *A Director of Louis Harris Public Opinion Polls: Machine Readable Data Files,* Louis Harris Data Center, University of North Carolina, Chapel Hill, 1985.

5. S. Migdal, R. P. Abeles, and L. R. Sherrod, *An Inventory of Longitudinal Studies of Middle and Old Age,* Social Science Research Council, New York, 1981.

6. R. C. Taeuber and R. C. Rockwell, *National Social Data Series: A Compendium of Brief Descriptions,* Social Science Research Council, Washington, D.C., 1982.

APPENDIX
B

List of Conference Participants

Participants:

Robert C. Atchley, Ph.D.
Scripps Foundation Gerontology
Center
Miami University
Oxford, OH

Richard V. Burkhauser, Ph.D.
Department of Economics
Vanderbilt University
Nashville, TN

Richard T. Curtin, Ph.D.
Institute for Social Research
The University of Michigan
Ann Arbor, MI

Greg J. Duncan, Ph.D.
Institute for Social Research
The University of Michigan
Ann Arbor, MI

Jersey Liang, Ph.D.
Institute of Gerontology
Wayne State University
Detroit, MI

Linda S. Mitteness, Ph.D.
Department of Anthropology
University of California at San
Francisco
San Francisco, CA

Marilyn L. Moon, Ph.D.
Urban Institute
Washington, D.C.

Leslie A. Morgan, Ph.D.
Department of Sociology
University of Maryland
Baltimore, MD

Linda K. George, Ph.D.
Duke University Medical Center
Duke University
Durham, NC

Barry J. Gurland, M.D.
Center for Geriatrics and
Gerontology
Columbia University
New York, NY

Marie R. Haug, Ph.D.
Department of Sociology
Case Western Reserve University
Cleveland, OH

Ronald C. Kessler, Ph.D.
Department of Sociology
The University of Michigan
Ann Arbor, MI

Martha Clare Morris
University of Iowa
Center for Health Services Research
Iowa City, IA

Angela O'Rand, Ph.D.
Department of Sociology
Duke University
Durham, NC

Martin S. Pernick, Ph.D.
Department of History
The University of Michigan
Ann Arbor, MI

Joseph F. Quinn, Ph.D.
Department of Economics
Boston College
Chestnut Hill, MA

Shulamit Reinharz, Ph.D.
Department of Sociology
Brandeis University
Waltham, MA

Virginia Reno, Ph.D.
U.S. Social Security Administration
Washington, D.C.

Lois B. Shaw, Ph.D.
Ohio State University
Center for Human Resource
Research
Worthington, OH

Kathleen Short
Population Studies Center
The University of Michigan
Ann Arbor, MI

John Turner, Ph.D.
U.S. Department of Labor
Washington, D.C.

Joan F. Van Nostrand, Ph.D.
U.S. National Center for Health
Statistics
Potomac, MD

Lois M. Verbrugge, Ph.D.
Institute of Gerontology
The University of Michigan
Ann Arbor, MI

Jennifer L. Warlick, Ph.D.
Department of Economics
University of Notre Dame
South Bend, IN

Sue Perkins Taylor, Ph.D.
Department of Anthropology
Wayne State University
Detroit, MI

Lillian Troll, Ph.D.
Department of Psychology
Rutgers University
New Brunswick, NJ

Deborah L. Wingard, Ph.D.
Department of Community and
Family Medicine
University of California at San Diego
La Jolla, CA 92093

Organizing Committee:

A. Regula Herzog, Ph.D.
Institute of Gerontology
The University of Michigan
Ann Arbor, MI

Karen C. Holden, Ph.D.
Department of Economics
University of Wisconsin
Madison, WI

Mildred M. Seltzer, Ph.D.
Scripps Foundation Gerontology
Center
Miami University
Oxford, OH

Ethel Shanas, Ph.D.
Department of Sociology
University of Illinois at
   Chicago Circle
Chicago, IL

Carol S. Hollenshead, M.A.
School of Nursing
The University of Michigan
Ann Arbor, MI

Conference Advisors:

Patricia J. Green, B.A.
Inter-University Consortium for
Political and Social Research
The University of Michigan
Ann Arbor, MI

Marcia Ory, Ph.D., MPH
Program Officer, Behavioral Sciences
U.S. National Institute on Aging
Bethesda, MD

Sally Powers, Ph.D.
The Henry A. Murray Research
Center
Radcliffe College
Cambridge, MA

Conference Staff:

Nancy H. Fultz, M.A.
Institute of Gerontology
The University of Michigan
Ann Arbor, MI

Jeanne E. Miller, M.A., A.M.L.S.
Institute of Gerontology
The University of Michigan
Ann Arbor, MI

Ginger Maggio, B.A.
Institute of Gerontology
The University of Michigan
Ann Arbor, MI

Diane K. Vinokur, Ph.D.
Institute of Gerontology
The University of Michigan
Ann Arbor, MI

Eloise R. Snyder, M.A.
Institute of Gerontology
The University of Michigan
Ann Arbor, MI

Diane M. Voss
Institute of Gerontology
The University of Michigan
Ann Arbor, MI

Julie Walton
Institute of Gerontology
The University of Michigan
Ann Arbor, MI

Laura H. Zarrugh, Ph.D.
Institute of Gerontology
The University of Michigan
Ann Arbor, MI

Jon Hendricks, from the Department of Sociology at The University of Kentucky and editor of the Baywood Series, Society and Aging, did not participate in the conference. However, the authors are highly appreciative of his continued assistance and support throughout the preparation and production of this volume.

Index

Author Index